The Elements of Peace

The Elements of Peace

How Nonviolence Works

J. FREDERICK ARMENT

McFarland & Company, Inc., Publishers

Jefferson, North Carolina, and London

LIBRARY OF CONGRESS CATALOGUING-IN-PUBLICATION DATA

Arment, J. Frederick, 1953–
    The elements of peace : how nonviolence works / J. Frederick
Arment.
        p.   cm.
    Includes bibliographical references and index.

    ISBN 978-0-7864-6854-6
    softcover : acid free paper ∞

    1. Nonviolence.   2. Peace-building.   3. International
relations.   4. Diplomacy.   I. Title.
HM1281.A67 2012
303.6'1— dc23   2012003271

BRITISH LIBRARY CATALOGUING DATA ARE AVAILABLE

On the cover: left to right: Wangari Maathai, Yale Club, New York
City, 2002, photograph by Martin Rowe (courtesy the Green Belt
Movment); Albert Einstein, 1931 (Library of Congress); Mother
Teresa, June 1982 in St. Paul, Alberta (photograph by Anne Georg);
Martin Luther King, Jr., 1964 (Library of Congress); background
images © 2012 Shutterstock

Manufactured in the United States of America

McFarland & Company, Inc., Publishers
  Box 611, Jefferson, North Carolina 28640
    www.mcfarlandpub.com

For my children,
John Collin and Emily Rose

Contents

Acknowledgments

The "nonviolent methods" concept was conceived in the spring of 2004 when I realized that most of the information about peace was framed in the context of violence and war. At the time, I was the director of the Dayton International Peace Museum and was having difficulty finding exhibits about peace. I began a personal odyssey into the expansive and often overlooked history of alternatives to violence that resulted in the concept for this book as well as an exhibit for the Museum.

I want to express my appreciation to the individuals who contributed during the process of compiling the alternatives and completing this book, including Irwin Abrams, Charles Chatfield, Richard Deats, Ralph and Christine Dull, Steve Fryburg, Wayne Wlodarski, Norm Cary, Peter van den Dungen, Kate Johnson, Joe Kunkel, Jim Hagan, Bill Shaw, Jim Malarkey, Meg Carver, Igor Golovcsenko, Bill Alexander, Mark Willis, Marlene Connor Lynch, Ed Davis, Viki Church, Sherreé Sundermeyer Etter, Chiai Lkuda, and Amy Achor. Thanks to Lisa Wolters for her suggestions and encouragement.

In addition, I am indebted to those whose stories are included as real-world examples of peacemaking. For their courage and ideas, for their virtues, for the legacy of their use of nonviolence, I give my esteem and gratitude.

... acts of love and service are much more common
in this world than conflicts and quarrels. — Mohandas Gandhi

Preface

Peace is the world dream. From a hungry child in Somalia to a billionaire on Wall Street, from a democratic leader in Myanmar to a silent general in North Korea, everyone's deepest desire is for a life of peace. To have a feeling of personal safety, prosperity for our families, and a quality of life that gives us personal inspiration are the illusive visions of peace we all hold in our collective dream.

Yet peace is controversial. The word has been bandied about and claimed by armies and dictators that have wreaked havoc on our world. Peace is the poster child of ambiguity. Is it the absence of war? The attainment of justice? Faith? Communion with nature? A healthy meal? Or is it simply a quiet morning to read the newspaper and contemplate the blessings of our life? Peace defies a complete description as surely as the elephant is denied totality to the blind man's touch.

When I was in college during the early 1970s, the world was reeling from a tumultuous decade when hopeful revolution had paled in the shadow of violence. Civil rights had made progress but there were five dead on Kent State University's lawn. Women's issues had made it to the public debate but drugs and assassination had taken the hallowed icons of a generation.

I was repelled by political corruption yet energized to work for electoral change. Vietnam was winding down but the global wars for oil had just begun. Proceedings from the high-profile Watergate Committee competed for media attention with the underground rants of the Black Liberation Army. Radical notions of all sorts vied with pragmatic, work-within-the-system approaches to win the minds of youth.

For those of us who came of age in the '70s — and had bought into the '60s mantra that the times were a changin' — found ourselves with a choice. We could choose to give flight to our frustration by cynically dropping out of society. We could add to the rancor of the angry, join a group like the

Weather Underground, and declare a "state of war." Or we could lick our idealistic wounds, fold seamlessly into society, and do what we could to make a difference.

Trouble was, either dropping out or blending in went against my grain, just as it did many of my generation. I didn't believe in the conspiratorial "them" or the uncompassionate "they." I didn't have a hardened or angry heart. I simply wanted to live and work in my own unique way and find this illusive peace.

Not that I presumed to know the answers. I was no Gandhi or King. Even then I understood that if I reached up real high I could almost touch the knees of a Nelson Mandela or Mother Teresa. Yet like them and everyone else in the world, I had a choice.

I sat down and considered. I put my thoughts on paper. As a naïve twenty-year-old college student in a sweat-browed hour of Socratic questioning, I ended up with a disjointed essay that cleared away the noise of history and showed me my path. In a prophetic touch of whimsy and droll, I entitled the two-page, hand-scribbled treatise "The Yea and Nay of Civil Disobedience."

"Change is inherent in governments and societies," I wrote as a pithy ending to the first passage. "Therefore even utopia could only be temporarily attained."

I pondered my postulate. "Since governments and societies are devised to allow us to live with one another," I continued with the seriousness of a history major, "systems should create stability. And violent civil disobedience entails instability."

At length, there seemed only one conclusion. "Therefore civil disobedience must be limited to nonviolent attempts to achieve gradual change in a search for stability."

It was my epiphany. It wasn't the Declaration of Independence or the Sermon on the Mount, but it was personal and definitive. Nonviolence would be my choice.

Indeed, we all make decisions about the way we approach the world. Deceit or honesty. Bully or advocate. Status quo or change. Fear or courage. My Socratic questioning may have been a playful expression of my college antiquities course, but those guileless postulates have stayed with me all these years. Nonviolence as a means of change is the choice that has always made the most sense to me.

Nonviolence. And I thought peace was controversial. The term nonviolence is caught in the same ambiguity. Do you have to be a pacifist to be nonviolent? Is nonviolence fine on a personal level but to be left at the border when it comes to national interest? There are seven billion people in the world and everyone, it seems, has a different idea about how to approach conflict.

That is the point that gave the first impetus, or reason, for this book. The world has billions of people, with different cultures and faiths, with strongly held opinions and beliefs, with starkly individual expressions and desires. The collective mind stops at the door of personality. Anyone who has gone to a political debate or even a family reunion or business meeting knows that the individual nature of peace is a fundamental truth.

As individuals, we have the right to find peace in our own way. My way is not, necessarily, your way. From this natural individuality springs the many ways, even billions of ways, to find peace.

Which brings me to the next reason for this book. The methods of nonviolence are many. The individual nature of our way to create peace in our lives spawns a variety of methods. From artistic endeavors to working for the environment or holding silence at a peace vigil, the many methods of nonviolence, the thirty surveyed in these pages, allow for every individual to find their personal way to work for peace.

Why are the methods of nonviolence so individual in nature? Now comes the third reason for this book. A study of nonviolence shows that the heroes who have made a difference in this world have within their characters the personal, individual qualities that drive their success. The virtues of peace, such as forgiveness and empathy, wisdom and a sense of fair play, are the values these famous men and women embody. The virtues of peace are the specific character traits that have allowed Bishop Tutu to achieve reconciliation in South Africa and César Chávez to lead the boycott of grapes that changed the lives of thousands of migrant workers. The methods of peacemaking are the manifestations of an individual's virtues.

As we contemplate the real-world examples of nonviolent peacemaking throughout history we are astounded and inspired. We see how from the fires of violence comes the progress of humanity, which is the fourth reason for this book. As a human society, we are slogging our way through the historical phases of slavery and dictatorship, through epochs of hunger and poverty, through centuries in the darkness of ignorance and abuse.

The real-world examples of progress surveyed in *The Elements of Peace* are testaments to the ways in which nonviolence has changed the world. These examples cannot help but give us hope and promise. Through civil rights abuses, colonialism, the slave trade and nuclear brinkmanship, the most intransigent problems that have plagued our history have been transformed by the work of peacemakers. The progress from where we've come, if really contemplated with clarity, is undeniable.

Which brings us to the fifth and final reason for this book. To fully embrace the progress we've made is one way to heal our wounds. Optimism can, indeed, be therapeutic. Like a hypochondriac who loves misery, we sometimes dwell on the negative. Yet doctors tell us that worry is not a prescription but rather part of the diagnosis.

To heal the wounds of the past, to see our way clear to the next level of human achievement, requires a clear, unadulterated consciousness of the progress we've made. The result of that clarifying healing comes the next step in our journey: the actionable component of peace, which is love.

To have love for ourselves, love for others, love for the collective human contingent of the needy and abused, is the reciprocal energy that creates the inner and outer peace we all seek. Love is the peace we make.

With that profound and oft-repeated insight, I want to convey my love and appreciation for those who have contributed to the making of *The Elements of Peace*. First and foremost are my family and friends who each, in their own way, are finding a better world through integrity, humbleness, and attention to their creative instincts. I also am deeply grateful to my colleagues and peers, many of whom are included in a more extensive acknowledgment in this book.

When all is said and done, though we collaborate and find warmth in those closest to us, we are alone in this world with our decisions. I have chosen to work for peace even with the knowledge that the knees of Mandela are above me and the mystical sense of Mohandas Gandhi is beyond my reach. Yet I know that peace could, actually, beyond all reason, begin with me. Such is the promise for us all.

Introduction: Real-World Methods of Nonviolence

From the local schoolyard to the global stage, we are constantly faced with a choice. Do I respond to a violent situation with more violence? Or do I find another way?

Evidence of people fostering peace is all around us: the nurturing of a child by a mother's love, acts of kindness from strangers, an organization's charitable contributions, and the extraordinary international airlifts of food and medicine to countries in dire need.

Indeed, through the centuries, humanity has made much progress toward a more peaceful world. From the days when the vast majority of people on this planet were slaves, we have evolved to a high degree of individual freedom, democracy, and rule of law. "Peace is a daily, a weekly, a monthly process," said John Fitzgerald Kennedy, "gradually changing opinions, slowly eroding old barriers, quietly building new structures."[1]

Yet the power of violence in our daily lives is also undeniable. In February of 2010, a remote tragedy in a small Massachusetts town shocked the consciousness of an entire nation. Fifteen-year-old Phoebe Prince, a recent immigrant to the United States from County Cork, Ireland, was found dead after a day of intense bullying by classmates.

The suicide of a vibrant and beautiful teenage girl was another chilling wake-up call for a world seemingly asleep to the reality that bullying is violent behavior and not just kids being kids. According to the U.S. Department of Education and leading bullying statistics, 77 percent of middle and high school students reported bulling. Over 280,000 students report being attacked in American high schools each month. About 160,000 children stay home each day out of fear. Bullying is one of the leading causes of death among 10- to 14-year-olds.[2]

Children are our canaries in a coal mine, sensitive indicators of the health of our society. When Phoebe Prince was found hanging in the stairwell of her mother's rental house, we sensed that a precious life had been cut short, at least in part, by the violent patterns that we sometimes accept as normal.

Unfortunately, many other indicators of a violent culture lie just below the surface of our daily lives, only to rise in the tragic news of the day. Many will remember when students Dylan Klebold and Eric Harris packed their duffel bags with explosives and tucked shotguns beneath trench coats for their assault on Columbine High School. Under the peaceful sky of Littleton, Colorado, their arsenal of homemade bombs and gun-show semiautomatic weapons soon ended the lives of one teacher and fourteen students, including Klebold and Harris.

Still, the seeds of peace are ever present. Hope was sprouting even as Columbine's macabre dance of teenage cynicism, anger, and grudging misunderstanding was televised to the world. Tales of courage began to filter out in the aftermath of violence, with staff and students acting heroically and empathically in the face of murder. Student Makai Hall, whose knee was splintered by a shotgun blast, grabbed an arriving pipe bomb and threw it beyond his wounded friends. He was soon aided by Patrick Ireland, who was then shot and fell unconscious until he revived and crawled to a window and dangled over the edge to the arms of police.

Patrick's escape was caught on camera and "the boy in the window" became a symbol of hope and perseverance in the face of violence. Years later, his friend Makai Hall would speak before a U.N.–sponsored peace conference and help start the Columbine Ambassadors of Peace program.

"It's good that it raised the consciousness level about the issue," Patrick Ireland said, referring to one of the shooters' reference to being bullied by athletes, "and that it might prevent or already has prevented bullying attitudes and actions from being condoned or remaining under the radar. But to simply foam at the mouth," he continued, "and buy into all the crap — sorry, I can't think of a better word — about athletes' attitudes proving some sort of 'excuse' for the killers? That's offensive."[3]

As Patrick alluded, there are no easy answers to what creates the disturbing dance of violence. The circumstances are many, the excuses finely wrought. Yet it is important that we try to understand the dynamics of violence because each year statistics tell of great suffering around the world.

According to the U.S. Center for Disease Control, each day in 2005 an average of sixteen U.S. children were murdered. Women in America were victims of nearly 200,000 incidents of rape and sexual assault. In 2007, worldwide terrorist incidents caused the deaths of 22,000 people.[4]

During the twentieth century, the century that started with U.S. President

Wilson's "war that ends all wars," worldwide conflicts broke their historical record with estimates of more than 167 million deaths.[5] From the trenches of World War I and the Holocaust of World War II, to the mass killings in Sudan's region of Darfur, the work of global bullies and the dance of violence is alive and well.

Violence

The use of force with intent to injure: including direct and indirect physical or emotional abuse, fighting, war, torture, killing, oppression, exploitation, marginalization, or intimidation.

We reach for answers and struggle with such statistics, but as "the boy in the window" challenged us, the problems of the world are not easily blamed on the excuses of the day. The bullies live in the same world and are subject to many of the same circumstances as the victims. And to defer blame to television and movies, or politicians and generals, is also an easy answer that removes from each of us the responsibility for violence.

Collectively, we create our culture. Each individual contributes to our future with thought and action. As philosophers and religious prophets have told us for millennia, the real challenge against violence is not without us, but within our individual hearts and minds.

Peace

A state of tranquility or serenity; harmony within or between people or groups.

How can we be peaceful in a world reeling from violence? We must start, undoubtedly, with clear perspective. We acknowledge there will always be conflict and people who resort to violence. We understand that targeting, or victimization, is very real. It can be on a personal level or within a society. The abuse can be physical, verbal, social, or relational. Bullying can be direct or indirect, overt or covert, sophisticated or clumsy. The ways and means of violence are diverse. Its effects are with us in our daily lives.

Yet to keep a clear perspective within this reality of violence, we must recognize that most of our days are spent in relative safety and security. We sometimes take for granted the wonderful peace we find in our friends and family, our hospitals and schools, our judicial system and faith-based practices. When we fully grasp the relative perspective of history and measure it with our modern daily lives, we can see that most of our circumstances are rich with prosperity, recreations, and freedoms.

The astounding advances in our quality of life over the centuries give us great hope. Even in areas of the world where high crimes are common against ordinary people, there are continual signs of hope. At the same moment that armed soldiers on camels were razing small villages in Darfur, there were hundreds of doctors, nurses, and journalists in refugee camps working to heal the wounds and make the genocide known.

In Sierra Leone, boy soldier Ishmael Beah escaped his captors and wrote a revealing book called *A Long Way Gone*. In Beah's autobiography, he brought tremulous light to the darkness as he recalled the horrors he had committed under the spell of war and his heroic rescue by the men and women of UNICEF.

If we can hold our clear perspective, if we can clear away the mesmerizing fear of violence and see the progress and beauty in the world, it is possible to find the courage to act peacefully. The journalists who risked their lives by telling the stories of refugees in Darfur undoubtedly saved thousands of lives. The choice of Ishmael Beah and all the other individuals who speak out and act in the name of peace gives us cause for cautious optimism.

Imagine for a moment the promise of peace: a schoolyard where conflict is settled in ways that prevent harm to our children; a society where emphasis is put on sharing resources to meet challenges common to all; a world where respect and forgiveness is extended to all forms of life. That promise is of a culture where the methods of nonviolence are valued above those of violence.

Too idealistic? Too good to be true? Fortunately, history proves otherwise.

The tried-and-true techniques of nonviolent action are well supported by examples in every part of the world. Diplomacy, mediation, arbitration, peacekeeping, all of the different nonviolent methods are stopping violence and saving thousands, even millions, of lives each year. Nonviolent actions are mainstays of peace in schoolyards and neighborhoods, in cities and among nations.

One serious challenge in keeping our clear perspective is that the history and modern instances of nonviolence are seriously under-documented. Each day, the peaceful actions of children and average people certainly go unheralded. On a grand scale, the history of humanity is brimming with the forgotten stories of courage that have escaped the written history of tribes, cultures, and nations throughout time.

In our modern era, nonviolent methods have worked time and again, from the fall of apartheid in South Africa to the People Power Revolution in the Philippines. Yet historians seem to write the history of humanity with the underlying assumption that a response to conflict with violence is a legitimate, though sorrowful, means to resolving disputes.

Chapter after chapter detail the personal and social struggles that are stopped, at least temporarily, with a "successful" war or surge of violence. The next chapter, the next violent episode in our history, always seems to trace its roots to the violence in the previous chapter, on and on.

The Story of Peace

The history of nonviolence has a different dynamic. The cycle of violence, proven by historical example after example, can be ended with the creative and consistent use of nonviolent methods. If we rely on solutions that are based on humiliation and subjugation, anger and hatred, vengeance and retribution, the roots of violence are only encouraged. On the other hand, if peaceful and just solutions are found through nonviolent methods, history teaches us that the seeds for renewed violence most often go unplanted.

For proof, take a deeper look at history. See the nonviolent revolutions in Poland and Serbia. Witness the nonviolent strategies of Martin Luther King, Jr., and the Civil Rights Movement in America. The noblest acts of humanity are, by necessity, nonviolent in nature. The best resolutions to conflict are those where a solution is found in common ground — the peaceful withdrawal of Britain from Hong Kong; the treaty with the Iroquois by William Penn; the embargo and statecraft of the Kennedy bothers that stopped the Cuban Missile Crisis.

When nonviolent alternatives, such as statecraft or humanitarian aid, stop a spiral of conflict, historians seem ill at ease in writing about the event. Though the facts are recorded for all to uncover, the times when violence was used seem to shine through the lessons we teach our children. Our glorification of violence becomes part of our collective consciousness, a powerful drive in our culture.

War and murder, rape and robbery, racism and oppression: such acts of brutal force and misuse of power are specific to each episode of hate and bullying. The overpowering focus on these acts of violence enters the general identification of what many believe is the main dynamic of our lives.

Yet even with such a stilted culture, each of us still has an individual choice. Are we people of violence? Or are we people of peace?

The bullies of the world have made their decision. They perpetuate acts of violence on a repeated basis. At the core of these bully/victim conflicts is the sustained belief that there is an imbalance of power. The bullies use it; the victims are abused by it.

Fortunately for those of us wishing to choose peace, we know that these imbalances of power are tenuous. They are constantly shifting and changing over time. They depend on all of us playing our parts. An imbalance of power exists only if the bully and victim, as well as others involved in the violence, accept it as so.

Everyone in the dance of violence — supporters and assistants, passive and active participants, outsiders who witness the acts — must hold this imbalance of power to be true for it to continue. The bullies have their henchmen, the victims their defenders. Even as outsiders to a conflict, we find ourselves in complicity with episodes of violence and the misuse of power.

The good news is that sometimes teachers and police, or on a global scale powerful organizations such as the United Nations, question this balance of power. After that questioning comes the demand for an end to the violence.

"Power is of two kinds," Gandhi is said to have postulated. "One is obtained by the fear of punishment and the other by acts of love. Power based on love is a thousand times more effective and permanent than the one derived from fear of punishment."[6]

The Virtues of Peace

The way to prevent these shifting imbalances from affecting our lives is not to fear them, but to react with courage and love. To expose an imbalance, to act against it, to refuse to believe in the status quo, is to puncture the myth that the bully/victim reality is necessarily so. To be people of peace is a form of concerted action. It is possible to use power in positive ways. Our daily lives provide a multitude of examples; our history offers firm and documented proof.

As outlined in this book, there are at least thirty nonviolent methods that can change the dynamics of power. These techniques of responding to violence are much the same in the schoolyard and workplace as they are in international relations. Conflict resolution, arbitration, artistic expression, and citizen diplomacy all have parallels on a societal and personal basis.

Yet what do these methods of nonviolence require of practitioners? They are direct expressions of the virtues people hold. Forgiveness, foresight, wisdom, and other such virtues reside at the core of nonviolent actions. They are the character traits, qualities, and values carried by those in our society we most honor and cherish. These virtues of nonviolence are the attitudes, beliefs, codes, conduct, conscience, ethics, ideals, integrity, morals, mores, scruples, and standards by which we live. They give us the basis for authentic actions that deliver us from the cycle of violence and move us toward a life of peace.

A person who chooses to be peaceful must possess a measure of the character traits that enables him or her to act in a nonviolent manner. Those who put their lives on the line to protest oppression must have courage. To reconcile the memory of atrocities in the wake of a victory, a person must surely possess the generous ability to forgive. To be successful at the methods of peacemaking requires us to embody the virtues that make the process authentic and strong.

With that said, the lives we lead together depend on the qualities we foster in our larger society, as well as those we manifest in our individual lives. To embrace peace as part of our consciousness requires a practical and hopeful mind that's open to the possibilities of nonviolence.

Rather than seeing conflict as negative, normal tensions become the natural result of legitimate disagreements. The way we handle conflict makes all the difference. For those who choose peace, for those who endeavor to foster the values of peace inside them, an array of nonviolent alternatives is available to change the growing patterns of violence. Real-world examples of nonviolent actions and examples of personal courage abound.

Even in the direst of circumstances, we find that nonviolent means are proven over and over again to work for long-term solutions. We need to inform ourselves about the successes of nonviolence. We need to teach succeeding generations. For the global stage to be more peaceful, the local schoolyard must be rife with the wisdom and practice of peace.

Nonviolence

A philosophy, practice, or technique of refraining from the use of violence; a strategy for changing the dynamics of conflict by peaceful means.

The undocumented history of nonviolent action, undoubtedly, goes back to prehistory when the first conflict between two human beings was solved without violence. Since then, from Jesus Christ's Sermon on the Mount to Mohammed's words in the Qur'an on the "establishment of peace," our collective cultural history and especially our religious experiences are alive with the ethics of nonviolence.

In modern history, the writings of Henry David Thoreau and Leo Tolstoy sowed the seeds of actions by Mahatma Gandhi, Martin Luther King, Jr., and Nelson Mandela. Since its philosophical beginnings, nonviolence theory has evolved from its nineteenth century association with passive resistance. Nonviolence is now about action — a small man in a dhoti standing against the British army; American teacher Jodi Williams stopping the blight of land mines; Lech Walesa, a Polish steelworker, scaling the shipyard fence.

Top left: In writings such as *The King-dom of God Is Within You*, Leo Tolstoy espoused the nonviolent principles that would later influence Gandhi and King. *Top right:* The writings of American Transcendentalist Henry David Thoreau provided early reasoning and inspiration for modern environmentalists and pacifists. *Bottom:* Mohandas Karamchand Gandhi, often referred to as the Great Soul, championed the philosophy of total nonviolence, or *ahimsa*, in the movement toward Indian independence.

The Elements of Peace is dedicated to the real-world examples and the courageous heroes that have found inside themselves the virtues of peace and the power of nonviolence. The methods of nonviolence are powerful tools that enable us to respond peacefully to the normal tensions and extreme conflicts that come into our lives. Simply put, this is how nonviolence works.

> *Non-violence leads to the highest ethics, which is the goal of all evolution. Until we stop harming all other living beings, we are still savages.* — Thomas Edison, American inventor

... nonviolence is not a cloistered virtue to be practiced by the individual for his peace and final salvation, but it is a rule of conduct for society.... To practice nonviolence in mundane matters is to know its true value. It is to bring heaven upon earth... — Mahatma Gandhi

1

The Art of Diplomacy:
Dayton Peace Accords
(1995)

Skillful negotiations between people or groups toward a solution where there is little or no ill will; the art of achieving tactical advantage in international relations, typically by a country's diplomats or representatives abroad.

In four years, from 1992 to 1995, over 100,000 people were killed in the Bosnian War, the bloodiest of all the Yugoslav regional conflicts. Nearly two million men, women, and children fled their homes as refugees from the horrors of murder, genocide, and rape.

Sarajevo, the capital of the breakaway republic of Bosnia and Herzegovina, was reduced to a bullet-ridden and deadly war zone. Like determined carrion on a high perch, Serbian forces took artillery positions in the mountains overlooking the city, shelling night and day until the buildings were in ruins.

Another Bosnian city fared even worse. Srebrenica had been declared a safe haven by the United Nations. In July 1995, over 8,000 Bosniak Muslims were executed in the worst massacre since World War II.[1]

The savage war in Bosnia was just one of a series of conflicts from 1991 to 2001 that decimated the culturally and religiously diverse Balkan Peninsula. The Yugoslav Wars came in the wake of a power vacuum created after the fall of Marshall Tito, who by strong-armed and brutal dictatorship had kept the historically antagonistic region together for decades.

After Tito's fall, Serbian ultra nationalists under President Slobodan Milosevic used a history of ethnic and religious tensions to inflame the Serbian people to dominate the region. When Bosnia and Herzegovina declared independence, Serbians considered it a civil war and gave the 31 percent Serb population military and financial support. Neighboring Croatia supported the 17 percent Croat population in Bosnia. The Bosnian Muslims, or Bosniaks, with a population of 43 percent, considered the conflict a war of aggression by both of the bordering regions.

After four extremely bloody years, the Bosnian War showed no signs of ending. News of rape, ethnic cleansing, and concentration camps began to gain international attention. As NATO's Operation Deliberate Force bombarded Serbian military forces, pressure mounted for a heroic and seemingly impossible effort to end the violence with a diplomatic push.

The Virtue of Tactfulness

The term *diplomat* dates back to the late 1700s when the French issued official documents for special privileges to people who represented and negotiated for the state. By the 1800s, the term was firmly associated with achieving tactical advantages toward a strategic end.

To be tactical in a diplomatic sense depends a great deal on the personal virtues of the negotiators. Tactfulness entails a multitude of skills, from sensitivity and discretion to decisiveness and forethought. It has been called the "intelligence of the heart," which means understanding the pressures on all parties and pushing the negotiations with delicacy when needed and strength when appropriate.

The negotiator's skill set is applied at different phases of the diplomatic effort. The first step is to assess the situation. The second is to respond with measured options. The third is to find a creative way forward that lessens the fears of all parties involved.

By using the virtue of tactfulness, negotiators can reduce tensions. When the parties' fears are taken into consideration, those involved can find a measure of trust to explore nonviolent ways to solve the dispute.

In 1995, at the height of the Bosnian War, President Bill Clinton and his State Department staff proved themselves to possess the virtue of tactfulness. Under intense political pressure to supply arms to the Bosnians in order to balance their military power against the Serbs, instead the Clinton administration chose to pursue a strategy of diplomacy.

Using his strongest negotiation point first, President Clinton invited, or strongly urged under threat of NATO bombing, the leaders of the three warring parties to come to the United States for serious talks. An unlikely place for an international stage, Dayton, Ohio, was chosen as the place for negotiations.

Dayton is home to Wright Patterson Air Force Base, part of the U.S.

Strategic Command. In addition to the obvious show of American power, the Dayton location was also selected for its low profile in order to keep negotiations at the bargaining table rather than played out in the international press.

The tactic of wooing the combatants to this little known city, away from the glare of the media, worked well. Participants in the conference were Serbian president Slobodan Milosevic, Croatian president Franjo Tujman, and Bosnian president Alija Izetbegovic. Diplomatic efforts were led by chief negotiator Richard Holbrooke and U.S. Secretary of State Warren Christopher.

Christopher and Holbrooke immediately assessed a critical element of the peace initiative. Key would be the delineation of the Inter-Entity Boundary Line, which was where the armies had entrenched. At first the leaders stubbornly postured, but Holbrooke used a step-by-step approach as well as a newly available technology — intricate satellite maps that showed clearly the lay of the land and the armies of occupation.

Meanwhile, the three warring presidents were wined and dined around the city of Dayton. They were feted with symphonies and visits to the local shopping mall. The citizens of Dayton became a positive part of the diplomatic environment.

Yet after weeks of negotiations, failure to make a deal became a real possibility. Holbrooke's team focused on a compromise in land allocation known as 51-49, which was the percentage of territory that would be split between the Muslim/Croats Federation and the Bosnian Serbs.

As pressure built for Milosevic to give up the last tiny disputed area, the Serbian leader dug in his heels. As the frustration of all parties reached critical mass, Holbrooke changed tactics. He took a big risk, which on another day might have ended in disaster. He and Warren Christopher started packing their bags. They ordered the U.S. negotiation team's plane to be readied for takeoff. Tact is knowing when to push and when to withdraw.

With little room to maneuver, still under the threat of NATO bombing and international condemnation, Milosevic asked for another meeting. The Serbian leader knew that failure would be blamed on him.

Reluctantly, the Serbians agreed to give up a sliver of land around the town of Orasje. That seemingly small compromise changed everything. It enabled the 51-49 land compromise to seal a deal.

The resulting agreement was signed in Dayton on November 21, 1995. The brokered treaty established the "political entities" of *Republika Srpska* to meet Serbian demands. It also created the Federation of Bosnia and Herzegovina within the overall country.

The Dayton Peace Accords are not perfect, of course, and at any moment violence could begin again. Yet negotiations were a textbook case of how the

The three warring presidents — (center, left to right) Slobodan Milosevic of Serbia, Alija Izetbegovic of Bosnia and Herzegovina, and Franjo Tudjman of Croatia — signing the 1995 Dayton Peace Accords, ending the Bosnian War (United States Air Force).

virtue of tactfulness can help end a war, even in an area with the most complex cultural, religious, and ethnic divisions.

The art of diplomacy has, undoubtedly, been used since the beginning of human history. Negotiations have been documented to the era of the Egyptian pharaohs. Today, when a co-worker steps back to gain perspective on another worker's aggressive actions, he initiates the first step in a diplomatic effort. When a child stops responding in kind to a bully's actions, they may be positioning for a diplomatic move.

The art of negotiation entails creativity from all parties involved. Much more than a splitting of the pie in fair and equal pieces, the process involves communication about each party's interests, fears, and goals. What first appears to each of the disputants as a final solution is simply the initial step in a sometimes long and grueling process.

Instead of equal and fair pieces of a single pie, the solution may involve bringing more considerations to the table. What are the hidden objectives? Where are the points of contention and how can areas of common ground be found? In what ways can the negotiation move the discussion from a zero-sum effort to one where all parties feel like they've won?

According to new theories of negotiations, as expressed by, among others, authors Hernandez and Graham in the book *Global Negotiations*, diplomatic negotiation is a highly creative process. In honing our diplomatic skills, we keep in mind the following:

- Establish goals for creative outcomes
- Gather background before and during the process
- Understand the culture of all parties involved
- Deal with the realities of the situation
- Connect with personalities and encourage relationships
- Facilitate the flow of information
- Use questions to open and drive the process
- Don't demand critical concessions until the end
- Agree upon a clear solution and path forward
- Continue the creative process during implementation

The Dayton Peace Accords was a highly creative work of diplomacy. After the Paris signing of the Accords in 1995, the hard work of making it a reality began. Several international organizations were established to implement and monitor the agreement. A NATO Implementation Force was deployed in December 1995.

As evidence mounted of atrocities that occurred during the war — and what many believe was genocide — the International Criminal Tribunal was established to prosecute war crimes. As a result, many Serbs have been indicted and prosecuted. In the Serbian election of 2000, which resulted from a non-violent political movement, Slobodan Milosevic was defeated and a new democratic leader won the presidency of that war-torn country.

The head of the Bosnia and Herzegovina Delegation to the U.N. has estimated "200,000 people were killed, 12,000 of them children, up to 50,000 women were raped, and 2.2 million were forced to flee their homes."[2] The human value of tact and the actions of diplomacy prevented more.

"You've got to end this war..."

Much of the success for ending the Bosnian War has been attributed to lead negotiator Richard Holbrooke. The diplomat had a long, distinguished, and storied career in civil service. In fact, Holbrooke's last words before an ill-fated surgery in 2010 were whispered in a good-natured jest to his doctor: "You've got to end this war in Afghanistan."[3]

Even to his final moments, Holbrooke exhibited the best qualities of a consummate diplomat: artful words, a sense of humor and irony, sensitivity and respect to those around him, and a gift for delivering the deep and subtle messages of a great negotiator. Richard Holbrooke was flush with the skills of a tactful negotiator.

When he died in 2010 at George Washington University Hospital of complications from a rare arterial illness, Holbrooke was serving as special representative for Afghanistan and Pakistan. He had begun working on one of the most frustrating problems in modern politics when President Barack Obama appointed him to that position in 2009.

Though he never achieved some of his greatest goals, such as being selected for the Secretary of State position or winning the Nobel Peace Prize, Holbrooke was important in what George F. Kennan called the "heroic effort" to end the bloodletting in Bosnia. In his remarks at the end of the successful Dayton negotiation, Holbrooke said, "Let us pledge, therefore, that this day in Dayton be long remembered as the day on which Bosnia and its neighbors turned from war to peace."[4]

Richard Holbrooke was a documented innovator in the tactful introduction of truth and consequences into some of the more intransigent diplomatic challenges of the late twentieth and early twenty-first centuries. He was a great believer in the historical importance of the Accords and often referred to the "Dayton Process" when speaking of global solutions. Whether it was the creative idea of using satellite maps to say a thousand words about borders, or knowing when to pack up and leave a process, Holbrooke will forever live in history as the essential negotiator that helped save thousands of lives by bringing an end to the Bosnian War.

> *If you want to make peace, you don't talk to your friend. You talk to your enemies.* — Moshe Dayan, Israeli foreign minister

> *All war represents a failure of diplomacy.* — Tony Benn, English politician

2

The Vision of Statecraft: The "Handover" of Hong Kong (1984)

Skillful management of state affairs by dialogue and negotiation between national leaders; finding solutions to issues of strategic national importance requiring great deliberation.

The history of relations between China and foreign nations is shadowed by millennia of war, domination, and conflict over territory. In the 1800s, China was a reluctant trading partner of Great Britain. In a clash of imperial power, the countries eventually fought in two conflicts called the Opium Wars.

At the end of the First Opium War, the 1842 Treaty of Nanking ceded to Britain the prosperous Pearl River Delta along China's southern coast. The English quickly established the New Territories as a Crown Colony. They named the capital of the sprawling island of Hong Kong Victoria City after the queen.

During the nineteenth and twentieth centuries, Victoria City developed as a major trading port and cultural hub. As an integral banking capital for East-meets-West financial interests, Hong Kong became the modern "jewel" of capitalist economic power in the East. Yet the inevitability of conflict over external domination was just below the surface of its success.

When Chinese nationalism rose in the latter half of the twentieth century, the call for a return of all historically Chinese land, including Taiwan and Hong Kong, became state policy. Gaining power in the late 1970s, Communist Party Chairman Deng Xiaoping demanded return of the Crown Colony with its nearly seven million people, who were mostly Chinese.

This public call from the leader of China for return of Hong Kong required a response by then–British prime minister Margaret Thatcher. In a speech during a state visit to China in 1997, Thatcher obstinately reaffirmed the validity of the Nanking treaty. With Hong Kong attached to China's southern coast, the leaders of the flagging British Empire began to realize that it was only a question of time before the rising world power forced the issue with a resurgence of military might.

The British began developing a risk management plan, in effect a withdrawal in the advent of a serious political or military situation. General Secretary Deng expressed interest in formal negotiations, but the issues seemed too difficult to resolve. The New Territories were on a 99-year lease that would end on the last day of 1997.

As the deadline loomed, the Chinese government became more adamant about letting the lease run out. Yet Hong Kong was considered so essential to the worldwide capitalist economy that the idea of it becoming a part of a communist state was, to the West, unthinkable. The British wanted, at least, to retain administrative authority even if political authority was turned over to China.

If both countries dug in their heels, there was a real possibility of armed confrontation.

The Virtue of Foresight

One attribute in approaching life from a nonviolent perspective is the ability to know when to leave a door open. Closed doors often disengage any communication and can result in stalemate and, ultimately, the intensification of an unresolved dispute.

Much like nations, from the moment we are born the disputes, disagreements, and problems in our interactions become commonplace with family and friends as well as co-workers and strangers. We often encounter bullies, or antagonists who take advantage, even abusers who can hurts us emotionally and physically. There is no question that we need to take a strong stand to stop victimization. Above all, we must take care of our interests and our well-being.

However, like in the relations between nations, a strong response in a violent manner, even when it relieves the problem temporarily, will not address the root causes of the conflict. As Martin Luther King, Jr., famously noted, "The old law of an eye for an eye leaves everybody blind."[1]

Whether done for "just" reasons such as preventing abuse or protecting property, violent reactions done without a measure of foresight will often simply add fuel to the energy of violence. Indeed, the root causes of violence that remain unaddressed will only lie dormant and, inevitably, rise again.

Such is the predicament of a visionary statesman. How can a leader prevent a short-term solution that does not really address the root causes from causing future wars and disputes?

The difference between a statesman and a diplomat is not only that the statesman is often the leader of a nation and the diplomat an emissary. Statesmanship is limiting the risk and having the ability to identify an opportunity for a long-term, practical solution that addresses the underlying problem. In this scenario, the two antagonists become linked as partners who must find a creative way toward a resolution that does not fuel future disputes.

Derived from the Dutch word "staatsman," the concept of statesmanship was a product of that seafaring culture which dominated the world for several decades during the early seventeenth century. The statesman (or in many circumstances more appropriately, stateswoman or statesperson) is poised at the helm of state, keeping accurate bearings, using his or her experience on rough seas, and steering the vessel of state toward safer waters.

The visionary statesman exhibits not only the tact of the diplomat, but also high levels of mental preparedness, insight, caution, discretion, and a demeanor of calm in the midst of storms. These individuals deal with major disputes that eclipse temporary tactical advantage.

Foremost among the skills of the visionary statesman is the lofty but necessary virtue of foresight. It enables a quality of leadership that sees a way through present problems to a future where nations can have lasting peace. Foresight is having the ingenuity to take advantage of an opportune moment to break through the present cycle of violence.

Such was the visionary moment for Margaret Thatcher. In an important speech, the conservative prime minister reiterated the sanctity of British treaties: "There are treaties in existence," she said. "We stick by our treaties unless we decide on something else."[2]

Chairman Deng also possessed the virtue of foresight in limiting the risk of a peaceful solution to Hong Kong's challenge. He realized that in Thatcher's seemingly defiant statement, she had left the door open for a compromise. Yet to avoid conflict would require continued statecraft from both national leaders.

The breakthrough in the stalemate between Britain and China came with a creative idea about administration and sovereignty. Chairman Deng amended a single clause in the 5th National People's Congress to include the visionary and ingenious concept of "one country, two systems."

Hong Kong, in Deng's view, would become a "special administrative region." That designation would allow a handover of the territory to China yet let the British retain limited sovereignty to continue financial operations. Hong Kong would be self-governing, maintain a capitalist economy within Chinese socialism, and retain a high degree of autonomy.

A Risk Well Managed

Both leaders of these great nations measured the risks involved with this strategy. Risk management is an important part of steering a nation, running a business, or living our personal lives. It is the process of limiting the negative effects of a difficult situation.

Risk management is also about positioning for a positive result. We do this by realizing opportunities that come with the uncertainty of present conditions. Managing risk involves several strategies, including avoidance of more potential for violence, reduction of its impact, moving the risk to another party, or even a strategic absorption of the negative consequences until a solution can be found.

The first step in risk management, for a nation or corporation, or an individual or group, is to identify and assess the risk of a state of violence. Succeeding steps are followed in order to apply creative thinking to the problem and coordinate resources to find a solution:

1. Identify the risks involved

2. Assess what areas the risks will impact

3. Determine the impact of the risks on each area

4. Strategize ways to reduce the negative impact

5. Look for opportunities to create a positive impact

6. Assess and prioritize the strategies

7. Act, evaluate, and modify as conditions evolve

"The handover" of British rule of Hong Kong to China, after much deliberation and negotiation, came on July 1, 1997. Amidst the celebrations in the streets were discussions and speculations about what would happen. Yet the risks associated, the fears which some held about the transfer of power, was abated when all the parties held to their agreements.

Today, the Hong Kong Administrative Region remains a capitalist center and part of China. The island is now known as one of the "Four Asian Tigers" and enjoys high status in the Index of Economic Freedom as having one of the freest economies in the world.[3] The visionary foresight of the leaders ruled the day.

The Iron Lady of Statecraft

The partnership of Deng Xiaoping and Margaret Thatcher is a case history in how statesmanship and risk management can prevent future violence. The creative approach of Chairman Deng was matched by Prime Minister Thatcher's ability to see an opportunity when it was presented.

Nicknamed by a Soviet newspaper "Iron Lady" because of her Cold War rhetoric, Margaret Thatcher had developed a reputation for standing firm in her beliefs. Her credentials as an anti-communist were not just words, but rather a policy alignment with then-president Ronald Reagan, whose 1980s anti–Soviet stand resonated with her views.

Yet both leaders, in the end, made compromises and helped lessen tensions with both communist powers, Russia and China. By the end of the 1980s, the world had changed. The Berlin wall had fallen, the Soviet Union had collapsed, and China was tentatively embracing new economic reform.

The stalwart ideology of the first woman prime minister had no small influence in these global events. In Britain, "Thatcherism" came to mean more than the prime minister's bold personal style, which ranged from uncompromising to *realpolitik*. In her 1979 Conservative Manifesto, Thatcher proclaimed, "This election is about the future of Britain — a great country which seems to have lost its way."

Finding the way forward for Margaret Thatcher meant the British people needed to have the foresight to see their way out of economic malaise. They needed to find their optimism, to revive their sense of nationalism and favor individualism over collectivism. "Yet success and security are attainable," she said, "if we have the courage and confidence to seize the opportunities which are open to us."

It was Thatcher's real and perceived sense of moral absolutism that gave her, as prime minister, the flexibility to deal with Communist China. She had railed against the high tax policies of her rivals as steps "not only toward Socialism, but towards Communism."

When Thatcher began negotiating with Chairman Deng, she was well accustomed to the long view. Like most British people, she wanted the Chinese to extend the lease. "But when this proved impossible," she said later in an interview, "I saw the opportunity to preserve most of what was unique to Hong Kong through applying Mr. Deng's [one country, two systems] idea to our circumstances."

"In fact, I complimented [Deng Xiaoping] on his brilliance," she said. "It's often a good idea to tell people with whom you negotiate that they were right all along."

Prince Charles wrote in his private diaries about what he considered the

"Iron Lady" Margaret Thatcher gained a reputation for anti-communist rhetoric and tough statecraft, in part due to her close working relationship with conservative U.S. president Ronald Reagan (The White House).

"Great Chinese Takeaway." Yet with hard-line credentials and skills of foresight to imagine a post–British Hong Kong, Thatcher expressed her practical vision of the future. "The Brits should not hang around," she said most practically at the time, according to Hong Kong businessman David Tang, "and must let the Chinese get on with it."[4]

> *If they want peace, nations should avoid the pin-pricks that precede cannon shots.* — Napoleon Bonaparte, Emperor of France

3

The Process of Reconciliation: Truth and Reconciliation Commission (1996)

Engaging with the past to enable friendlier relations; giving voice to victims and an opportunity for atonement from perpetrators in order for former disputants to coexist.

One of the quintessential heroes of nonviolence during the last of the twentieth century is Nelson Mandela. Like a tall oak, Mandela withstood the indignities of imprisonment and isolation and came to embody integrity and justice in the movement to free South Africa from the violence of institutional racism.

Yet this oak of nonviolence did not stop his peacemaking with the victory of democracy in South Africa. He knew that the most telling work of freedom comes after a conflict ends and peace begins, which is why Mandela is so important to the world.

The story begins in the sixteenth century. Located at the southern tip of Africa, Cape Town was a significant port as ships traveled between the Indian and Atlantic oceans. In 1562, the Dutch East India Company established a commercial enterprise at the Cape Colony to provision European ships on their way around the Cape of Good Hope.

Racial and ethnic conflicts soon arose between the Xhosa and Zulu, the indigenous peoples, and the Afrikaners, who were transplanted Europeans that had colonized southern Africa for generations. Added to these social and territorial tensions was the discovery of gold and diamonds. The huge opportunity for wealth eventually triggered the Boer Wars as Britain tried to annex the independent farming territories settled by Dutch, Flemish, German, and French farmers (Boer is Dutch for farmer).

After many bloody battles, the Boers were defeated and in 1910 South Africa became a British dominion. Fifty-one years later, the country gained independence and became the Republic of South Africa.

Yet lost in these geopolitical conflicts were the indigenous blacks who suffered under racial segregation established hundreds of years before. In 1948, the system of "apartheid," or "separateness" in the language of the Afrikaners, became the law of the land. People were classified by racial groups — black, white, colored, and Asian — which determined the jobs, areas to live, and activities open to each race.

As protests and violence naturally increased, Afrikaners responded with brutality and repression. They stripped blacks of citizenship and cordoned them into *bantustans*, or "homelands." Black leaders, including Nelson Mandela, established the African National Congress (ANC) to change the political system. At first a leader of the military arm of the ANC, Mandela initially chose violence and was sent to prison for his participation in an armed attack.

During the long years in the Robben Island prison, Mandela was to experience a personal transformation. Embracing the pragmatism of Thoreau, Gandhi, and other prophets of nonviolence, he began to see the world in a "mature way," where the oppressed and the oppressor must both be liberated.[1]

Mandela's imprisonment and his transformation to nonviolence drew the world's attention to South Africa's injustice. In the 1990s, citizens and nations across the globe began to respond. An embargo was put in place by Western powers that began to cripple the South African economy. International pressure became so intense that the ruling National Party under F.W. de Klerk began to slowly repeal the laws of apartheid.

President de Klerk could see the historical writing on the wall. He realized that Nelson Mandela had become an extremely powerful leader of a worldwide movement against South Africa's institutional racism. If the country was to avoid a descent into chaos, de Klerk and the entrenched white government needed a fair partner.

The government lifted its ban on political organizations, including the African National Congress, and negotiated with Mandela for the dismantling of apartheid and a path toward democracy. After twenty-seven years, Mandela was released from prison. In a celebrated democratic election in 1994 that saw twenty million multiracial votes, he ascended to the presidency.

Yet Mandela understood that the new South Africa, even with changes in the political system, was not beyond violence. The legacy of apartheid had joined South Africans in a collective nightmare of anger and hate. The Group Areas Act of 1950, which had driven nearly 600,000 people from their homes, was still fresh in their memories. Many families were forced to reside in slums, and untold thousands were subject to torture, murder, and rape.

As the sad history of many revolutions throughout history foretold, the country was now free to indulge in the historical precedent of retribution. Accusations and blame, vigilantism and punishment, even a bloodbath was not out of the question. Where was the precedent for nonviolence in a situation of such nightmarish proportions?

The Virtue of Forgiveness

Forgiveness would not come to the minds of many in South Africa who had experienced the emotional, physical, and spiritual ravages of violence. To give up the right to punish, to endeavor to pardon, to pass over such grave offenses was, seemingly, an unreasonable request. Yet Mandela knew that more violence would not heal the country's wounds.

The root of forgiveness in Old English is "forgiefan," to give or grant. To give up punishment, to cease to feel resentment, would take an act of spiritual transcendence, especially with the millions of people who had lived through a hellish time.

Mandela decided that vengeance could not be the foundations of the new South Africa. The country needed to overcome the hostility and distrust. It needed the means to resolve, to get past the violence, to come together for the sake of their children. The country needed a way toward forgiveness and away from the resentment that festers and breeds more hate.

With his commitment to nonviolence as the guiding light, the new president along with the new South African congress conceived of a method of conciliation that might bring together victims and perpetrators. Learning from the truth commissions of Latin America and other historical precedents, an innovative reconciliation commission was commissioned that included amnesty at its base.[2]

After centuries of violence, the Truth and Reconciliation Commission would allow injustices to be stated and acknowledged without resorting to retribution. This technique for restorative justice and forgiveness was given credibility and spirit by the well-known bishop of Cape Town, Desmond Tutu.

With victims and perpetrators together in the courtroom, the proceedings televised, testimony and evidence of human rights abuses such as murder and rape were publicly aired and acknowledged. Confessions of crimes committed during apartheid earned many of the perpetrators amnesty from prosecution, thereby reducing the potential for a renewed cycle of violence.

The Question of Amnesty

Giving amnesty is a government act that restores to a state of innocence those who are guilty of an offense. Derived from the word for "oblivion," amnesty obliterates any legal obligation or remembrance of the act. It is similar to a pardon yet a pardon only removes the punishment but does not absolve the crime.

Amnesty has been used on many occasions and in a variety of situations. American president Jimmy Carter granted amnesty to draft "dodgers" in order to heal the wounds of the Vietnam War. Today in many countries, there is an international debate surrounding the granting of amnesty to illegal aliens.

There are many advantages to using amnesty as a nonviolent solution to the carry-overs of anger

Nelson Mandela, of South Africa and icon of nonviolence and reconciliation (Government Communications, Republic of South Africa).

and hate that come with the cessation of brutal wars. Amnesty can be an incentive to combatants laying down their arms. Amnesty can reduce the cost of prosecutions in countries where the economy has been shattered.

The greatest advantage of amnesty may be that it can lead to reconciliation between the victims and perpetrators and lead to a more peaceful society. The Truth and Reconciliation Commission in South Africa made amnesty a part of the process. Three committees were established to do the work:

1. Human Rights Violation Committee to investigate abuses
2. Reparation and Rehabilitation Committee to restore a measure of dignity to victims and assist with rehabilitation
3. Amnesty Committee to consider granting amnesty to those who committed politically-motivated human rights abuses

The debate on the merits of amnesty continues to cause controversy. Many people in South Africa were not satisfied to simply hear testimony and reports of abuses and crimes. There was a call for retribution, especially in high profile cases of murder such as that of Steven Biku.

In the end, nearly 1,000 people were granted amnesty. Over 5,000 were refused. Yet the numbers do not tell the whole story. The real power in the Commission and its offer of amnesty was in the act of forgiveness. The Commission gave voice to the victims and an opportunity for remorse to the abusers. It offered an end to the cycle of violence that comes from the repetitive motion of abuse and retribution.

Since the success of South Africa's Truth and Reconciliation Commission, many other countries have opted for truth and reconciliation rather than retribution and bloodbaths. Nelson Mandela, Desmond Tutu, and the long-suffering people of South Africa institutionalized forgiveness as a wise and proven method to resist continued violence and endeavor toward peace.

The Elders

Nelson Mandela and Bishop Tutu are considered two of the greatest men of our time. With their actions and insights regarding the transition in South Africa, they became possibly the first universally acknowledged leaders of our human tribe.

Wisdom on issues of great importance has always been attributed to the elders in society. Those who have weathered the tides of history and flourished are respected and given a decision-making, idea-generating power that reflects their value to society. The reality of our worldwide connectivity and the issues that affect us all has given rise to the need for a new council of elders on a global scale.

The idea for the Global Elders developed out of a conversation between musician Peter Gabriel and the chairman of the Virgin Group of businesses, Richard Branson. Could the world benefit from the experience, intelligence, and peacemaking spirit of recognized leaders to engage and, perhaps, solve some of the more difficult challenges that global interdependence has given rise?

Nelson Mandela, Bishop Tutu, Kofi Annan, Jimmy Carter, Li Zhaoxing, Muhammad Yunus, and Aung San Suu Kyi were some of the founding members of what has become a force working toward reducing human suffering and grappling with regional conflicts. In the tradition of respect for those who have proven their maturity of character and skill, the Elders hold no office and are not affiliated with politics in general.

The group is simply charged with using their positions as celebrities of peace to give voice to the voiceless, to engage in the challenges of our time, and to work for change where the world most needs it. Perhaps the Elders' most powerful tool is the combination of their individual voices with an organization committed to finding the truth and letting it rise above the din of complexity and polarization.

Results from the Elders' work is already apparent though only convened in 2007. They are working in Zimbabwe, Burma/Myanmar, the Middle East, Cyprus, and other areas where conflict and human rights abuses are rife. They have called for an end to all justifications, whether religious or societal, for discrimination against girls and women. They are engaged in peacebuilding and development in Sudan. The group speaks boldly and is involved in the drive for the elimination of all nuclear weapons.

"Together we will work," said Nelson Mandela, "to support courage where there is fear, foster agreement where there is conflict, and inspire hope where there is despair."[3]

> *The practice of peace and reconciliation is one of the most vital and artistic of human actions.* — Thich Nhat Hanh, Vietnamese Buddhist monk

> *Without forgiveness there can be no future for a relationship between individuals or within and between nations.* — Desmond Tutu, South African Anglican bishop

4

Mediation Techniques:
The Good Friday
Agreement (1999)

*Resolving disputes indirectly with a non-binding agreement by the help of a
third-party intermediary; solving disputes between nations by involving
another power as a go-between.*

On January 30, 1972, twenty-six protestors in Belfast lay dead or dying
on the street. The oldest was fifty-nine. Among the youngest were six
seventeen-year-old boys. They were protesting against the occupation of their
homeland by British troops. That day is now known as Bloody Sunday.

Separated by a thin channel of the Irish Sea from England, Ireland has
a long history tied to its relationship to the larger island to the east. In 1707,
the British Act of Union formalized Britain's dominance of Ireland, creating
the United Kingdom, which already included Scotland and Wales.

Over the centuries, the Irish often rose in rebellion, and in 1916 the
bloody Easter Rising saw a number of cities come under Irish Republican
rule. As with previous attempts for succession, the new uprising was brutally
crushed and most of its leaders executed.

In 1922 after decades of civil war, the British parliament passed the Partition of Ireland Act. The legislation attempted to maintain for the dominant
British and Protestant citizens the northern part of the island. In the south,
the Act created the Irish Free State, which was mostly Roman Catholic and
covered five-sixths of the land.

The 1922 Partition planted more seeds of conflict between the Catholic
Nationalists and the Protestant Unionists in the North. The Free State became
the Republic of Ireland, a sovereign country, while predominantly Protestant
Northern Ireland remained part of the United Kingdom.

During the 1960s, militants opposed to the partition formed the Irish Republican Army (IRA) and began the Troubles, a fierce armed rebellion of Catholic nationalists. A political party closely associated with the IRA, Sein Fein, was able to gain seats in the Republic of Ireland's parliament and in the Northern Ireland legislature as well.

At the end of the twentieth century, there was an increase in car bombs and armed skirmishes with British troops. The historical failure of direct negotiations between British and Irish nationalists made it apparent that a third party might help break the impasse.

In 1995, U.S. president Bill Clinton brought the moral authority of the United States to bear on the problem. With consent of the disputing parties, Clinton dispatched special envoy George Mitchell, a former senator from Maine and majority leader for the Senate, to help mediate the stalled negotiations. Mitchell had also served as chancellor of Queen's University in Belfast, so he was familiar with the goals and differences of the two factions.

From the start, Mitchell knew that the basic principles of nonviolence were core to creating an environment for negotiation. As a first step, Mitchell managed an agreement where the parties would work toward resolution in an "exclusively peaceful and democratic means." Once agreed, the group was then able to go to work on the more sticky issues of political power, police reform, prisoner release, human rights, and citizenship.[1]

Envoy and international mediator George Mitchell (U.S. State Department).

The Virtue of Integrity

The bloody and chaotic Troubles had lasted for thirty years. It is estimated that 3,254 died as a result of the rebellion.[2] It seemed the rest of the world could only stand by as gruesome acts of violence continued in vivid broadcasts on the evening news.

This feeling of being a bystander, simply witnessing the violence, is familiar to anyone who has seen violence in their house, or school, or neighborhood. As bullies and victims face off, those who witness are necessarily involved. Many bystanders, unfortunately, just stand back and let the violence continue.

A notorious case happened in New York City during the early 1960s. According to a report by the *New York Times*, in front of an audience of thirty-eight people, a young woman named Kitty Genovese was stabbed to death on her street. Not one single witness intervened to prevent the murder.[3]

The "bystander effect" is a topic of study by sociologists, psychologists, and criminologists. Reports and studies show that many third parties feel useless. They believe they have little or no effect on the situation. Other bystanders feel a "diffusion of responsibility" where they believe someone else will do the work for them.

Third parties to violence between aggressors and victims fall into many bystander roles. Some assist or reinforce the bully. Others defend the victim. Still others are outsiders and beyond the immediate proximity of the violence.

Yet many bystanders can go beyond their role-play and have a positive effect. One way is to step in and offer mediation of the dispute. Whether the violence is a family abuse case or a national tragedy such as the Troubles, the bystander turned mediator must first overcome the profound mistrust that comes from being an outsider to the violence.

All parties involved must trust or at least accept the personal integrity of the mediator. The word integrity comes from the root for integer, or undivided whole. A person with the virtue of integrity has a soundness, or wholeness that gives the parties in the dispute a reason to trust in the process of mediation.

In Northern Ireland, it seemed that George Mitchell had spent a lifetime preparing for this duty. The former senator was the embodiment of integrity. After hundreds of years of war, the negotiators involved in the dispute would have to overcome intense historical polarization. Mitchell leveraged his personal reputation and called upon the full prestige of the United States to encourage compromise from all parties.

The commitment to "exclusive and peaceful means" that served as a precondition for negotiations is part of the "Mitchell Principles." A second innovation that Mitchell used in this mediation was the "sufficient consensus" clause, which allowed parties that didn't agree with particular sections to agree to the overall pact.

"Sufficient consensus" allowed intense negotiations to continue through many sticking points that had caused other processes to fail. Mitchell was able to set a firm deadline to prevent escalating violence. When a power-sharing agreement was finally drafted, it created a Northern Ireland assembly and ended the Republic's claim on the North.

The Agreement repealed the hated Government of Ireland Act of 1920, thereby affirming the Irish people's rights to their future. On some of the most contentious areas such as disarmament, vague wording described as "constructive ambiguity" ensured that all parties could agree in principle and move on.

The Belfast Peace Agreement of 1998, called the Good Friday Agreement, effectively ended centuries of violence. The deadline of disarmament in 2000 was missed, yet further talks have solved most issues. The process of peace in Ireland, like all negotiated settlements, needed constant attention and the evolution of a nonviolent process for settling further disputes.

Mediator Code of Conduct

U.S. envoy Richard Haass replaced George Mitchell for the final negotiations. Haass' credentials and actions maintained the integrity of the process. The mediator's main responsibility is to assist the disputing parties in their negotiations, rather than imposing a solution as in arbitration.

The mediator seeks to keep the dialogue open and remain impartial to the discussions. Creating a safe, neutral environment is a necessity. Ground rules must be established and the process must be clear to all parties. The mediator should watch for signs of intimidation in order to reduce the participants' emotional anxiety.

The International Mediation Institute has issued a Code of Professional Conduct, which attests to the importance of trust in the mediation process. Some of the tenets of the Code follow:

- A mediator must reveal any information that compromises their ability to be neutral and impartial.
- A mediator must explain the mediation process to all parties in the dispute and agree upon any compensation.
- A mediator will conduct the mediation with fairness, ensuring that all parties have the opportunity to be heard.
- A mediator will ensure confidentiality of the process unless compelled to disclosure by law.

- A mediator will ensure each party's right to counsel before agreeing to any resulting non-binding agreement.

In 1998, George Mitchell was awarded the Liberty Medal for his work in mediating the Agreement. He was tapped by President Barack Obama as an envoy to the Middle East in 2009. Though he resigned that commission in 2010 with little overt progress, Mitchell will never be forgotten for his work in Ireland. Though hard times have came back during the global recession, in 2005, according to the *Economist* magazine, the Republic was named the best place to live in the world.

The Peace People

For successful mediations like that in Ireland, more than a good mediator is needed. The parties involved must have courage and be willing to come to the table. Often outside influences, such as media coverage or activist group pressure, have an important impact on the parties involved.

In Ireland during the mid–70s, television broadcasts of the horrors of violence were beginning to bring world opinion to bear on the conflict. On a local front, one particular incident, and one particular woman's witnessing of a single violent act, became the wrenching heart of a people.

On the tenth of August 1976, an Irish Republican Army fugitive had been fatally shot in Belfast by British authorities. As Danny Lennon's car came careening around a corner, the Maguire children were walking with their mother. Lennon's car plowed into the children, killing three.

Betty Williams was not far away. She was driving home with one of her two children when she heard the gunshots. Turning the corner, she saw the Maguire children and their hysterical mother.

"A deep sense of frustration at the mindless stupidity of the continuing violence," Ms. Williams later said, "was already evident before the tragic events of that sunny afternoon of August 10, 1976. But the deaths of those four young people in one terrible moment of violence caused that frustration to explode, and create the possibility of a real peace movement.... As far as we are concerned, every single death in the last eight years, and every death in every war that was ever fought represents life needlessly wasted, a mother's labour spurned."[4]

Betty Williams acted. In a few days, she had 6,000 signatures on a petition to stop the violence. She and Anne Maguire's sister, Mairead Corrigan Maguire, co-founded an organization, Women for Peace. Later with Ciaran McKeown the group became The Community for Peace People.

Soon, the women organized a peace march that gathered 10,000 frustrated and war-ravaged citizens. The following week, a second march drew 35,000 and was instrumental in not only honoring the death of the children but also in demanding that the parties mediate their differences and put an end to the violence.

The first declaration of the Peace People is a "simple message" to the world: "to live and love and build a just and peaceful society."[5]

Sadly, the children's mother, Anne Maguire, committed suicide in 1980. Williams, Maguire and McKeown went on to work for peace. They earned the Nobel Peace Prize in 1976. When the parties to the Northern Ireland conflict convened at the bargaining table in the late 1990s, the heart-wrenching memories of the Maguire children were present at the table.

Meditation brings wisdom; lack of mediation leaves ignorance. Know well what leads you forward and what holds you back, and choose the path that leads to wisdom. — Siddhartha Gautama, *the Buddha*

5

Arbitration Techniques: The WTO TRIPPS Agreement (1995)

The hearing and determination of a dispute by a third party arbiter; an imposed settlement technique agreed to by the disputants or referred by a court or legislature.

As new medicines are discovered, tensions naturally grow between those needing expensive pharmaceuticals and those selling the products. The multinational corporations that own the patents feel justified in recovering research expenses and delivering a fair return to stockholders. Yet many in the world believe that everyone, even those too poor to afford the cost, should benefit from life-saving discoveries.

Conflicts between private and communal rights have always been a source of tension, from land ownership to water rights. These disagreements are most heart wrenching when it comes to the sale and distribution of medicines that will prevent millions of deaths, such as those addressing HIV/AIDS.

In the 1990s, 76 percent of HIV/AIDS deaths occurred in Sub-Saharan Africa.[1] As the death toll mounted, developing countries such as South Africa and Côte d'Ivoire naturally began calling for lower prices on vital drugs.

The pharmaceutical companies dug in their heels. Patents for the most common anti-retroviral drugs such as AZT were held by the British-based pharmaceutical company GlaxoSmithKline (GSK) and German-based Boehringer Ingelheim (BI). They held that continuing the research for improved drugs for a wide range of diseases, including potential pandemics, depends on income generated from current drugs.

Those on the side of communal rights argued that to restrict the flow of anti-retroviral drugs for HIV/AIDS increased new cases of AIDS. High prices, they said, contributed to more people dying and spreading the disease, especially those in poverty conditions.

Both sides in the controversy had legitimate moral and legal claims that resulted in a continuous impasse. As the world debated, thousands continued to die. To make matters worse, a fair and just solution was hampered by outdated organizations that could no longer deal with concerns that were increasingly technical and global in scope.

The General Agreement on Tariffs and Trade (GATT) was a post–World War II relic. In the early 90s, GATT tried responding to the dispute with the Agreement on Trade-Related Aspects of Intellectual Property Rights (TRIPPS). The TRIPPS agreement set minimum standards for property right protection. It covered copyrights for performers, sound recordings and broadcasts, designs for integrated circuits, new plant varieties, trademarks, and other "creations of their minds," including pharmaceuticals.[2]

Yet GATT lacked full arbitration authority and the TRIPPS agreement fell short of a solution. As tension and polarization increased in the pharmaceutical dispute, the vacuum created by the world's indecision provided for increasing animosity between nations and a rising condition for violence.

The Virtue of Decisiveness

The late fourteenth century French word for arbitrate is to "decide" or "to cut off." Often a professional arbiter, or objective decider, is brought in to have a full airing of the sides in a dispute. After the adequate presentation of an issue, the arbitrator cuts off debate, then makes an objective decision based on their personal expertise or judicious character.

In the early '90s, the world found itself without the means for decisiveness on a complex global issue. In recognition of that untenable situation, the international community formed a new body, the World Trade Organization (WTO), to correct some of the problems with GATT. Created in 1994, the WTO had the power to make its arbitrated decisions count. If a member nation has an internal law or action by citizens that counteracts a WTO agreement, the WTO can authorize trade sanctions against that nation.

When the HIV/AIDS drug debate was brought before the Geneva Ministerial Council of the WTO, worldwide attention was focused on the painful realities of the issue. After much deliberation, expert testimony, and the development of some very creative language, the Council managed to hammer out an agreement to solve the critical pharmaceutical dispute.

The WTO agreement included the means for both sides to achieve many of their goals. Yet the arbitrated agreement, on the whole, was a victory for

World Trade Organization headquarters, Geneva (World Trade Organization).

developing countries. It allowed for fast track licensing and parallel importing of generic drugs to the countries of Sub-Saharan Africa. The patent-holding companies would receive reduced royalties of up to 5 percent on the net sale price of their "innovative" health products to that region.

The World Trade Organization now has over 150 member nations and decisions in global disputes are made by consensus. The WTO is not only responsible for global trade agreements but also for policing member nations. As with any nonviolent solution, attention to the process continues after the solution is found.

In the case of the TRIPPS treaty, increasing concerns of poorer nations about strict interpretation by pharmaceutical companies demanded an additional resolution. The DOHA Declaration in 2001 added an idealistic clarification that the agreement should "promote access to medicines for all."[3]

America's Favorite Pastime

There are four main forms of arbitration. Judicial Arbitration is simply a court process for small claims, especially in the United Kingdom. Bracketed Arbitration is where an agreement has been reached but a third-party arbitrator will determine the compensation between an agreed upon amount. A Non-

Binding Arbitration, the most common of the types, is intended to facilitate but not bind the parties in an agreement. If the parties do not agree with the award, they may continue their claims in another venue.

The fourth type of arbitration is called Pendulum Arbitration and is useful for trade union disputes. It has come to be known as Baseball Arbitration because of a very high-profile settlement in the world of sports.

Since 1842 when baseball took the form of an organizational sport between baseball clubs, compensation for ballplayers has been an issue of contention. In the beginning, players paid dues to be in a club that rented a playing field, such as the Elysian Fields in New Jersey where in 1845 the New York City club the Knickerbockers convened in some of the original play.

In another development in the history of baseball, the Cincinnati Redstockings in 1869 were the first team to acknowledge that their players were paid. Two years later, the first formal league was established and competition for players began to rise. When teams began to raid players from other teams, the owners struck a practical bargain to "reserve" players before the seasons began.

The "reserve clause" worked well for the next century. However, as baseball ascended to become America's favorite pastime, players began to negotiate for higher compensation. By the 1970s, labor disputes had taken on the form of labor unions and strikes. As high-profile compensation packages were negotiated, the disputes began to tarnish the game's reputation from the old days when players, as the saying goes, played "for the love of the game."

In 1972, the situation took a turn for the worse. Team owners refused to negotiate with their players. The ballplayers responded with a league-wide strike. As the regular season started with no game played, the owners reluctantly came to the table with major concessions.

With that success by players, the stage was set for yearly strikes when contracts came up for renewal. As part of the negotiations in 1973, the owners agreed to submit to a system of arbitration for contract disputes. Owners and players would provide to arbitrators a "final offer" over salary disputes. The arbitrator would consider both sides and choose one of the packages. Both parties were bound by the agreement.

In 1975, the reserve system was severely tested when players Messersmith and McNally went a full season without signing a contract. When their teams automatically renewed their contracts, the dispute was turned over to arbitrator Peter Seitz. The decision sided with the players and struck down the reserve clause, which created a new "free agent" system.

Around the same time, pitcher Catfish Hunter entered a salary dispute with his team, the Oakland Athletics. The case was turned over to an arbitrator who voided Hunter's contract and made him a free agent. When Hunter decided to sign with the New York Yankees for a substantial salary increase, Hunter set the stage for decades of huge compensation packages.

By the 1980s, desperate team owners agreed to a system of collusion, much like the reserve clause, where they agreed not to bid on other players contracts. The players again responded by testing this "gentleman's agreement" in court and the owner's lost much of their bargaining power.

Strikes and salary arbitration continued until 2002, when teams and players reached an agreement for the first time without a strike. The arbitration technique between labor unions and corporations are now referred to as Baseball Arbitration, a form of Pendulum Arbitration.

In these "last offer arbitration" cases, the arbitrator's decision is limited to choosing between two alternatives with no leeway for altering the settlement. Still, arbitration's influence on America's favorite pastime continues to evolve with strong opinions by fans, owners, and players alike, year after year.

The Global Fund

There are some disputes that require more than a mediated or arbitrated settlement, such as the global AIDS epidemic. The fact that a problem is global in nature, and requires a global solution, does not make it any less local and personal in effect. The AIDS/HIV epidemic is so pervasive that the empathy of the world is required to stem the tide of person-to-person contractions.

"All i [sic] could think about now are my kids," wrote a mother in Africa with a healthy attack cell (CD) count of a dangerously low 54. "My doctor said is gonna put me on treatment immediately. I dont know if i should be happy or worried for the treatment because i think it might be too late. I love my kids soo much n i dont want to leave them all alone in this world."[4]

The international funding organization The Global Fund was established while the world waited on an arbitrated solution to the distribution of medicine. The Fund's creation was a unified attempt by private and public institutions, as well as financial companies, to prevent millions of new stories like this mother's in Africa.

With over $21 billion committed to date, The Global Fund is working in 150 countries on large-scale prevention programs AIDS treatment for AIDS treatments, anti-tuberculosis medicines, and insect-treated nets to stop the ravages of malaria. It is estimated that the programs have saved 6.5 million lives and prevented even more devastating statistics from the spread of AIDS.

Today because of treatment options and programs like The Global Fund, though more people are becoming infected, fewer people are dying of

AIDS/HIV. The strong arm of arbitration, combined with the helping hand of generous spirits, have helped turn the tide.

> *Gentlemen, I fervently trust that before long the principle of arbitration may win such confidence as to justify its extension to a wider field of international differences.* — Sir Henry Campbell-Bannerman, English prime minister

> *Do I believe in arbitration? I do. But not in arbitration between the lion and the lamb, in which the lamb is in the morning found inside the lion.* — Samuel Gompers, founder of the American Federation of Labor (AFL)

6

Peacekeeping: East Timor Independence (1999)

To create a safe condition for peace in areas torn by conflict; the maintenance of a truce between nations or communities by an international peacekeeping force.

During the oppressive military occupation of Timor by Indonesia, conflict-related deaths from killings, hunger, and resulting illness are estimated at over 60,000.[1] In a sustained and bloody campaign from 1975 to 1999, the ragtag guerrilla resistance force Falintil battled the well-armed and increasingly brutal Indonesian army.

Located in Southeast Asia just northwest of Australia, the tiny island of Timor is one of over 17,000 islands in the huge Indonesian archipelago. Ruled by Portugal and the Dutch since the sixteenth century, Indonesia was occupied by Japan during World War II. Two days after the Japanese surrender, the islands declared their independence and appointed strongman Sukarno as president of a unified country.

Yet many islands felt little loyalty to the central government in Jakarta, and in 1975 East Timor declared its independence. When Indonesia reacted by invading the island with military forces, the people of East Timor resisted with a guerrilla campaign.

Several political parties, some pro–and some anti–Indonesian, emerged as leaders in the Timor provincial government. After Indonesia declared and banned the pro-independence party of East Timor as a communist plot by China, a civil war erupted.

The United Nations Security Council called for an end to the occupation, but the United States, an ardent ally of anti-communist president Suharto, who succeeded Sukarno, blocked sanctions. In the wake of Vietnam, the "domino effect" was still a pillar of U.S. policy. When one domino fell to the communists, the theory maintained, others such as Indonesia would follow.

In the last decades of the twentieth century, East Timor's guerrilla resistance ramped up to where thousands of innocents were dying from battles and collateral damage. The Santa Cruz Massacre, in which 180 people died, exposed the brutality of the Indonesian military.[2] Television cameras filmed footage of soldiers beating citizens and reporters, which horrified the international community and led to widespread condemnation of the occupation.

The Virtue of Calmness

When thousands of people are dying, a cessation of violence is not necessary for diplomatic efforts to take place. Yet a state of relative calm clearly helps prepare the ground for a peace process. The parties in East Timor, reeling from horrible atrocities and repression, needed a glimpse of calm to see beyond the fog of war.

The word calm is derived from the Latin "cauma," a time when there is relief from the hot sun. In war, a time out of the heat of violence allows tensions to release and reason to gain the upper hand.

In 1999 the United States and Australia changed policy and allowed the United Nations to pass an act of self-determination for East Timor. With the threat of a large international peacekeeping force in East Timor, Indonesia was forced to stop the brutality and allow a popular referendum.

A large majority, 78.5 percent of voters, chose independence. The Indonesian military and militias responded with increased brutality. Yet the people of East Timor had spoken with nearly one voice.

A regional U.N. peacekeeping contingent of mainly Australian forces landed in Timor to restore the calm. Pushing the militias into West Timor, the INTERFET peacekeepers forced the Indonesian army to withdraw. INTERFET was soon replaced by a U.N. international police force, which was also led by regional power Australia.

A U.N. Crime Scene Detachment (UNTAET) began investigating wartime atrocities. In 2000, the parties in the dispute convened in a working meeting to revise strategies and identify how to move forward.

José Ramos-Horta, in exile from his homeland, was a man of calm and determination, having received a master's degree in peace studies at Antioch College in the United States. He had received international attention for his peacework during exile and, because of his urging for a peaceful solution in Timor, he received the Nobel Peace Prize in 1999 with his fellow countryman, Bishop Ximenes Belo.

When the U.N.–sponsored workshop was convened, Ramos-Horta returned to lead the East Timorese delegation. Under his steadfast leadership, the peace conference etched out a blueprint for a joint administration of the state by contending political parties.

On May 20, 2002, the Transitional Cabinet was created. Due to international pressure, strong leaders like Ramos-Horta, and the will of the people, East Timor gained full independence.

The Call of a Leader

Since the Democratic Republic of Timor-Leste was created, political battles have continued to shake the sovereign island, including an assassination attempt in 2008 on President Ramos-Horta.

In 2006, a disgruntled soldier mounted a coup attempt and instigated riots in the town of Dili. Before Australia and other regional states intervened with peacekeeping forces, forty people were killed, including the rebel leader.

Two months after rebel gunmen shot José Ramos-Horta in the lung, the embattled president of East Timor stood in front of a press conference with one message: we must achieve peace and end the violence.

"I don't want anybody to die," he said, holding back his tears. "Gastao should surrender to justice and hand over his weapons."[3] He felt a little naive to believe the rebels would lay down their arms, but that was the conundrum of a Nobel Peace Prize winner thrust into the belly of violence.

There were many times when Horta wanted to shun public service and pursue his dream of writing a novel and having a life of calm and serenity. Yet his history is a microcosm of the colonial history, struggle, and personal tragedy of East Timor.

His Portuguese father had been exiled by the Salazar dictatorship to Timor, which was then a Portuguese colony. His Timorese mother experienced the loss of four children killed by the Indonesian military. Young José was educated at a Catholic mission in the small village where he would later found the Revolutionary Front for an Independent East Timor (FRETILIN).

At only twenty-five years old, Ramos-Horta became spokesperson in exile for the independence movement. For ten years in New York and other cities he kept the struggle alive in the minds of the world with a persistence and personality that engendered support. "People were more sympathetic to me than to the cause itself, in a sense. Because by then they knew me and they liked me. They were prepared to put up with me, listen to me, but I don't think they believed much in the cause itself, in the sense that for them it was a lost cause. A lot of them would vote with the resolutions because of me, not because they believed in the issue."[4]

When he was elected president of the new Democratic Republic of Timor-Leste, Ramos-Horta brought the country's history with him. From colonization and dictatorship to exiled governments and war for independence, he embodied the hopes of a people dealing with the reality of mixed and often opposing cultures. Indigenous Austronesian and Melanesian roots with influences of Portuguese, Roman Catholic, and Malaysian domination, the democratic story of East Timor owes no small debt to those like Horta with the disposition of calm and balance.

"I never accept being locked in an ideological straitjacket," he said. "I see good and bad in all sides. The left cannot claim to have all the virtues. The left has failed miserably over the decades. And the right don't have a monopoly on virtues, or on evil."[5]

In the assassination attempt that put bullets in the president's lung, two of the rebels were killed and one of Ramos-Horta's guards was wounded. Flown to a medical facility in Australia, Horta was put on life support and rendered unconscious by induced coma. When he awoke, he said he remembered every detail of the shooting. All of the emotions of violence undoubtedly ran through his mind: anger, bitterness, revenge, even a desire to kill his adversaries.

Yet, characteristically, he chose calm in the midst of violence. Even when his fellow countrymen were dying, he was steadfast for peace. "I have been sending messages to Timor saying 'no violence, no violence.' I don't want to see one Indonesian or one collaborator harmed. [Civil war] will take place only if Indonesia foments it, which they are likely to do. But if they don't do it, I don't see why there would be civil war. An overwhelming majority of the people will vote for independence."[6]

Blue Helmets the World Over

The calm that enabled a democratic movement in East Timor to take root has also made it possible in many other countries around the globe. The United Nations peacekeeping operation is a direct result of the lofty goals of the United Nations. As stated in the originating documents, the organization is intended to achieve world peace.

The organization was formed in 1945 in the wake of World War II and the failure of a weakened League of Nations. Today, with offices and actions around the globe, the United Nations comprises over 190 nations. Its committees, agencies, and missions have had and continue to have a profound impact on global issues such as health, security, international law, economic vitality, social conditions, and the human rights of women and children.

United Nations peacekeeping forces arrive in Abyei on the border of Sudan and the
new country of South Sudan (U.N. photograph, used by permission).

The General Assembly debates the great issue of the day at its headquarters in New York. The Security Council, which has the five permanent members of China, France, Russian Federation, the United Kingdom, and the
United States, as well as ten rotating members, decides resolutions in matters
of peace and security. The Economic and Social Council, the Secretariat, the
International Court of Justice, and the Trustee Council each provide services
in support of the main goal of world peace.

In addition to high profile and important work of such organizations as
the World Food Program (WFP) and the Children's Fund (UNICEF), the
United Nations maintains security forces in some of the most troubled spots
in the world. The "Blue Helmets," as the international forces are called, keep
warring armies apart and enforce peace agreements on a daily basis. During
this century, U.N. peacekeepers have been sent on missions to the following:

- Sierra Leone civil war
- Eritrean-Ethiopian war
- Burundi civil war
- Democratic of the Congo war
- war in Central African Republic and Chad
- humanitarian and police missions in Haiti
- elections in Tajikistan

- Abkhazian war
- Bosnian war
- Previaka territorial dispute
- Iraq-Kuwait Gulf War

Current deployment of United Nations peacekeeping forces, as of this writing, include the following:

- Second Liberian civil war
- civil war in Ivory Coast
- Sudanese civil war and the Darfur conflict
- Second Congo war
- South Kordofan conflict
- Haiti rebellion
- Afghanistan war
- Libyan civil war

It is an understatement to say that not all of the United Nations peace-keeping missions have had full support from the international community. Many resolutions for deploying Blue Helmets have been vetoed by one or more members of the Security Council for diverse reasons. Many issues of the day have strategic implications for the political and national interests of one or more Council members.

During the 2011 Arab Spring uprisings, a contentious deployment resolution was made regarding the Libyan Civil War. The president of Libya, Colonel Muammar Gaddafi, came to power in a coup in 1969 and ruled for over forty years. During the Arab Spring when rebel forces mounted a campaign to depose Gaddafi and install a democratic government, loyal troops as well as mercenaries promised a brutal and potentially genocidal retribution.

To prevent another Rwanda, where the world watched as over 800,000 people were killed, U.S. president Obama, French president Sarkozy, Italian prime minister Burlesconi and others, including some leaders of Arab nations, unified in their condemnation. United Nations Security Council Resolution 1973 demanded a ceasefire and called for the international community to establish a no-fly zone to keep Gaddafi's air force from destroying towns and killing civilians in rebel strongholds.

The United States used high-tech weaponry to decimate the Libyan air force. NATO forces took command of the operation but the war bogged down for logistical and political reasons. Soon the original resolution seemed insufficient to remove Gaddafi. Civilians were dying not only because of Gaddafi's forces but also because of NATO bombing.

The Libyan resolution is a case history of the challenges facing any armed mission the United Nations decides to initiate. When do military operations by the United Nations contribute to the mission of achieving world peace? And when do such military interventions simply become another confusing and deliberate act of war?

Such questions are for the consideration of the General Assembly and the Security Council. The long and distinguished history of the Blue Helmets will not be diminished by the complexity of current issues, but the world needs to be vigilant that the United Nations does not go the way of the League of Nations.

The success of United Nations missions in areas like the Indonesian archipelago gives the world hope for the future. Four peacekeeping missions have been mounted in East Timor. Forces were first sent during the 1990s in response to the Indonesian invasion and occupation. The continuing mission is to support the transition to independence.

Today, Timor-Leste is a success story among the community of nations and a member in good standing of the United Nations. It holds elections in the relative calm supported by the Blue Helmets.

U.N. peacekeeping operations are now increasingly complex and multi-dimensional, going beyond monitoring a ceasefire to actually bringing failed States back to life, often after decades of conflict. — Kofi Annan, Ghanaian diplomat, U.N. secretary general

Peace is a fulltime job. It's protecting civilians, overseeing elections, and disarming ex-combatants. The U.N. has over 100,000 Peacekeepers on the ground, in places others can't or won't go, doing things others can't or won't do. Peace, like war, must be waged. — George Clooney, American actor, U.N. messenger of peace

7

Economic Aid: Economic Aid to Africa (2008)

Monetary or other kinds of non-military help provided during a humanitarian crisis or to achieve a socioeconomic objective; also termed international aid, overseas aid, or foreign aid.

Every second of every day one person dies as a direct or indirect result of hunger. One child dies every five seconds.[1]

Though world food production is estimated to be enough to feed twice our current population, hunger and poverty continue to fuel serious humanitarian needs. The funds that nations allocate for economic aid seem fairly minimal when compared to the hundreds of billions spent on military arms and operations.

Yet the spirit of giving, fortunately, is a fundamental part of the human character as well as many national creeds. In the first part of this century, for instance, American aid to Sub-Saharan Africa doubled to over $4 billion. During the same period, European countries increased their aid to over $21 billion.[2]

Economic aid is a relatively small but important part of each nation's budgetary debate about priorities, which have changed significantly since September 11, 2001. Global military spending reached $1.6 trillion in 2010, of which the U.S. provides over 40 percent.[3] Much of that U.S. total, over $700 billion, went to the Department of Defense, security-related issues, and to fund the wars. Three billion of the U.S. budget was committed to what was termed the Economic Support Fund and the Millennium Challenge Corporation, which distributed aid to "encourage economic freedom." Those monies were tied mostly to security issues in areas such as Israel, Pakistan, Jordan, Egypt, and small oil producing nations such as Kuwait and Libya. Over one

53

An 18-month-old girl is spoon-fed a ready-to-use therapeutic food at a food distribution site in Niger (UNICEF/NYHQ2010-1584/Pierre Holtz).

billion went for infrastructure rebuilding in Afghanistan and Iraq as part of the Global War on Terror.

The Global HIV/AIDS initiative received $7.5 million, a paltry amount when compared with defense expenditures. Economic Aid programs received only $6.5 million. The debate of "guns or butter" in what choice is better for our global security continues with the latter ever losing the contest.

The money that nations do spend on foreign aid has always been steeped in controversy due to the difficulty in measuring results, especially in Africa where problems seem intractable. With their vast reservoir of natural resources, from iron and manganese to platinum and diamonds, African countries are theoretically some of the richest nations. However, much of these nations' resources have been "colonialized" and taken out of the country to create wealth for those in more developed nations. As testament to the situation, 40 percent of the people in African countries live on less than one dollar a day.

The roots of Africa's economic problems, arguably, are linked to historical tribal wars and an abusive colonial past. Rampant corruption and inefficient distribution systems are also to blame. In addition, debt servicing from international loans takes much of many nations' exporting profits. Together with plunging commodity prices, these conditions keep Africa one of the poorest continents on the globe.

The Virtue of Generosity

Until the roots of poverty and hunger are eradicated in all countries, the need for individual, group, and governmental generosity will be high. Derived from the Latin for "of noble birth," generosity calls to the highest values of humanity and of national consciousness.

Alms-giving, charity, hospitality, philanthropy — the synonyms for humanity's generosity of spirit ring with the long history of noble actions. Through the centuries, help in the form of monetary donations, volunteer service, and in-kind products have come from individuals as well as nations.

In modern times, wealthier countries provide two main types of economic aid. Humanitarian aid is offered in emergency situations such as famine and natural disasters. Development aid is used to foster a sustainable economy in areas that have a pattern of poverty or instability.

Bilateral aid is when one country gives directly to another. When multiple countries combine resources to solve a particular problem, it is called multilateral aid. An international agency, such as the World Bank or the European Development Fund, is usually the medium for multilateral aid.

No matter where you live, the ravages of poverty and hunger are apparent to those who will open their eyes. According to the United Nations, "Fundamentally, poverty is a denial of choices and opportunities, a violation of human dignity."

Around the world, nearly two billion of our seven billion mass of humanity are living without clean water, adequate nutrition, health care, or simple clothing and shelter. Even in the largest economy in the world, the United States of America, around 17 percent of citizens live below the federally established poverty line.

Another measure of the great need in the world for aid is a full appreciation of those who go to bed hungry. Malnutrition is caused by improper diets, which leads to disease and sometimes death. Starvation comes from exhaustion of the body due to lack of food and often precedes death.

When most of us go into a grocery and see the amount of food on the shelves, it is hard to believe that famine exists in many parts of the world. Famine is the scarcity of food that results in malnutrition, starvation, widespread epidemic, and high rates of mortality.

A year 2000 International Food Policy Research Institute report cautioned, "About 167 million children under five years of age, almost one-third of the developing world's children, are malnourished." The good news is that the world is taking better care of its own. "The most startling and important finding is that improvements in women's education have contributed by far the most, accounting for 43 percent in the reduction in child malnutrition between 1970 and 1995, while improvements in per capita food availability contributed about 26 percent."[4]

Non-Governmental Organizations (NGOs)

A modern innovation of generosity is the proliferation of nongovernmental organizations (NGOs) that serve needy populations all over the world. NGOs are U.N.–sanctioned organizations that are created specifically to provide humanitarian services. These nonprofit, charitable foundations, often with faith-based backing, help with food and water distribution, building homes and wells, and providing health care or financial support.

Nongovernmental organizations operate independently and do not have government status or an overt political agenda. Recognized by the United Nations in 1945, NGOs support health centers, schools, water projects, and thousands of other life-saving efforts.

There are over 40,000 international NGOs operating internationally with untold thousands working nationally and locally. The benefit of being independent allows the organizations to innovate and work in areas where the political situation would preclude another governmental organization from breaching borders. NGOs do charity work, provide essential services, and encourage and empower women and children at great risk of disease and famine.

Without the millions of volunteers who have been called to serve through NGOs over the past decades, the world would certainly be a bleaker place. "The door that nobody else will go in at," said Clara Barton who founded the Red Cross, "seems always to swing open widely for me."[5]

At the heart of volunteerism and economic aid is an altruistic motive to reduce suffering and make the world a better place. However, the urge to use financial support to change policy or gain allies in geopolitical struggles has often caused economic aid to be mired in controversy. Peace comes not from the roots of avarice and ambition, but rather from an open heart and understanding.

Often the stories of their success are both heart wrenching and inspiring. The NGO Save the Children tells the story of Deepchang, a fourteen-year-old orphan who lives in the slums of New Delhi. Two hours before dawn, the boy rises from his sleeping bag to pick through yesterday's trash for plastic bottles and metal cans to sell for a few *paise*. His sleeping bag is made from the same plastic bag he uses to pick up the trash.

A rag picker, Deepchang is not unlike other unschooled children in India. It is estimated that ten million young people are at risk, many spending twelve-hour days in factories, mines, and restaurants, or collecting trash in the heaping piles around the slums.

Even amidst such hardship, Deepchang still has dreams of receiving an education. Fulfillment of those dreams depends almost entirely on the Aviva Street-to-School Centre, a program run by Save the Children. "It's hard to teach them at times," said teacher Pradeep Kumar, "they're so exhausted."[6]

The Aviva school's mission is to teach the basics, from holding a pencil to sharing, in order to prepare them for a mainstream school.

Save the Children's worldwide programs are in 120 countries and support sixty-four million children. The organization is one of the largest nongovernmental organizations in the world. Along with such international entities as World Vision, the International Red Cross, and the Art of Living Foundation, Save the Children serves as a conduit between those who want to give money or volunteer to help some of the most destitute of humanity.

Personal Philanthropy

In addition to governments and NGOs, many private individuals and organizations provide philanthropic aid for a variety of motivations and goals. One of the highest profile organizations, the Bill and Melinda Gates Foundation, has a potential endowment of $60 billion, including most of the fortune of financier Warren Buffett.

Yet everyone can find a way to be generous. Domestic and foreign aid are not the exclusive domains of the wealthy. There are many things individuals without a great deal of money can do to help those in need. There are many practical ideas in books and on the Internet. Some are listed below, but there are many more creative ways to help put into practice by millions of concerned citizens.

- Participate in community service programs at work. Many corporations allow employees to choose a charity to help on company time
- Donate a vehicle and possibly earn a tax deduction
- Donate to the Red Cross (www.redcrossblood.org)
- Register with the National Marrow Donor Program to help those with bone marrow disease (www.marrow.org)
- Become an organ donor
- Donate your time as well as extra building and repair supplies to Habitat for Humanity (www.habitat.org)
- Some athletic shoe companies turn old shoes into playgrounds and ball courts (www.nikereuseashoe.com)
- Donate your wedding dress and unused gowns to combat metastatic breast cancer (www.makingmemories.org)
- The World Medical Relief organization redistributes old medicines to those in need (www.worldmedicalrelief.org)
- Donate canned goods to food pantries and homeless shelters
- Recycle old computers and phones for use in developing countries
- Donate old coats and clothing to charities to be distributed locally and globally
- Advocate for increased economic aid by calling or e-mailing your local representative

Most faith-based institutions, global NGOs, and local charities have innovative and easy ways to make a contribution. Citizens can volunteer at local food banks and shelters. Political pressure can be put on representatives to increase economic aid, especially when put in context of its impact on reducing global conflict and suffering.

> *Peace is the work of justice indirectly, in so far as justice removes the obstacles to peace, but it is the work of charity (love) directly, since charity, according to its very notion, causes peace.* — Saint Thomas Aquinas
>
> *Poverty is the worst form of violence.* — Mahatma Gandhi

8

Fair Trade: Fair Trade Certification Mark (1997)

Buying or selling goods and services under just and appropriate circumstances; a social movement or market-based approach to promoting sustainability for local economies.

On the upside, globalization has increased market opportunities for small producers by opening larger markets for farm and handicraft goods. On the downside, increased competition from multinational mega-farms has crunched prices to the point where small and medium-size farmers can barely scrape out a living.

For modern producers of handicrafts, cocoa, sugar, tea, bananas, honey, cotton, wine, fresh fruit, and in particular coffee, fair trade has become a matter of survival. According to the Quaker relief group Oxfam, coffee prices are at their lowest value in a century.

Over a hundred million *cafeteleros*, or coffee farmers and their families, have been reduced to poverty and hunger through unemployment or loss of markets. Coffee is a $70 billion industry but a sack of coffee worth $13,000 at the marked-up retail cup price in New York or London is only worth $70 to farmers.[1]

If a society seeks a higher level of morality, the pursuit of fairness cannot stop with protectionist strategies designed to keep only domestic products and producers earning a fair wage. With the increase in civil wars and regional conflicts, which affects everyone, wealthy countries cannot retreat within their borders and disregard the plight of the world's poor.

Reducing poverty, especially in troubled regions, is about global connectedness. Proponents of fair trade believe that ethical practices and policies can reverse the conditions of violent conflict caused by anger from inequalities

59

of commerce. The benefit of fair trade is a vibrant local economy for families, which has positive repercussions for peace in the world.

The Virtue of Justice

Trading between groups and communities goes back to prehistoric times, yet the concept of "fair" trade is fairly recent. A sense of justice in the marketplace reflects the evolution of a twelfth century word for the vindicated right of reward or punishment. Fair play, equity, and square deal, the common words for fair trade, establish a moral principle of economic justice that requires us to assure equitable return for a person's labor.

It wasn't until the 1940s that the fair trade movement began in earnest. Religious and social groups began to form organizations, such as the Mennonite Central Committee and SERRV International, to import handicrafts to help developing countries.

The fair trade movement has focused on the need to support marginalized farmers and workers before they are forced into decisions that have a rippling effect for the stability of their region. The movement's associations and policies help growers and artisans move from poverty to economic security through fair pricing and contracts.

Since the 1990s, sophisticated organizations have been developing standards for verifying and certifying fair trade goods and producers. Fair trade coffee producers must be small, family-based growers in democratic associations that encourage environmental stewardship. Coffee importers must agree to minimum pricing and cooperative financing.

The Fairtrade Labeling Organizations International (FLO), which formed in 1997 to inspect and certify producers, now works in over fifty countries. The European Fair Trade Association (EFTA) is a large network of traders that imports products from hundreds of disadvantaged groups in Africa, Asia, and Latin America. International aid organizations such as Catholic Relief Services and Oxfam also support the fair trade movement with funds and training.

Organizations for profit are also finding the fair trade culture is good for business. In 2006, Starbucks changed strategies and became the world's largest supplier of Certified Fair Trade with contracts for over forty million pounds in 2009.[2] In cooperation with Fairtrade Labeling Organizations International, Starbucks made a multi-year commitment to equitable sourcing.

In 2006, millions of small producers took advantage of fair trade funding, assistance, and development projects, with over two billion in sales of fair trade goods. Fair trade pricing and contracts now contribute to protection from commodity crises, stabilize communities, reduce poverty and displacement, and stop the roots of unrest and war.

Civilization Thriving Without War

Trade, simply put, is the transfer of goods and services from one person or group to another. In ancient times, a system of barter created the means of commerce. As precious metals and tokens of exchange were replaced by paper money and digital transactions, trade has in some ways become more complex with stock markets, government issuance, and financial institutions providing intermediaries between producers and consumers.

Yet trade between peoples is a prehistoric phenomenon. Exchanges of flint during the Stone Age and jewelry during the age of pharaohs shows the importance of trade in early societies. The Phoenicians were prolific traders on the Mediterranean Sea. The Greeks and Romans sold textiles on the coast of France and Spain.

Roman roads turned into highways, Nordic long boats turned into freighters, railroads ushered in delivery by air, and technological advances

Starbucks and other coffee retailers are moving toward an expanded offer of free trade coffee.

have now made trade on the Internet as important as local stores. The flow of goods and services between peoples has always increased communication and provided the basis for a relationship between cultures and nations.

What is the effect of trade on peace and war? In the Barranca province of Peru, archaeologists uncovered in 1948 the ancient city of Caral. Part of the Norte Chico civilization, Caral was thriving nearly 5,000 years ago. It is thought to be the oldest urban center in the Americas. With 60-foot pyramids, holy temples, and common houses, the metropolis spread out to over 150 acres.

What is important about Caral is that archaeological evidence showed that the society lived without warfare. The excavations found no weapons or battlements. There were no bodies from the violence we have all been pre-conditioned to expect — mutilations, sacrifices, or executions.

Caral was a society that thrived on a relatively extensive system of trade. Peruvian archaeologist Ruth Shady Solís has found evidence that the town served as a major trading center from the Amazon to the Andes. Fragments of the plant *achiote* from the rain forest and necklaces of snails point to commerce between distant civilizations. Trade with fishermen possibly included producing the cotton plant needed to make nets.

With no evidence of warfare, Caral has archaeologists questioning one of the most deeply held beliefs — that early civilizations were based on security and warfare. With Caral flourishing as a trade center during the third century B.C.E., the theory of violence many believe to be the primary pre-condition for civilization may, in fact, be wrong.

A system of free trade among peoples must be based on the free flow of commerce across boundaries. Whether between tribal cultures or complex modern nation-states, free trade is a choice that both societies make to let trade become mutually beneficial.

With limited interference from local governments, free trade relies on natural supply and demand to determine production and prices. Proponents of free trade point to the negative aspects of trade-distorting protectionism. The positive effects of the free movement of labor, capital, and the resulting products and services result in many potential advantages:

- Lower prices through competition
- Increased production resulting from more sales
- High efficiency production due to specialization
- Increased customer satisfaction from higher quality
- More innovation due to entrepreneurship
- Increased wages due to increased exporting
- More efficient allocation of local resources

- Increased communication between countries and cultures
- Decreased tension between nations

On the other hand, protectionism is used by nations to protect the advantages of trade for its citizens. Tariffs, quotas, and other forms of trade barriers give a domestic advantage on many commodities and products, from steel and precious metals to oil and automobiles.

- Prevents unfair competition when other nations give subsidies
- Prevents dumping of below-cost goods to gain advantage
- Prevents a negative balance of trade
- Protects new technologies or infant industries
- Encourages and protects strategic industries
- Extends the life of declining industries
- Protects domestic employment

The Gravity of Globalization

Any serious debate about fair trade and free trade practices inevitably involves weighing of the benefits and ills of globalization. Former U.N. secretary-general Kofi Annan quipped, "It has been said that arguing against globalization is like arguing against the laws of gravity."[3]

With accelerated and pervasive means of transportation and communication, world trade has reduced the dependence and in some ways the importance of localities. The United States ships steel from China and fruit from Brazil. Remote islanders listen to the BBC News. And villagers around the world watch movies from Hollywood. Whether it is a medical supply, or an agricultural product, or a technological innovation, products, ideas, and raw materials routinely flow from country to country with increasing rapidity.

The benefits of globalization, in the view of many, are lifting the world out of isolation and poverty. As trade barriers such as tariffs and quotas between national borders are abandoned, proponents tout the efficiencies of competition and specialization in driving prosperity and choice.

Yet increased capital flow and labor migration, investment by multinational corporations, and the proliferation of technologies come with huge challenges for local populations. Societies, economies, and cultures are not only becoming interwoven but also homogenized.

"The negative side to globalization," said Australian sociologist Peter L. Berger, "is that it wipes out entire economic systems and in doing so wipes out the accompanying culture."[4]

Unification of the world's economies and acculturation of ideas, languages, and cultures has caused uncertainty and anxiety for localities competing in a world economy. Indeed, some believe that globalization actually increases the potential for conflict and war. The shift to outsourcing, for instance, can affect local jobs and lower wages. The growing incidence of worldwide economic crises puts local economies at the whims of global financiers. And the shifting needs for labor present new opportunities for exploitation of children.

As the debate continues over whether globalization is a natural and evolutionary model of human relations, the world must endeavor to understand the human element and the potential violence that comes in its wake. "It is people who are the objects of globalization and at the same time its subjects," said former president of Finland Tarja Halonen. "What also follows logically from this is that globalization is not a law of nature, but rather a process set in train by people."[5]

Globalization, according to this view, is a choice just as are decisions on whether we choose to create violence or peace. In the end, fair trade is a choice of individual consumers. Ethical consumerism is a conscious decision to buy goods and services that have minimal exploitation to people, animals, or the environment.

Such decision-making within a complex global economy requires a great deal of information. Consumers who consider themselves ethical, whether it be to "go green" or to practice fair trade buying, try to understand the interconnectedness of producing products.

Having a grasp on raw material acquisition, employment wages and conditions, environmental design, and other factors can be difficult. Yet for ethical consumers and those who value fair trade the drive to limit the violence of consumerism is a moral obligation.

Justice and power must be brought together, so that whatever is just may be powerful, and whatever is powerful may be just. — Blaise Pascal, French mathematician

The sort of peace in which we believe, and which we pursue, is comprehensive, just and lasting. It would enable the peoples of the region to realize total development, to improve their standard of living in the framework of stability, and to live in security and dignity. This is the peace which the peoples make, and defend with conviction. — King Hussein I of Jordan

9

Boycott: The "No Grapes" Boycott (1965–1975)

Withdraw from commercial or social relations with a country, organization, or person as a punishment or protest; legal sanctions to bring economic or social hardship in order to effect change.

The hardship of farm workers in the United States during the 1960s reflects the bittersweet journey of immigrant populations in many countries. To leave a homeland for one with better economic opportunity, only to be prevented from the promise of a better life, is a demoralizing experience amidst a dream of plenty.

The plight of farm workers in the bountiful fields of the southwestern United States had its roots in the Great Depression of the 1930s. As unemployed workers fled the Dust Bowl of the Great Plains for productive farmlands of California, wages plummeted and working conditions quickly deteriorated.

Through the '40s and '50s, as the Depression era became a distant memory, the demand by a prosperous nation for produce from the Southwest increased. In the wake of a shortage of American workers to harvest the crop, Congress passed Public Law 78 to encourage growers to hire Mexican workers.

These Hispanic *braceros* came from relative poverty and were willing to work for lower wages, longer hours, and in harsher conditions. Moving from town to town, state to state, these *braceros* "migrated" to where they could get work. In contrast to the millions benefiting from the American Dream, many migrant families lived in rundown shacks with no running water or electricity. Others lived in tents or under bridges.

In response to the degenerating state of workers, César Chávez and Dolores Huerta formed in 1962 what became the United Farm Workers Asso-

Founded in 1962 by Chávez and Huerta, the United Farm Workers of America continues to organize in major agricultural industries, forging contracts that have saved lives and benefited families (United Farm Workers, Jocelyn Sherman).

ciation. Born in Arizona, Chávez had labored in the fields around Delano, California, and was deeply moved when he saw migrant families barely surviving. As a rising leader of the movement for better wages and conditions, Chávez organized marches and protests to raise attention for the migrant workers' plight.

The Virtue of Discretion

Whether people accept the status quo when it is obvious there are injustices around them, or they decide to act according to their beliefs is a matter of personal choice. To have discretion, or to discern or make distinctions between right and wrong, is a precondition for action amidst injustice.

The value of discretion gives people a power over their lives. It allows them to make decisions, either to act or to abstain. Boycott is the societal version of personal discretion. With the power of one's attention, or money, people combine with others to have a larger effect on the world.

In 1965, Chávez and the United Farm Workers Association called for people to make a choice. They organized a strike against the powerful Schenley Liquor Company, partly to gain national attention and partly to increase membership in the union. Schenley owned most of the vineyards in the San Joaquin Valley so the work stoppage had a major impact on the harvest. The strike ended when growers were forced to sign contracts for better wages and benefits.

Optimistic with this success and expanding union membership, Chávez initiated the "No Grapes" boycott in the mid–1960s. Protesting deadly pesticides used in the fields, the boycott received national attention and significantly decreased sales of table grapes across America.

Chávez staged a personal hunger strike for twenty-five days to further increase public awareness. A Harris pole in 1975 found that seventeen million Americans were boycotting grapes.[1]

Under intense public pressure, Congress passed the Agricultural Labor Relations Act, which reaffirmed farm workers' rights to organize and bargain for contracts. Even the largest growers were forced to sign agreements with workers that standardized hours and improved living conditions.

The use of boycotting tactics has a long history of both failure and success. The term comes from the Irish land wars of the 1880s. Irish farmers demanded that Captain Charles Boycott, agent for an absentee English landowner, reduce high land rents. When Boycott evicted the troublemakers, the farmers stopped work, which forced Boycott to leave his post.

Another successful example of boycott was the Montgomery Bus Boycott of 1955, which resulted in the U.S. Supreme Court declaring Alabama's segregationist bus laws unconstitutional. In addition, the international "divestment boycott" of the 1980s eventually led to the breakdown of apartheid in South Africa.

A modern form of boycott is the "sanction," which is a penalty or reward instituted by a legal authority such as the U.N. in order to prevent or demand certain actions. For instance, the United Nations places sanctions on countries trying to develop weapons of mass destruction or that intended to commit genocide of a minority population.

From personal discernment, to societal choice and government policy, the virtue of discretion at the basis of boycott is continuously changing the world.

Newton and the Active Consumer

The principles behind consumer activism are in a very direct way based on the laws of physics. To take away the money or interest from an oppressive or abusive system will eventually bring down the system.

According to the first law of thermodynamics, all systems have energy. They obey the law of conservation of energy. Unless you put more energy into the system, it cannot continue. A system cannot create energy in and of itself.

The second law of thermodynamics states that the energy in a system will experience entropy. Again, unless you put more energy in, the system will become disordered or random. Eventually, it will collapse.

Like other forms of energy, the energy of violence and abusive trade needs to be constantly supported if it is to continue. Consumer activism is a method of making changes in that support. The goals of consumer activism are many, from ensuring the rights of citizens under oppression to fighting for the right to have healthy food.

The point is to make a change to a system of government, our economy, or even the social systems of our collective morality. If people withdraw support for a dictator, as history shows us, the regime will eventually fall. When laws are passed that prevent child labor in the workforce, the abusive energy of underage exploitation is taken away. In cases of mass boycotting, whether it be taking up the cause of migrants or advocating for more sustainable environmental practices, the energy of support for unfair practices disappears.

The history of consumer boycotts and activism can be categorized in three overlapping phases. The first was "consumer activism," which in the United States dates back to pre–Revolutionary War and the Boston Tea Party. Tactics for consumer activists included boycotts and protests, as well as lobbying for consumer laws and promoting objectives in the media.

The second phase is the "consumer movement," which focused on an attempt to create a consumer protection agency (CPA). Just when all hopes of creation seemed to be gone, U.S. president Barack Obama and Congress established the U.S. Consumer Financial Protection Bureau (CFPB), which is responsible for consumer protections. Whether this bureau will stand the test of time is debatable but precedent has been set.

The third phase is consumerism, which is an interesting development made possible by the availability of consumer products. This form of activism focuses on the actions and implications of consuming. The theory states that increasing consumption is good for the economy. We make decisions on our purchases and those decisions change the way our society works.

Today, with the explosion of new communications tools such as the Internet and social networking, consumer activism is becoming a powerful force for change. Consumer activists use the Internet for communicating information and creating spontaneous blogs and groups for special concerns.

These virtual activists try to make informed buying decisions based on a match between their values and research. To begin the work of consumer activism is a matter of becoming informed about where products come from and what products do. Indeed, the number of pressing issues and concerns can be daunting. There are hundreds, even thousands, of boycotts and consumer alerts happening at any one time around the world.

For those who become consumer advocates, there is usually a special issue that draws our attention. We hear about something, maybe animal rights or a health risk to the planet, then begin to research the topic. Usually there is an organization dedicated to improving things. In the case of animal rights there is People for the Ethical Treatment of Animals. In the case of environmentalism, there are the Sierra Club and the Nature Conservancy.

Once one is informed and connected, then comes the decision making. What do you buy? What stores do you frequent? Which companies are worthy of your purchasing stock? Do they value corporate responsibility?

The habit of making informed decisions is not only a skill to be developed but also a way of living. Many of us write positive letters to good companies and negative letters to those that need improvement. We discuss with our friends the issues. We let our families know that what they buy and support can make a difference.

The Truth Force of Consumer Activism

Consumer activism includes many tactics, including boycotting an unwanted law. Legislation and adjudication have profound effects on the morality and ethics of a society. Yet each law, each assault on the freedom and welfare of individuals, becomes a rallying point for change.

One such law was devised by the British parliament, which ended up creating a rallying point for a boycott that led to an increased call for independence of India. In the tradition of the original term named from the Irish farmer's nonpayment of Lord Boycott's rents in Ireland, boycott of rents and taxes can have a profound effect on the legitimacy of colonialism and occupation.

Such was the strategy of Mahatma Gandhi, who was one of the important leaders in the Indian independence movement in the 1930s when he conceived of the idea of the Salt Satyagraha. Meaning "truth force," Satyagraha conveys the principles of nonviolence that Gandhi based on the writings of Leo Tolstoy and others.

The Satyagraha action boycotting payment of the British salt tax is the specific action that is most associated with the collapse of England's occupation of the Indian peninsula. Mohandas Gandhi had studied the philosophy of Thoreau and Tolstoy and firmly fixed the Indian independence movement on a course of nonviolence with this much publicized, yet bloody March to the Sea.

To entrench their domination over the population and extend their monopoly of salt production, the British passed a law making it illegal to make salt unless a tax was paid to the Raj government. The Purna Swaraj declaration of independence had just been signed by the Indian National Congress on January 26, 1930.

Gandhi declared that he would boycott the law and make salt without paying the tax. He said, "Next to air and water, salt is perhaps the greatest necessity of life."[2]

The March to the Sea began with seventy participants near Gandhi's base of operation near Ahmedabad in February 1930. By the time the 390-kilometer march ended at the coast, the throngs had grown to hundreds of thousands.

When Gandhi scooped up the sand that contained the salt, he declared the tax morally wrong. The group, of which 80,000 were jailed and many killed, continued to make salt along the coast toward where there was to be a major protest at the Dharasana Salt Works.

Gandhi was arrested before he reached that British-controlled operation but his objective was already won. The world community had been alerted to the protest and opinion was shifting to the cause. Negotiations between the Raj and the Indian National Congress eventually resulted in Indian independence. The salt tax was repealed only with ascendancy of the interim presidency of Jawaharlal Nehru.

> *The consumer boycott is the only open door in the dark corridor of nothingness down which farm workers have had to walk for many years. It is a gate of hope through which they expect to find the sunlight of a better life for themselves and their families.* — César Chávez, American founder of the United Farm Worker's Association

> *Someday they'll give a war and nobody will come.* — Carl Sandburg, American writer

10

United Action: Poland's "Solidarność" Movement (1980)

Joining together for a common purpose or a common feeling to achieve an aim; to organize in a way that brings the energy of the many to bear on a problem or concern.

When the horrible Nazi menace was soundly defeated in 1945, the Soviet Union established a series of satellite states across a weakened Eastern Europe. One of these "Soviet Bloc" states was the bordering country of Poland.

After the fighting stopped, a communist government was quickly established. As had East Germany, Czechoslovakia, Hungary, Romania, Bulgaria, and Albania, Poland slid under oppressive and sometimes brutal Soviet control.

As the decades progressed, the power of the Soviets to hold the Bloc together began to wane. Poland's trade unions had gained the respect of citizens as a force for reform against the policies of the Communist government. In the 1950s and 1960s, there had been a series of strikes in Polish cities to protest working conditions and despotic rule. These rebellions were brutally crushed but laid the foundations for later actions against the puppet regime.

A shipyard electrician, Polish union worker Lech Walesa became a minor participant in a strike during the 1970s that resulted in four workers being killed by riot police.[1] Walesa was identified with the reform movement and accused of gathering signatures to memorialize the killed workers. He was fired from his job and found himself without employment and needing support from friends.

Finding courage in the solidarity of his co-workers, Lech Walesa and other activists soon formed the Free Trade Union of the Coast. The electrician turned trade union leader was arrested several more times for distributing leaflets and organizing an "anti-state" organization. During a 1980s action in the Lenin Shipyard of Gdansk, Walesa showed his determination and courage by scaling the wall of the shipyard. He soon became known as a major leader of the strikes that were increasing across Poland.

Under intense economic and political pressure from a nationwide general strike, the communist government under General Wojciech Jaruzelski grudgingly allowed unions to organize legally. Walesa took advantage of the new law by co-founding a free trade union called "Solidarność," or "Solidarity," which means "union of purpose."

Strikes continued at an increasing rate and an alarmed Jaruzelski declared martial law, reversed his decision, and outlawed the Solidarity union. Authorities arrested Walesa for "anti-social behavior" and he was sent to prison. After eleven months Walesa was released and returned to his job at the yard. Yet even after his imprisonment, the unrepentant organizer continued to agitate for reform.

The Virtue of Cooperation

It takes more than one man, no matter how courageous, to change a nation ruled by a despotic government. Walesa was one among many activists combining for a common purpose in Poland, but he became the face of the movement for millions. His organization was named Solidarity to acknowledge the power and value of combined vision and cooperation.

Walesa and his fellow activists knew that to change the status quo of a country or culture, especially one supported by a strong military, requires thousands, even millions, of people working together. Such mutual effort or joint action is needed to create the alliances, coalitions, and collaboration necessary to build a power base strong enough to challenge the structure of society.

Though the word collaboration took on a negative meaning during the great wars of the twentieth century — meaning collaborating with the enemy — the process of collaboration has become crucial for cooperative united action. Collaboration simply means working together toward a shared goal. With more people, resources, and creative ideas put to work, change can come faster and with a larger consensus for the outcome.

The Advantage of Collaborative Action

In Poland, the collaborative process took place through trade unions. Yet collaboration is a powerful peacemaking process used for everything from deposing dictators to planting gardens. People use many techniques to work together efficiently and effectively in support of their common goals.

Those who work in small or large collaborative processes can choose to have a leader or they can work in egalitarian groups or democratic committees. With the goal of improved performance and outcomes, collaborative groups are a creative process that taps into the collective experience and imagination of members.

Today there are sophisticated technologies for collaboration. Corporations and organizations, indeed peace groups, use collaborative workgroups to communicate, plan, and put actions into place. The use of collaborative software has enabled face-to-face meetings online with immediate access to charts, documents, graphs, and other helpful data for developing strategies and checking progress.

The process of collaboration has some distinct methods that increase its chances of success. The following is a brief overview of steps:

- Convene interested or required participants
- Choose a collaborative model
    Leadership roles
    Parity among participants
- Establish how decisions will be made
    Democratic or delegated
    Majority vote, consensus, or unanimous
    Steering committee and subcommittees rules
- Establish a functional plan
    Communication methods
    Expectations and accountability for members
    Additional resources and support needed
    Engagement and involvement processes
    Feedback and change procedures
    Reward and recognition methods
    Time and place for meetings
    Provision for disagreements and dissent
- Fine tune goals
    Establish objectives
    Identify significant milestones
    Apply resources to the objectives
- Evaluate progress
    Measure outcomes
    Identify further goals for group or individual action

The value of collaboration is in the synergy created through teamwork. The time put into defining the relationship between members will be well-spent. Collaborative groups must have a fundamental basis in goodwill. Members who have not bought into the process will eventually hinder achievement of the final goal. Collaboration depends on the trust and cooperation of participants, especially when meeting goals is difficult or, in Lech Walesa's case, potentially harmful to life and limb.

As events played out during the 1980s in Eastern Europe, Solidarity began to gain membership and the synergy of cooperation within Poland began to change the dynamics of power. Striking workers, not only in Poland but also across many of the Soviet Bloc states, began to receive attention from the international press.

Lech Walesa's name was increasingly associated with the Soviet Bloc's wider drive for freedom. In 1983, in recognition of his courage and actions, the former shipyard worker was awarded the Nobel Peace Prize. However, he was unable to leave Poland to receive it. Though officially treated by the Polish government as a regular worker, he was put under virtual house arrest until 1987.

The trade union Solidarity was becoming a powerful political party in Poland and a touchstone for world opinion. In the shadows of the declining influence of communism and Soviet rule, many of the satellite states began to introduce political and economic reforms.

Walesa was instrumental in forming a coalition government, the first in the Soviet Bloc that was not fully aligned with the communist party. Roundtable Talks began between trade union leaders and the Polish government. After tough negotiations, a breakthrough resulted in a government compromise and an agreement to hold semi-free elections.

In 1989 as the world press watched, Solidarity members swelled the election polls and the party won the majority in Parliament. Walesa was elected as president of Poland and served for five years. The shipyard electrician helped turn the communist nation toward a market-based economy with increasing political freedoms.

Today, the democratic nation of Poland is a member of the European Union. The formation of the Solidarity movement that unified Poland is considered an important milestone in the fall of the Soviet Bloc and communism throughout Eastern Europe.

Bad Guys Also Collaborate

The story of Poland is not unlike many other countries that used unity of action to break Warsaw Pact domination. Czechoslovakia, East Germany, Hungary, Romania, Bulgaria, Yugoslavia, and Albania all had vibrant anti–Soviet movements and moved toward democracy after the fall of the Soviet Union in the late 1980s.

What kept these nations under communist rule for four decades? Unfortunately, unity of action can be used in the hands of dictators to perpetuate violence. The communist party's Front of National Unity closed ranks around their satellite's puppet leaders, who used military action, internal spying, and propaganda to keep their populace under control. Unity of action became a tool of violence, its power used as a means of coercion instead of cooperation.

In Poland's case, the tools of power were in the hands of General Wojciech Jaruzelski. Born to the Polish gentry, schooled in a Catholic school, Jaruzelski was captured by the Soviet army and sent to work in the labor camps in the coal mines of Russia. Often shown covered by dark sunglasses, Jaruzelski's eyes were damaged by snow blindness from his experiences in the North.

When the Germans and Soviets clashed during World War II on the Eastern Front, Jaruzelski joined the First Polish Army, gaining the rank of lieutenant. After the war, he rose in the ranks to become Minister of Defense even though he had fought his Soviet masters. During this time he showed his changed loyalties by participating in anti–Semitic campaigns and the suppression of strikes.

An unlikely partner in the eventual peace process of the 1980s, Jaruzelski relied on what he had learned from his experiences in war. He resisted labor union advances by instituting martial law but the forces of nonviolent resistance had grown too strong. Jaruzelski had no choice but to agree to negotiations, which resulted in round table talks. A legislature and office of the presidency was created. Jaruzelski won the office by one vote, but as the pressure to share power grew, he resigned in 1990 and was replaced by Walesa in the first truly democratic election.

When unity fails because of weak cooperation by those falsely creating the unity, the power of unified action shifts from being a tool of tyrants to a method of nonviolent change. In such cases, men with ambivalent loyalties like Wojciech Jaruzelski often back-pedal on their decisions. For his support of the Warsaw Pact invasion of Czechoslovakia in 1968, the humbled dictator said it was a great "political and moral mistake." Such is blind unity in the hands of those ambivalent about the point of violence.

Liberty is not only a right, but also our common responsibility and duty.—
Lech Walesa, Polish founder of Solidarity Trade Union

Democracy is an objective. Democratization is a process. Democratization serves the cause of peace because it offers the possibility of justice and of progressive change without force.— Boutros Boutros-Ghali, Egyptian diplomat and former secretary-general of the U.N.

11

Civil Disobedience: The Civil Rights Movement (1955)

Refusal to obey laws in order to influence legislation or make changes in government; employment of nonviolent techniques to force concessions; in the past, called "passive resistance."

In the mid-twentieth century, Jim Crow laws and other forms of institutional racism were holding back the advancement of African Americans in the most prosperous nation in the world. Segregationist statues not only prevented the descendants of black slaves from achieving the American Dream but also from making a decent living and supporting their families.

Those laws began to be questioned and tested in ways that would change not only America but inspire the world. In 1955, Rosa Parks, a secretary for the National Association for the Advancement of Colored People (NAACP), drew attention to discrimination by refusing to comply with the Jim Crow law that prevented blacks from sitting at the front of a city bus. That same year, a young Baptist minister, Martin Luther King, Jr., began the Montgomery Bus Boycott that brought commerce in Montgomery, Alabama, to a standstill.

The boycott lasted over a year and tensions mounted, but the tactics of the fledgling Civil Rights Movement, such as sit-ins and protests, were making progress in bringing attention to abusive laws. A suit before the U.S. District Court resulted in a ruling that racial segregation on Montgomery city buses must finally end.

In 1957, the Reverend King helped found the Southern Christian Leadership Conference (SCLC) to energize black churches. Individual and group actions of civil disobedience increased throughout the South, as violence against black protestors was televised to a shocked nation.

King was arrested in 1963 and incarcerated, where he penned his famous

"Letter from a Birmingham Jail." Now considered an icon of American literature, the letter showed the influence on King of many African American leaders, including theologian Howard Therman and activist Bayard Rustin, who encouraged him to choose nonviolent methods. Therman and Rustin had studied the writings of Mahatma Gandhi, Thurman visiting Gandhi before the Indian leader's death.

With the help of the American Friends Service Committee (AFSC), King went to India in 1959 to meet Gandhi's family. The experience had a profound effect on his philosophy. He realized there were many examples of civil disobedience working to dismantle unjust laws and effect great changes, including

The Rev. Dr. Martin Luther King, Jr., leader of the American Civil Rights Movement, made an early decision to advocate nonviolence as the powerful strategy that could truly effect change (National Archives).

the creation of India and Pakistan after independence from Britain in 1948.

At the basis of the philosophy of nonviolent strategies is a moral power. When people resist oppression in a nonviolent manner, their energy becomes stronger than the immoral power of despotic rule. In choosing the nonviolent strategies of Jesus, Leo Tolstoy, Henry David Thoreau, and Mahatma Gandhi, Martin Luther King, Jr., took a courageous stand. By that choice, he ensured that those in the Civil Rights Movement in their historical quest for change would use the moral power of nonviolent marches, boycotts, and protests instead of the self-defeating power of violence.[1]

The Virtue of Dissent

The refusal to obey certain unjust laws or the demands of a government is at the core of nonviolent resistance. George Bernard Shaw once said, "The reasonable man adapts himself to the world; the unreasonable one persists in trying to adapt the world to himself. All progress depends on the unreasonable man."[2] Nonconformity may be an uncomfortable state of existence, yet for some to conform to laws that oppress and abuse is even more discomfiting. To dissent, or to register personal disapproval, hails from the fifteenth century Scottish word for differing in sentiment, or to feel or think differently.

Dissent takes on many forms with variations being used successfully in thousands of situations. From the Critical Mass bicycle celebrations that clog city streets to individual school protests by students protesting clothing rules, people use the tried-and-true methods of nonviolent civil disobedience to effect change:

- Street protests by individuals
- Protest marches by groups
- Pickets outside a business
- Sit-ins or die-ins in public spaces
- Sing-ins of protest songs
- Lockdowns to structures with chains and locks
- Public speeches and shouting

By 1963, more people in the United States had become uncomfortable with the status quo in the South and were putting pressure on the central government to act. With rising violence, including the bombing of Martin Luther King Jr.'s home, the Movement became an increasingly federal issue.

President Kennedy was fully prepared to use National Guard troops to ensure Federal laws were upheld. When Alabama governor George Wallace stood on the steps of the University of Alabama to keep two black students from enrolling, federalized troops made the governor step aside.

In that same historic year, at the March on Washington for Jobs and Freedom, King delivered his iconic "I Have a Dream" speech. To an estimated crowd of 250,000, the civil rights leader advocated and envisioned a world of the future that would dwell in racial harmony.

Following these events, President Lyndon Johnson pushed civil rights legislation, which the late President Kennedy had championed through a divided Congress. With King in attendance, Johnson signed the Civil Rights Act of 1964. That groundbreaking legislation was followed in 1965 by the National Voting Rights Act, which reiterated every citizen's right to vote.

The Rev. Dr. Martin Luther King, Jr., was awarded the Nobel Peace Prize in 1964 for his work to end racial segregation through nonviolent means. He continued to give inspiring speeches and lead marches until he was assas-

President Johnson signing the Civil Rights Act of 1964, with members of Congress and the Rev. Dr. Martin Luther King, Jr., looking on (National Archives, Cecil Stoughton, photographer).

sinated in Memphis, Tennessee, on April 4, 1968. King was posthumously awarded the Medal of Freedom in 1977. Martin Luther King, Jr., Day became a national holiday in 1986.

The Arab Spring

On December 10, 2010, a street vendor named Muhammad Bouazizi set himself on fire to protest his humiliation and anger with conditions in his homeland of Tunisia. As his body was engulfed in flames, he could not have know that his act of self-immolation would send waves of anger across the entire Middle East and result in the deposing of powerful and oppressive dictators.

After Bouazizi's act of civil disobedience, Tunisians began filling the streets. They protested high unemployment and food prices, lack of free speech, and human rights violations, as well as corruption and political oppression. Many of the protestors were young people with computers and smart phones connected to Facebook and Twitter pages and texted messages that urged action.

As thousands more Tunisians poured into the streets, President Zine El Abidine Ben Ali and his family fled the country. A caretaker government that included opposition leaders was formed, reformed, and finally began the rigor of governing after the revolution.

In Egypt, protests began in January 2011 and continued for eighteen days. The government of Hosni Mubarak shut down the Internet and allegedly encouraged anti-protestor bullies to fire into the crowds. The momentum of revolution was too great for Mubarak to stay in power. In February, he ceded power and left for one of his summer houses. The Egyptian army, respected by many of the protestors and pro-government groups, took power, lifted the nation's thirty-year continuous emergency laws, and promised free elections within six months.

"Days of rage" in other mostly Muslim countries around the Arab world were often planned for Fridays after the noon prayer. The organizing power of the call to prayer became an asset of demonstrators, driving the greatest number of people into the streets. Though considered a non-sectarian revolution, the Muslim influence over the resulting changes worried a Western world that would prefer secular democratic governments.

After Tunisia and Egypt, the world looked on as the popular revolt moved from Algeria and Jordon to Yemen and Bahrain. When Libyans took to the streets, the dictator Colonel Muammar al-Gaddafi and his supporters dug in their heels and promised to wipe the threat of revolution from the country with major bloodshed. As rebels began to take over much of the country's territory, Gaddafi made good on his promise and sent his air force, army, and paid mercenaries to kill the rebels and any citizens who supported their cause.

The United Nations, at the urging of many Security Council members such as France, Italy, and the United States, passed Resolution 1973, which was intended to prevent Gaddafi from massacring his people. When the dictator held onto power, NATO warplanes and American drones pummeled the capital of Tripoli and increased their intervention.

The risk associated with Western military support for rebels in Libya, even though many of the Arab states agreed to the initial Resolution, prevented open outside intervention intended for regime change. The West applied sanctions and made supportive statements and, in the end, increased military support until the dictator was driven from power.

Many countries in the wider area were affected. Sudan's president Omar al-Bashir bowed under the added pressure to his being indicted by the International Criminal Court and announced that he would not seek re-election.

In Jordan, King Abdullah appointed a new prime minister and charged him with forming a new government. The president of Yemen, Ali Abdullah Saleh, first announced he would step down, then backed out of the offer, causing further unrest. In Kuwait, the emir gave citizens 1,000 dinars ($4,000). In Bahrain, a group of petitioners called for universal suffrage and reform of the Federal National Council.

In Lebanon, thousands took to the streets and called for Hezbollah to disarm and for the rule of law to take precedence over rule by weapons. In Mauritania, protestors and a public self-immolation forced the mayor of Awjeft to resign. In Qatar, the ruling regime worked to prevent social networking sites from fomenting revolutionary fervor.

In Syria, President Bashar Al-Assad took military action to stop the rising revolutionary fervor. Following the footsteps of his father, Hefez Al-Assad, Bashar quickly began a brutal retaliation that killed thousands of his countrymen. For decades, the Assad family had kept the Baath Party in power by use of an extensive network of secret police and tactics of imprisonment and torture.

In Saudi Arabia, with a huge reservoir of oil needed by the West, the army endeavored to keep the status quo. Demonstrators were arrested and security in several areas was tightened to prevent the House of Saud from going the way of other Arab regimes. The "Women2Drive" movement, where courageous women broke laws by driving cars, drew much attention to the plight of women in much of the Arab world.

In the Palestinian territories, things changed rapidly. The competitive governments of the Palestinian Authority, led by Mahmoud Abbas, and Hamas, led by Ismail Haniyah, announced a reconciliation agreement for power sharing. Concurrently, nonviolent protests began in several areas, including East Jerusalem and Hebron. When protestors breached barriers and entered the Golan Heights, the Israeli army fired into the crowd and killed thirteen protestors.

The face of the Middle East has continued to change beyond this writing. In all the uprisings of the Arab Spring, there have been amazing acts of courage. Unfortunately, there were also unrestrained killings and the use of fear tactics against the family of any protestor caught on camera or detected using the Internet for revolutionary communication. Such is the risk of civil disobedience and such is the drive for freedom.

> *An individual who breaks a law that conscience tells him is unjust, and who willingly accepts the penalty of imprisonment in order to arouse the conscience of the community over its injustice, is in reality expressing the highest respect for the law.* — The Rev. Dr. Martin Luther King, Jr., American Protestant minister and civil rights leader

12

Conscientious Objection:
Desmond Doss (1945)

An action or a refusal to act, according to a sense of what is right or wrong; refusal to participate in military service because of moral or religious beliefs.

As a soldier in the U.S. Army during World War II, Desmond Doss (1919–2006) refused to carry a gun, citing his beliefs as a Seventh-day Adventist. Instead of accepting a deferment, he enlisted as a private and was assigned to a medical unit with the 77th Infantry. Doss worked as a medic in the War's Pacific theater where on Okinawa Island, at great risk to his own life, he saved the lives of many other men. According to his medal of Honor citation:

On May 21, in a night attack on high ground near Shuri, he remained in exposed territory while the rest of his company took cover, fearlessly risking the chance that he would be mistaken for an infiltrating Japanese and giving aid to the injured until he was himself seriously wounded in the legs by the explosion of a grenade. Rather than call another aid man from cover, he cared for his own injuries and waited 5 hours before litter bearers reached him and started carrying him to cover. The trio was caught in an enemy tank attack and Pfc. Doss, seeing a more critically wounded man nearby, crawled off the litter; and directed the bearers to give their first attention to the other man. Awaiting the litter bearers' return, he was again struck, by a sniper bullet while being carried off the field by a comrade, this time suffering a compound fracture of 1 arm. With magnificent fortitude he bound a rifle stock to his shattered arm as a splint and then crawled 300 yards (270 m) over rough terrain to the aid station. Through his outstanding bravery and unflinching determination in the face of desperately dangerous conditions Pfc. Doss saved the lives of many soldiers.[1]

Desmond Doss received America's highest gift for courage, the Medal of Honor. He is one of the few conscientious objectors to have received the award. A humble man from Lynchburg, Virginia, Doss always preferred the term "conscientious cooperator," reflecting the conflicting view of what conscientious objection means.

The history of the choice undoubtedly goes back to prehistory, but legal status is fairly new. Today, many nations give official conscientious objector (CO) status and offer noncombatant roles or a civilian service during times of military conscription.

Many individuals choose to make their claim of refusal for military service at the time of their induction. Others develop a conviction for conscientious objection after they become a part of a military service. The United Nations Commission on Human Rights acknowledged that people in the military might become conscientious objectors due to experiences and thoughts that caused a change of heart.

One of the most famous advocates of conscientious objection is the American transcendentalist Henry David Thoreau. In his book *Walden*, Thoreau expressed individuality and a moral philosophy that is best expressed in his poetic words, "If a man does not keep pace with his companions, perhaps it is because he hears a different drummer."[2]

Thoreau wrote his famous essay "Civil Disobedience" when he was in jail in July 1846. The local tax collector, Sam Staples, had asked the writer to pay six years of unpaid taxes. Thoreau openly refused and argued with the government official, citing a personal opposition to slavery and the Mexican-American War.

The essay "Civil Disobedience," some of which has been excerpted here, has become one of the most famous antiwar documents in American literature. His argument for individual resistance to government is based on a decision of his conscience, a moral opposition to unjust laws and policies of the state.

The Virtue of Conscience

The word conscience comes from the French word for knowledge within oneself, or a moral sense. That no other person can determine what you think is a power all of us possess, to use or not. This inner sense of right and wrong, this quiet voice of principles and qualms, is available to determine our most important thoughts and actions.

In the end, conscientious objection is a highly personal conviction. Governments, charged with protecting their people and possessions, have had a difficult time dealing with conscientious objectors. For thousands of years, objectors were imprisoned or executed for their beliefs.

In modern times, especially with the resolutions of the United Nations, conscientious objection has achieved recognition in the documents and laws of freedom. It has never been enough for a person to claim exemption due to a disagreement with government policy. The conviction must be based on a deeply held belief that killing is against his/her moral principles.

Since morality is difficult to define, governments have used various ways to determine the depth of belief. During World War II, the United States sent potential registrants for the draft a questionnaire.

The DSS 47 Form by the U.S. military is now obsolete but its questions give insight into the information a government needs in order to understand whether conviction is convenient or deeply held. The following is a paraphrase of those questions that might provide a basis for understanding personal belief when considering the choice of conscientious objection:

- What is the nature of your conviction as a conscientious objector?
- From what source have you derived your conviction?
- Do your religious beliefs contribute to your conviction?
- To what creeds, beliefs, or doctrines of opinion do you ascribe?
- Who are the persons that have guided you in your conviction?
- With what organizations are you affiliated?
- Have you associated with organizations that condone violence?
- Have you exhibited behavior that demonstrates your conviction?
- Have you expressed your conviction in public?
- When do you believe the use of force is necessary?

Individual acts of moral conscience have been played out in the heroism of conscientious objectors throughout time. Examples are well documented in history, including Austrian Roman Catholic Franz Jägerstetter who refused to serve in the Nazi army and was executed in 1943.

Another famous CO came to public attention during the Vietnam War. Heavyweight champion boxer of the world Muhammad Ali applied for status as a conscientious objector. Ali famously declared, "I ain't got no quarrel with them Viet Cong."[3]

In addition to individuals, organizations such as the Quaker American Friends Service Committee and Amnesty International actively support the moral choice of conscientious objection. The United Nations Office of the High Commissioner on Human Rights recognized in 1998 that "persons performing military service may develop conscientious objections."[4] These COs have gained status legally and alternative ways of fulfilling their duty is sometimes called "discretionary armed service."

The Disobedient Soul

The American Transcendentalist Henry David Thoreau is often attributed as a profound influence by icons of nonviolence such as Tolstoy, Gandhi, and King. In 1848, Thoreau spoke at the Concord, Massachusetts, Lyceum on "The Rights and Duties of the Individual in Relation to Government."

In that lecture he outlined his strategy of tax resistance as a form of nonviolent protest against unjust governments. Together with other American Transcendentalists, such as famed Concord residents Bronson Alcott and Ralph Waldo Emerson, Thoreau strived to live a philosophy of moral imperative and right action.

Refusing to pay the poll tax in protest to his government's use of the money, Thoreau spent only one night in jail, a friend having paid the tax. Yet the repercussions of that single event have rippled through the justification for civil government for over 150 years.

Spurred by his disgust with the Mexican-American War and slavery, Thoreau focused on the independent nature of people, their consciousness, and their duty to fulfill the promise of a just spirit. In his impassioned essay he laid out the justification for breaking the law:

> If the injustice is part of the necessary friction of the machine of government, let it go, let it go; perchance it will wear smooth — certainly the machine will wear out. If the injustice has a spring, or a pulley, or a rope, or a crank, exclusively for itself, then perhaps you may consider whether the remedy will not be worse than the evil; but if it is of such a nature that it requires you to be the agent of injustice to another, then, I say, break the law. Let your life be a counter friction to stop the machine. What I have to do is to see, at any rate, that I do not lend myself to the wrong which I condemn.[5]

Thoreau wrote succinctly about the rationale for nonviolent action and juxtaposed it with the violence of governments. He defined the basis for a "peaceable revolution" and called for people of conscience to seize the power that the minority has through united action.

> Under a government which imprisons any unjustly, the true place for a just man is also a prison. The proper place to-day, the only place which Massachusetts has provided for her freer and less desponding spirits, is in her prisons, to be put out and locked out of the State by her own act, as they have already put themselves out by their principles. It is there that the fugitive slave, and the Mexican prisoner on parole, and the Indian come to plead the wrongs of his race, should find them; on that separate, but more free and honorable ground, where the State places those who are not with her, but against her — the only house in a slave State in which a free man can abide with honor. If any think that their influence would be lost there, and their voices no longer afflict the ear of the State, that they would not be as an enemy within its walls, they do not know by how much truth is stronger than

error, nor how much more eloquently and effectively he can combat injustice who has experienced a little in his own person. Cast your whole vote, not a strip of paper merely, but your whole influence. A minority is powerless while it conforms to the majority; it is not even a minority then; but it is irresistible when it clogs by its whole weight. If the alternative is to keep all just men in prison, or give up war and slavery, the State will not hesitate which to choose. If a thousand men were not to pay their tax-bills this year, that would not be a violent and bloody measure, as it would be to pay them, and enable the State to commit violence and shed innocent blood. This is, in fact, the definition of a peaceable revolution, if any such is possible. If the tax-gatherer, or any other public officer, asks me, as one has done, "But what shall I do?" my answer is, "If you really wish to do anything, resign your office." When the subject has refused allegiance, and the officer has resigned his office, then the revolution is accomplished. But even suppose blood should flow. Is there not a sort of blood shed when the conscience is wounded? Through this wound a man's real manhood and immortality flow out, and he bleeds to an everlasting death. I see this blood flowing now.[6]

Thoreau's "Civil Disobedience" lays out in plain yet elegant narration a theoretical basis for nonviolent action. In doing so, he reveals the conflicted yet determined soul of the conscientious objector.

That government is best which governs least. — Henry David Thoreau, "Civil Disobedience"

And so the non-violent resister never lets this idea go, that there is something within human nature that can respond to goodness. — The Rev. Dr. Martin Luther King, Jr.

13

Spiritual Practices: Penn's Treaty with the Delaware (1693)

To seek inner peace or to do good works based on a nonmaterial, soulful approach to the world; the ideal that peace starts within yet is connected with the larger whole.

One of the best examples of applied love through nonviolence is the experience of the Religious Society of the Friends, or as they have come to be known from their "trembling at the word of God," the Quakers. The history of the Quakers is replete with examples of individual peacemaking, including the legacy of William Penn, who was "Absolute Proprietor" of the seventeenth century British colony that later became Pennsylvania.

As a close friend of the Society's founder, George Fox, William Penn believed in the Quaker value of peacemaking. A proponent of religious freedom and nonviolence, Penn subscribed to the Quaker Peace Testimony, which was composed of pacifist ideas that Fox began developing as early as 1661.

The Peace Testimony in various forms urges humanity to end wars and fighting, one proclaiming, "All bloody principles and practices, we ... do utterly deny, with all outward wars and strife and fightings with outward weapons, for any end or under any pretence whatsoever."[1]

As head of the government in Pennsylvania, William Penn was in charge of relations of the indigenous people whose land had been ceded by Royal Charter. Influenced by Fox's writings on peacemaking, Penn met with the Delaware Indians without taking any weapons or guards. This compassionate diplomacy was a risky and innovative tactic that has precious few parallels in the history of colonization.

The Virtue of Compassion

Compassion comes from the Latin phrase for "sympathy" or "to feel pity," yet to "suffer with" is its more active form. Putting compassion into relationships and daily associations brings to our lives a level of humanity that encourages peace both externally and internally.

Inner peace, or peace of mind, is a state of being that gives a person the ability to be calm or serene in the face of outside influences, including the potential for violence. That humans, through an increasing sense of compassion, are on a progressive path toward a better world is the lofty ideal behind spiritual evolution.

How we reach that ideal in our personal lives comes from many personal beliefs. For some, the state of inner peace is achieved with a deep knowledge and understanding of the self. For others, it is achieved through divine intervention. For others still, in their compassionate actions toward others they find a deep source of personal inspiration.

William Penn endeavored to put compassion into his relations with the Delaware Indians. He learned their language and treated their leaders with respect. Though most of his Colonial peers would not think of including indigenous people in a discussion about land rights, Penn followed his beliefs and sought a fair conclusion to boundary disputes.

The actual treaty that was agreed to between Penn and the Delaware did not survive through the centuries. Yet tradition holds that Penn paid the tribe a fair value for land that had been given to the Quakers by the English monarch. The tenets of the treaty, memorialized in an engraving in the state capitol rotunda, survived for several decades until the policies later came under control of the Pennsylvania legislature.

Penn's use of his personal beliefs in state dealings with the Delaware is an act of spirituality applied. Many people think of spirituality as closely tied to religion, but it also describes a wide set of beliefs, such as love and compassion, that are commonly held.

For spirituality's metaphysical reference, peace comes from the belief in something greater than one's self. It is that which gives us the ability to love and have compassion for other human beings as well as for ourselves. Love is an intense feeling of affection for others and the self, which provides one of the strongest motivations to work for peace.

In *Fruits of Solitude*, William Penn wrote: "All Christians are to mind God and Christ's teaching, who teach Christians to love one another, yea, enemies...."[2]

The *"Just War"* Theory

With the long and bloody history of religious wars, it is difficult to keep in mind that faith is intended to be a basis for peace. People often become so impassioned with their belief that they feel the need to bring the good news to everyone. In other cases, they fear an alternative religious practice or sect might corrupt the "true" faith and so suppression or death seems to be a just cause.

The "Just War" theory has been called upon by leaders since the beginning of human society to justify the killing and savagery resulting from armed conflicts. The theory holds that certain conditions provide the basis for military action. Most religions have a history, including a doctrinal legacy, of justifying war and suppression.

In Christianity, theologians often point to Saint Augustine who defined a defensive war with the central motive of peace. He wrote that war should not be self-interested or a grab for power. Rather it must be for a good purpose and only exercised by a legitimate government. Individuals, he contended, must practice pacifism but when the state is pursuing peace through war the teachings of Christ must be understood in the context of a just war to restore peace.

In a 1983 pastoral letter from the U.S. Catholic Bishops,[3] the conditions for defense of a nation by use of military forces exist:

- when damage by an aggressor is "lasting, grave, and certain,"
- when everything else has been tried,
- when there is a good chance for success, or
- when using force does less harm than the aggression.

It is easy to see how virtually any war can be justified on this basis. For wars of religion, the aggressor can be an entire religion, a splinter sect, or simply another government that uses its religion as a motivating device to rally its citizens to war. The examples are many and only a few are listed below:

- The Crusades — Christianity's attempts over six centuries to regain dominion over Jerusalem
- The Muslim conquests of the seventh through ninth centuries — attempts to suppress sects and bring the faith to unbelievers
- The French wars of religion — sixteenth- and seventeenth-century power plays between the established Catholics and the Protestant Huguenots that were inspired by the theology of John Calvin
- The twentieth-century Irish struggles for independence — conflicts entangled in divisions between Irish Catholic and Irish Protestants.

- The fight for Jerusalem — a confluence of three major religions, Judaism, Christianity, and Islam, which continuously contest for possession of the Holy Land and the right to worship in peace

In all of these wars and conflicts, there are religious actions that invest the faithful. Several Popes called the crusaders into action. Many rabbis have pointedly expounded on the struggles detailed in the Bible. Catholic priests accompanied French troops into Russia while Orthodox priests accompanied the opposition. Mullahs teach the faithful about their interpretation of Minor Jihad. Each battleship is launched with interdenominational prayers.

It seems that the Divine is on everyone's side. As long as the war is deemed just, the slaughter can begin. Yet there is a glimmer of hope in the theory of just war. Whether religious, or political, or philosophical, these war justifications come with a caveat. War is abhorrent. That's an underlying consensus. With the need for serious justification comes an acceptance of "war as the last resort."

Nonviolent alternatives then become inherent in any debate about just war, especially those with a spiritual factor. One of the criteria to consider in the decision to go to war, illusion or not, is the possibility that a nonviolent solution could actually prevent war. In effect, there is always an alternative to be tried before complete justification can be ascribed.

The Spirit of Peace

Yet war does not define religion, nor spirit. The deep feeling and expressions of spirit are creating peace in families and in communities. The compassion we feel and the passion we express are the ways we find inner peace and work for outer peace in the world.

The spirit moves people to have empathy for themselves and for others and seek inner peace. Spiritual practices, such as meditation, prayers, fasting, and pilgrimages give a sense of well-being and connect the individual with the whole.

When people feel compassion for others, they suffer with their fellow beings and seek outer peace with the world. Through charity and relief work, by committing our lives to education and innovation, by giving solace and understanding, we do the work of spirit.

The following three prayers and excerpts from the sacred texts of the three Abrahamic religions speak to the peacemaking traditions of formal religion. First is the Prayer of St. Francis, which expresses our desire to be made an instrument for peace:

Lord, make me an instrument of your peace.
Where there is hatred ... let me sow love

Where there is injury ... pardon
Where there is doubt ... faith
Where there is despair ... hope
Where there is darkness ... light
Where there is sadness ... joy
O Divine Master, grant that I may not so much seek
To be consoled ... as to console
To be understood ... as to understand
To be loved ... as to love
For it is in giving ... that we receive,
It is in pardoning ... that we are pardoned,
It is in dying ... that we are born to eternal life.

The second sacred wish is the Jewish Prayer for Peace, which is a direct excerpt from the book of Isaiah 2:4.

Come, let us go up to the mountain of the Lord,
to the house of the God of Jacob.
He will teach us his ways,
so that we may walk in his paths.
The law will go out from Zion,
the word of the Lord from Jerusalem.
He will judge between the nations
and will settle disputes for many peoples.
They will beat their swords into plowshares
and their spears into pruning hooks.
Nation will not take up sword against nation,
nor will they train for war anymore.

The third convocation of spiritual conviction is the Muslim Prayer for Peace, which is based in part on the text of the Qur'an 8:61.

In the name of Allah, the beneficent, the merciful.
Praise be to the Lord of the Universe who has created us
and made us into tribes and nations,
That we may know each other, not that we may despise each other.
If the enemy incline towards peace, do thou also incline towards peace,
and trust God, for the Lord is the one that heareth and knoweth all things.
And the servants of God,
Most gracious are those who walk on the earth in humility,
and when we address them, we say "peace."

For those who consider themselves spiritual but not associated with a formal religion, the words of peace and peacemaking are just as beautiful. The Lebanese poet Khalil Gibran gave a toast to tolerance and embracing that comes from the spiritual domain: "Say not, 'I have found the truth,' but rather 'I have found a truth.'" "For the soul walks upon all paths."[4]

14

Pacifism: The Russell-Einstein Manifesto (1955)

Moral opposition to war and violence; the principle that peace can be maintained by adjusting differences instead of resorting to violence and war.

In the world today, there are thousands of nuclear warheads much larger than those dropped in 1945 on Hiroshima and Nagasaki.[1] Add to that all the chemical, biological, and other forms of weapons and we realize the globe is a virtual arsenal.

The first nuclear bombs were built during World War II in the secretive American Manhattan Project. Soon afterward, the Soviet Union developed nuclear technology and the global arms race was on.

Today, the tragic game continues with an ever more destructive cocktail of weapons designed to broadcast target humans and cities, be deployed above ground and below, and proliferate across the earth and into space.

Yet in the early years of atomic weaponry, many scientists from around the world — including Albert Einstein, who developed the formula that expressed the potential for such weapons — began to call for a more reasoned approach than the competitive, brinkmanship strategy of unbridled nuclear proliferation. Einstein wrote that the "unleashed power of the atom has changed everything save our modes of thinking and we thus drift toward unparalleled catastrophe."[2]

In 1955, the famous British physicist and philosopher/pacifist Bertrand Russell issued a warning about the dangers of nuclear weapons. The Russell-Einstein Manifesto urged governments to consider the dire nature of nuclear weapons and to find other ways to resolve differences.

"In view of the fact that in any future world war," the Manifesto stated, "nuclear weapons will certainly be employed, and that such weapons threaten the continued existence of mankind, we urge the governments of the world to realize, and to acknowledge publicly, that their purpose cannot be furthered by a world war, and we urge them, consequently, to find peaceful means for the settlement of all matters of dispute between them."[3]

The Virtue of Morality

In the view of Einstein, Russell, and other prominent scientists, untold millions could die from bad decisions made by generals and politicians faced with what was, in essence, a moral choice. To continue on the path of potential destruction, they believed, was simply immoral.

Though the meaning of morality as "goodness" is a late derivative from the 1950s, the Latin root *moralitatem* means manner or character. To these gentlemen and ladies of science, the question of whether to continue with the arms race was one of individual and societal moral or virtuous behavior, an attention to the rules of right conduct.

Devastation in Hiroshima, Japan, August 6, 1945, after the atomic bomb "Little Boy" was dropped from the *Enola Gay*.

Though a strong sense of morality is not the sole virtue of the pacifist, those who take an incisive moral stand against war are often considered pacifists. The word pacifism was coined in 1901 at the International Peace Congress held in Glasgow, but it has a long history of both individual courage and the work of peace groups such as the Quakers and War Resistors International.

The definition of pacifism has expanded in recent years as anyone who is "working to create or perpetuate peace."[4] Still, those who proclaim themselves pacifists must suffer the skepticism of many in the general public who see alternatives to violence and war as simply the dreams of idealists.

The strongly held argument that only overpowering force can actually stop those who would use violence is at the core of this perception that pacifists are only dreamers. That the ends justify the means, pacifists protest, and that violence is the only practical method is a myopic view. Violence, they contend, only creates the seeds of more violence. They also note that the use of violence in one situation, such as conventional weapons against an army, makes it easier to use in other situations, such as in a nuclear attack against an entire people.

The principles of pacifism are illuminated in the concepts of non-aggression and nonkilling. The non-aggression principle is a moral axiom that contends the initiation of aggression by physical force is not a legitimate action. It is not an entirely pacifist doctrine because, in some interpretations, it allows the use of self-defense.

The non-aggression principle is linked to the timing and conditions of an act of violence. John Locke in his work *Second Treatise on Government* said, "Being all equal and independent, no one ought to harm another in his life, health, liberty, or possessions."[5]

Pacifism is linked to the freedom and sanctity of self-possession. Herbert Spencer believed that every man "is free to do that which he wills, provided he infringes not the equal freedom of any other man."[6]

The principle of nonkilling, on the other hand, is an entirely pacifist doctrine. In his 2002 book *Nonkilling Global Political Science*, Dr. Glenn D. Paige introduced the term nonkilling. The concept allows us to investigate and try to abolish the root causes of violence. Nonkilling not only covers the absence of actual killing, but also includes threats to kill as well as the conditions that are conducive to killing.

A society that would embrace nonkilling would be a pacifist society with far reaching goals for wiping violence from our lives. It would entail the elimination of the psychological causes such as deprivation and hunger. Such a society would advocate elimination of the structural conditions such as the death penalty and military force.

Paige suggests that a higher evolution of thought is required to embrace the tenets of pacifism and nonkilling. First, we would need to move from the idea that killing is imperative to questioning that reality. From this questioning, we would begin to see killing as a problem for society. Only then can we explore alternatives and methods to achieve a consensus that a society without killing is, indeed, possible.

The paradigm shift from a culture of violence to a culture of peace is required for societies to embrace the concept that killing is not necessary as a means of organization. The following Action Principles of nonkilling have been compiled by the Global Center for Nonkilling:[7]

- Draw strength from life-respecting inspiration, whether religious or humanist. Respect your own life and the lives of others.
- Seek the well-being of all. Killing divides; nonkilling unites.
- In conflict, from beginning to end seek reconciliation not humiliation, degradation, predation, or annihilation.
- Join in constructive service to remove conditions of suffering of those in need.
- Be creative. It has taken great creativity to reach present conditions of technological and structural violence. It will require greater creativity for nonkilling transformation.
- Adopt an experimental approach to change. Seek successive approximations of nonkilling societies, learning from successes and failures.
- Respect both individual and large-scale social action, from the influence of moral example to mass nonkilling to people's power.
- Be constructively courageous. Withdraw support from violence and commit it to strengthen nonkilling alternatives.
- Walk lightly upon the earth; reduce demands upon nature and fellow human beings that contribute to killing.

Commitment to pacifism may be grounded in the emotional dimension of a person's morality, but it also has specific practices. To do without war and violence demands a more thoughtful approach, a more creative solution. It requires practice of the methods of nonviolence that are the alternatives highlighted in this book.

Two years after the pacifist Russell-Einstein Manifesto of 1955, a global conference of twenty-two scientists and eight signatories was held at the small city of Pugwash in Nova Scotia, Canada. The Pugwash Conference on Science and World Affairs continues today as a platform for ways to settle disputes through nonviolent means.

Forty years after the Manifesto was issued, Bertrand Russell and conference organizer Joseph Rotblat were awarded the Nobel Peace Prize for their contribution to the moral conversation about war and weapons.

Albert Einstein

Throughout the world, the word Einstein is synonymous with genius. The actual flesh-and-bone man achieved that honor on his merits both scientific as well as his lesser-known ideas on morality and the human condition.

Born in Germany in 1879, young Albert famously had difficulty with formal education. He said later that rote learning took the creativity and passion out of learning. He was born to be his own man with his own thoughts, ideas, and a strong sense of personal moral conscience.

Einstein is considered the father of modern physics and is best known for his theories initially conceived during his "miracle year" in 1905. Working in a patent office in Bern, Einstein's job was to evaluate electromagnetic devices. The job and his PhD work at the University of Zurich gave him the ability to fully comprehend the classic mechanical physics of Isaac Newton, which the young scientist found wanting in light of the new laws of electromagnetics.

In that one year, Einstein published four astounding papers on four subjects: the photoelectric effect, Brownian motion, special relativity, and the equivalence of matter and energy. The latter paper gave us the formula $E=mc^2$ and unleashed the conquest for a way to harness the capacity of turning matter into an explosive device that would change the potential destruction of war forever.

Later, Einstein developed the general theory of gravitation, which established the principles behind the spacetime continuum. His formula on gravitation spawned new visions of

Physicist, pacifist and activist Albert Einstein.

our physical world in terms of particle and wave theory as well as insights such as the Big Bang and black holes.

Yet the physicist's genius had another personal dimension that diverted him from his theories of physics into the realm of moral reasoning. Albert Einstein was a pacifist, indeed, an impassioned pacifist.

> I am not only a pacifist, but a militant pacifist. I am willing to fight for peace. Nothing will end war unless the people themselves refuse to go to war.[8]

It is ironic that the man who discovered the possibility of nuclear weapons would work so hard to keep them from being used. His fears that his German colleagues were developing a nuclear weapon that could destroy the Allied forces during World War II caused him to write then-president of the United States Franklin Roosevelt and inform him of the possibility of a weapon so destructive that it would dwarf all other weapons.

The resulting Manhattan Project delivered two atomic bombs in 1945, dubbed Fat Man and Little Boy, which were dropped on Hiroshima and Nagasaki. One can only imagine the horror that pacifist Einstein felt with the news of the deaths of over 100,000 people in a single act of war.

When in 1955 Einstein joined with Bertrand Russell and Joseph Rotblat to sign the Russell-Einstein Manifesto, his famous and respected name was used to add public credibility to the call for restraint:

> It looks as if the ruling statesmen of today were really trying to secure permanent peace. But the ceaseless piling-up of armaments shows only too clearly that they are unequal to coping with the hostile forces which are preparing for war. In my opinion, deliverance can only come from the peoples themselves. If they wish to avoid the degrading slavery of war-service, they must declare with no uncertain voice for complete disarmament. As long as armies exist, any serious conflict will lead to war. A pacifism which does not actively fight against the armament of nations is and must remain impotent.[9]

Always searching for a better way, Einstein's later years were spent trying to combine the four forces of the universe into a single description of reality, or Unified Field Theory. Considered a failure in that quest, Einstein's search for unity has inspired modern physicists to search for a theory of everything and the sage continues to gain respect for his work concerning that effort.

Einstein's idealistic quests did not stop with science. He called repeatedly for a world government. Though he feared the power of such an institution, he believed that only through unity and the wisdom of the many could the world survive the advent of increasingly powerful weapons. From an acceptance speech for receiving the World Award in 1948, he tried to rally the world.

> A tremendous effort is indispensable. If it fails now, the supranational organization will be built later, but then it will have to be built upon the ruins of a large part of the now existing world. Let us hope that the abolition of the existing international

anarchy will not need to be bought by a self-inflicted world catastrophe the dimensions of which none of us can possibly imagine. The time is terribly short. We must act now if we are to act at all.[10]

Perhaps the reason Albert Einstein did not share the Nobel Prize for Peace with pacifist colleagues Rotblat and Russell was that his work in physics overshadowed his work for peace. Yet to have the name synonymous for genius associated with pacifism gives peacemaking a measure of authority that denies those who would give it short shrift.

> *The pacifist's task today is to find a method of helping and healing which provides a revolutionary constructive substitute for war.* — Vera Brittian, English writer

15

Cultural Exchange: "Ping-Pong Diplomacy" (1972)

Travel to or communication with citizens of other countries to increase good-will and understanding; to cultivate peace through an exchange of art, literature, sporting events, or other pursuits.

Cultural exchange is carried on daily by thousands, even millions, of individuals working to advance the cause of peace. Today with such global options as student exchange programs as well as the proliferation of social networking, the ways to communicate and increase good will have become possible for everyone, no matter their status or location.

Fundamental to this peacemaking method is the recognition that understanding the cultural dynamics of a foreign country is paramount for identifying and rectifying differences that can lead to violence and war. One of the most famous examples of cultural exchange was when the Chinese table tennis team toured the United States in 1972.

China has a long history of isolationism rooted in centuries of foreign intervention. The Great Wall was begun in the fifth century to repel invaders, but it was an inefficient guard. From the Mongolians to the European nations who carved up "Cathay" into spheres of influence, interference from foreigners is the subtext of Chinese history.

Even in the beginning of the nineteenth century, as China began to understand the significance of the rest of the world, the Qing Dynasty adopted a defensive posture towards the Europeans. Just as the Chinese began opening to foreign trade and missionaries, opium produced by the British colony of India began flowing into China. The resulting trade-based Opium Wars with Britain served to weaken the Qing emperor's control over outside influences.

The deep isolationism of China that resulted from these centuries of

U.S. President Nixon and Chinese Premier Chou En-Lai, February 1972 (U.S. State Department).

invasive experiences with foreigners lasted until the late twentieth century. An opportunity to reopen China to the world occurred in the 1970s when President Richard Nixon made a historic visit to Beijing and met with Chinese premier Mao Zedong.

Following Nixon's trip, arrangements were made for an unconventional cultural exchange. The world-renowned Chinese table tennis team would travel to the United States. Termed by the popular media "Ping-Pong Diplomacy," the resulting exchange of sports teams would work to further thaw relations between the two countries.

The Virtue of Friendship

As diplomats worked the halls of government, the table tennis teams embarked on an initiative to invoke the oldest method of making peace — friendship. Companionship, accord, affinity, agreement, and alliance, the synonyms for friendship are the very definition of living in peace with our fellow human beings.

From its Old English roots of "to love" or "to favor," friendship has a social dimension that elevates it to a tool to foster world peace. A friend is someone with whom you have an attachment or affection, a person who gives support, or with whom you are on good terms.

"Each friend represents a world in us," the writer Anais Nin said, "a world possibly not born until they arrive, and it is only by this meeting that a new world is born."[1]

As the U.S. and Chinese table tennis teams got to know each other through friendly competition, they fostered understanding and lessened the suspicion and fear that often creates unnecessary tensions between nations. The major sporting event for cultural exchange is, of course, the Olympic Games. Since the Olympic torch was rekindled in 1894, thousands of contestants and millions of spectators have communed on the playing fields in a cultural exchange that has had positive repercussions on world peace.

Today cultural exchanges through international and regional sporting events is common, yet in the 1970s it took the full tool bag of nonviolent methods to thaw the historical ice that had formed between China and the Western world. The feeling of friendship garnered from Ping-Pong diplomacy played a very important part and contributed to the establishment by 1979 of full diplomatic relations between the United States and China.

Many types of organizations now contribute to increased understanding between cultures but all depend finally on the actions of individuals. The Friendship Force, for instance, is a cultural exchange organization founded in 1977 by Wayne Smith to encourage people-to-people interaction through travel.

The Presbyterian minister and former missionary to Brazil believed that "a world of friends is at peace."[2] Since Smith's home was in Georgia, he gained the backing for his new organization from then-president Jimmy Carter, one of the state's favorite sons. The Friendship Force grew quickly by promoting global friendship, goodwill, and understanding. Members from all over the globe offered home-stay exchanges to other members, creating a cost-effective way of traveling and promoting peace. In one year alone, over 5,000 friendship ambassadors traveled between nearly sixty countries.[3]

One good example of a Friendship Force exchange occurred soon after the Dayton Peace Accords in 1975, which ended the bloody war in Bosnia. In 1996, the Dayton, Ohio, Friendship Force organized a trip to Sarajevo to celebrate the successful treaty that was signed in Dayton. As with other Friendship Force exchanges, members of the Dayton group stayed with host families in the war-torn region. Dayton and Sarajevo are now Sister Cities, a formal program where communities around the world establish friendships and exchanges for mutual benefit.

Student Exchange Program

Another formal cultural exchange that has exploded with promise over the last few decades is the student exchange program. Students from the secondary schools and universities from one country apply to study abroad while the other country provides the same opportunities for their students.

The reciprocal benefits to young people in these student exchange programs impact their lives immediately and for the rest of their lives. The hosting country is able to show foreign students their history and culture. Students studying in a foreign land are able to benefit from learning about other traditions and receive academic instruction as well as the possibility of training and employment.

Often times, students live with a volunteer host family in their home, or students can find apartments or houses through scholarships or loans. The programs provide a safe environment for serious study as well as activities such as sports, music, and making the social acquaintances that enrich all concerned.

The student exchange program began in earnest after World War II and has flourished, especially in recent years. General objectives include increasing a student's understanding of the world and creating more peaceful relations between countries, as well as specific objectives as follow:

- Provide rich educational opportunities for students
- Strengthen friendships and networking
- Broaden students' perspectives on the world
- Allow students to explore alternative cultures
- Help preserve languages and multilingualism
- Balance the gap between nations for educational quality
- Reduce the fear and prejudice toward other peoples

The student exchange program puts international youth on the path toward solving some of the global problems that seemed unsolvable by the older generation. When students return to their families, the experiences and learning naturally help foster understanding and tolerance throughout their community. Often the friendships made during the few months abroad continue to provide benefits for a lifetime.

Beyond Borders and Boundaries

The rise of social networking as a method of cultural exchange is important not only as a way to encourage friendship but also as a tool for revolution.

During the Arab Spring, the Internet, social networking sites, as well as mobile phones provided a hyper-connected form of communication that helped rally dissidents and confounded the ability for security forces to contain their movements.

Social networking sites such as Facebook and Twitter were particularly important during the spring of 2011. The cultural exchange inside and outside of all national boundaries has begun to create a global community, especially to those who have grown up with these new digital tools.

The technology for social networking entails the computer chip as well as a networking structure. Like-minded or interdependent individuals and organizations can spontaneously create a wide network of digital nodes. Whether it's a student exchange group or a family connection, whether the information is personal or public, whether the communication is financial or romantic, social networking makes immediate for the first time in history a connectivity that reduces the effects of time and location.

During the recent uprisings in Tunisia and Egypt, the regimes that brutally repressed movements for half a century found that they had less understanding of digital media than their citizens. To prevent the usual fear tactics of divide and conquer, revolutionaries used new technologies to bypass state control and create unity between remote groups.

When the Mubarak regime in Egypt acted to cut off the Internet, net-savvy users found ways to use proxies to keep the flow of information flowing. Soon the protest groups were using the Internet to disperse information, mobile phones to take photos and films of repression, and social networking to send maps and locations of mass demonstrations. World opinion, kept informed by citizen news feeds to diverse media outlets such as Al Jazeera, put pressure on the regime to give way to the demands and dreams of its people.

The exchange of information now possible through social networking has revolutionized the relations between citizens. No longer held within borders, the thoughts, actions, and ideas of individuals have eclipsed the status quo that depended on the historical technologies of expensive phone calls and slow transportation. Now participation in cultural exchange and peacemaking requires only a few clicks of the mouse or the upload of a cell phone video.

At this printing, there are fifteen virtual communities with millions of users online and the number is rising. From Facebook and Twitter, to Gmail and LinkedIn, the avenues for promoting understanding and communication have reached the level where such communities are becoming boundary-less countries with only a few degrees of separation where everyone is more closely connected.

The profound reality of such connectivity grew out of a game devised by Hungarian author Frigyes Karinthy in a story called "Chains." Karinthy proposed that any two individuals could be connected through five friends or acquaintances, or five degrees of separation. Through the decades, mathematical models pushed that figure to six degrees, but now more data is pointing toward a smaller scale. Even in 1929 when Karinthy's book was published, technological advances were interconnecting and shrinking the world. That everyone is only a few steps away in terms of connection from every other person on the globe is further proof that our seven billion human brothers and sisters are closer than we imagine.

In the future, cultural exchange between nations and cultures will adapt to the porous nature of global communication. With virtual communities rapidly developing, serving a purpose, and moving with updated needs and technology, the crisscrossing of geographical, social, and political boundaries has great potential to give freedom the edge.

> *When you're finally up on the moon, looking back at the earth, all these differences and nationalistic traits are pretty well going to blend and you're going to get a concept that maybe this really is one world and why the hell can't we learn to live together like decent people?*— Frank Borman, American astronaut

16

Citizen Diplomacy: Monitoring of Palestinian Elections (2006)

Citizens not officially sanctioned by a government who are engaged in dialogue and exchanges with other citizens, groups, and nations for the purpose of increasing understanding or gaining a specific political end.

The agonizing and heartbreaking conflict between Israel and Palestine has complex roots that go back millennia. Today, as the fortunes of politicians and political parties fluctuate, democratic elections have been one of the few consistent and relatively stabilizing forces in the region.

The Palestinian National Authority (PLA) was conceived during the low-profile, back-channel negotiations of the Oslo Accords in 1993. The resulting Israeli-Palestinian Interim Agreement of 1995 charged the PLA to organize elections. Within the Middle East environment of siege and civil war, fair and transparent elections would be difficult and hard-won. In order to increase the world's trust in their democratic process, the Palestinian Authority asked one of the most trusted private citizen organizations to observe the elections.

The Carter Center was founded in 1982 by former U.S. president Jimmy Carter and his wife Rosalynn two years after they left the White House. The nonprofit Carter Center is located in Atlanta but its work for human rights, disease control, and democracy is international in scope.

The stature and respect that Jimmy Carter enjoys is in large part due to his brokering of the 1978 Camp David agreement between Israel and Egypt. With that legacy as well as his constant work for human rights, Jimmy Carter's presence in any election increases worldwide confidence in the process.

Since the 1990s, the Center has monitored many elections, including the 2005 election when Mahmoud Abbas of the political party Fatah won a majority. Fatah success was short-lived as charges of corruption caused the organ-

President Carter gained credibility as a peacemaker by brokering the Camp David Accords with Egyptian president Anwar El Sadat and Israeli prime pinister Menachem Begin. Left to right: Aliza Begin, President Carter, Jihan El Sadat, Menachem Begin, Rosalynn Carter, Anwar El Sadat (U.S. State Department).

ization to lose much of the support of its people. This meant that the 2006 parliamentary elections would be wide open and requiring the same level of confidence in the process.

In partnership with the National Democratic Institute, the Carter Center was part of an 86-member team deployed into Gaza, the West Bank, and Jerusalem. Members met with Palestinian officials on election procedures and processes, including voter education. On the morning of the election, serious problems arose.

Officials found irregularities in voting lists and the credibility of the process came into immediate questioning. The State of Israel controlled East Jerusalem's polls and had created the lists to handle voters in the manner of "absentee ballots."

Yet that morning, the voting lists at the region's six area post offices did not match those that came in to vote. The situation had potential for spoiling the election and sending the region back into chaos.

The Virtue of Initiative

The need for citizen diplomacy increases during times of impasse between nations or peoples. When representative governments fail and third-party authorities make no headway, the personal initiative of citizens often holds higher authority than standard channels of communication.

The phrase "that which begins," from the Latin *initiatus*, is the essence of what brings enthusiasm and new optimism to a struggling impasse. To begin anew, to change the players, to provide new eagerness and vigor to a bogged down process, can change the dynamics of stalemate. New channels of communication, new ideas, new parties to a negotiation will often allow the intransigent to step back, consider, and endeavor to find a way forward.

As an avid proponent of human rights, Jimmy Carter had used his status as a former U.S. president to form initiatives to help in many areas of the world. The Center's programs have helped to eradicate the ravages of Guinea worm disease. They have established a village-based health care system in thousands of villages in Africa.

In Palestine, one of the most important days for the organization came in that 2006 election. The serious problem of legitimate voters not being on the voter lists was taken to the head of the monitoring team, Jimmy Carter.

Knowing its importance for worldwide as well as Palestinian trust in the elections, Carter immediately contacted both Israeli and Palestinian officials. Many voters were being turned away and the situation was intensifying. Within a few hours, the Commission ruled that any Palestinian who showed proper documents to the foreign observer teams would be allowed to vote.

With that quick resolution in place, the monitoring team continued to ensure the day's voting was fair and that ballots for every area of Palestine would be tabulated. The political party of Hamas, which had nurtured popular support through their network of social programs, won 74 of the 132 seats in the legislature.

To the disappointment of many outside Palestine, the winning party's platform refused to recognize Israel's right to exist. Many cried foul, but the Carter Center's participation ensured the election's legitimacy. There was a peaceful and democratic transfer of power in one of the more contentious areas of the world.

To date, the nongovernmental employees and volunteers at the Carter

Center have monitored elections in more than seventy elections in twenty-seven countries, including three in Palestine (1996, 2005, and 2006).[1] For his citizen diplomatic work to find peaceful solutions to international conflicts, Jimmy Carter received the Nobel Peace Prize in 2002.

Back-Channel Diplomacy

Citizen diplomacy in political negotiations can involve a variety of human resources, including officials from the public sector as well as non-officials from the private sector. Track II diplomacy is the process of negotiating informally so that governments can avoid highly public or fixed positions. Retired government diplomats and military personnel, out-of-office elected officials, academic professors and scholars, mediation professionals, and celebrities have all been involved in such below-the-radar meetings.

When the individuals or organization have no affiliation with a government, or are even working in defiance, the discussions are called Track III diplomacy.

There are many examples throughout history of such back-channel involvement. In the late 1960s, thousands were dying in a bloody civil war when the southeastern province of Nigeria seceded from the union. The Nigerian-Biafran War was mainly the result of a British colonial decision to combine diverse ethnic groups into one larger country. In addition, the discovery of oil in the region put intense pressure on the tenuous relations between regional groups.

After many blood battles and retaliations, the conflict entered a stalemate and blockade. The disruption in the supplies of food and medicine to the people in ravaged and isolated areas caused a horrible humanitarian disaster.

Enter Adam Curle, a former British officer and peace studies academic. Curle had a long career in human rights education and participated in several Nongovernmental Organizations. Among other positions, he served as professor of education at the University of Ghana and was the first professor of peace studies at the University of Bradford in England.

Together with the head of a Quaker mediation team, Kale Williams, Curle gained the trust of the disputants and encouraged the Biafrans to come to the table. Proving that "they could be trusted with sensitive information, including the personal disappointments and fears of men in power,"[2] the Quakers were able to influence the creation of formal peace talks. They made outside diplomats aware of the sensitive issues while opening lines of communication between the parties.

Estimates of deaths in the Nigerian-Biafran War, due to killing plus famine, are over one million people. The direct results of peace talks were hard to determine but the Biafran leader, Odumegwu Ojukwu, eventually agreed to a ceasefire. The secessionist state rejoined the larger nation and the Igbo people were raised from the specter of hunger from war and blockade.

As in the Nigerian-Biafran War, when a conflict is considered intransigent, or when two conflicting parties have reached an impasse with regular diplomatic efforts, there are other ways to find understanding. Track II diplomacy is away from the public view, sometimes in secret, sometimes with little publicity.

With separation from a direct government involvement and payroll, informal talks and meetings can achieve a low-key environment that is safe for the parties to offer ideas. The process tends to be constructive rather than judgmental, open rather than coercive.

In the most successful occasions, the parties in conflict are open to a resolution but simply can't negotiate with the opposition. The leaders are aware that the dispute can get out of control if left without a diplomatic effort. Third parties often initiate the meetings but, in the end, it depends on the parties directly involved.

Track II diplomacy has been successful many times as one part of a multi-track diplomatic effort that involves many different diplomatic efforts. From national leader summits, where presidents meet directly, to state department meetings, to third-party offers of intervention, diplomacy has a wide range of options. Serious negotiation processes will involve every possible means to find a solution or at least limit the violence born from conflict.

The Oslo Agreement

A more recent example of Track II diplomacy was the secret negotiations held in Oslo, Norway, during the early 1990s. The Arab-Israeli Conflict has a long history of mutual distrust and demonizing of the parties involved. Since the Camp David Accords in 1979, when Egypt and Israel signed a bilateral peace agreement, there had been little progress in a comprehensive solution.

Building on the Madrid negotiations of 1992, several individuals set up a meeting between Ahmed Qurei, a Palestinian Liberation Organization representative, and an Israeli history professor, Yair Hirschfeld.

These Track II negotiations provided the Israelis and Palestinians with a means of sitting down to discuss the seemingly intractable issues that had prevented progress since the Camp David Accords. After intense deliberations, Israeli prime minister Shimon Peres, Palestinian leader Yasser Arafat, and U.S. negotiator Dennis Ross and President Clinton got involved in the discussions.

The result was the Oslo Accords, which were signed in Washington D.C. on September 13, 1993. The principles of the Accord included the creation of the Palestinian National Authority but fell short of a comprehensive agreement. Unfortunately, since the start of the *al-Aqsa intifada* in 2000, the Accords have not achieved the necessary backing of the majority of the people in the region. Yet in some quarters, the introduction of democratic elections is considered a major accomplishment of Oslo's Track II negotiations.

> *Citizen Diplomacy is the concept that the individual has the right, even the responsibility, to help shape U.S. foreign relations, "one handshake at a time."*— U.S. Center for Citizen Diplomacy

> *I like to believe that people, in the long run, are going to do more to promote peace than our governments. Indeed, I think that people want peace so much that one of these days governments had better to get out of their way and let them have it.*— Dwight D. Eisenhower, American president

17

Environmental Activism: The Green Belt Movement (1977)

Advocating and/or working to protect the earth from harm; the philosophy or social movement linking a healthy natural environment to civilization, wellness, and peace.

In the twentieth century, environmentalism in the public mind was not so closely aligned to peace as it is today. Most environmentalists put the emphasis on preventing pollution to our planet, which they understood was under great threat of consumption and booming population.

Modern environmentalists have expanded the notion of advocating and working to stop unsustainable practices and create a more peaceful world. They put the emphasis on the violence directed toward humans and the earth by pollution, overuse, and misguided laws and controls.

In this connective reference, peace and environmentalism are inextricably linked. The two are intimately connected in a circle of harmony and dependence that creates a reciprocal necessity for acting. For environmentalists, social upheaval, violence, and war put added stress on the environment and cause resource depletion. For peace advocates, threats to our natural environment create conditions such as hunger, poverty, and disease that threaten human peace.

The Nobel Peace Prize of 2004 forever merged these two necessities. With the nomination of a Kenyan activist Wangari Maathai, the Nobel Committee made the link between peace and environmentalism, thereby validating the delicate balance of life.

An environmentalist and political activist, Maathai founded the Green Belt Movement in 1977. The groups planted over thirty million trees throughout Kenya in order to prevent soil erosion and depletion.[1] Such stewardship

protected traditional lands, resources, and ways of life from unbridled globalization and commercialization.

Born in the village of Ihithe in the Nyeri District of Kenya, Wangari
Maathai received a master's degree from the University of Pittsburg before
returning to Kenya. She worked as a professor of veterinary medicine before
turning her attention to the plight of the indigenous farmers working to make
a living on Kenyan soil.

According to writer Norman Myers, "There is a new phenomenon in the
global arena: environmental refugees. These are people who can no longer
gain a secure livelihood in their homelands because of drought, soil erosion,
desertification, deforestation and other environmental problems, together with
associated problems of population pressures and profound poverty."[2]

By the mid–1990s, it is estimated that there were approximately twenty-
five million environmental refugees. A combination of political and environmental mismanagement has created an unsustainable world, and a new type
of nightmare for parents and children.

The Virtue of Sustainability

To "hold up," to support, to maintain — sustainability is the capacity to
endure. It is a reciprocal relationship with the earth that enables the planet
and all things on it to thrive.

The Brundtland Commission of the United Nations defined in 1983 the
challenge: "Sustainable development is development that meets the needs of
the present without compromising the ability of future generations to meet
their own needs."[3]

The environmental movement covers the spectrum of reformers and radicals. Reformers work within the system. They mount campaigns to change
laws and elect sympathetic politicians. Many radicals, on the other hand,
believe that to achieve harmony with our environment we need to overhaul
our political, economic, and social systems. Only with radical changes, these
environmental radicals contend, can we achieve a more sustainable society.

Environmentalists such as Wangari Maathai work on many fronts to
ensure sustainability and the human rights that are so tied to the stewardship
of the earth. Maathai was instrumental in saving the Nairobi Uhuru Park by
stopping the construction of a sixty-story business complex. Often working
outside the confines of government channels, she is among a group of environmental pragmatists who use reform and radicalism to best effect. Maathai
was imprisoned and attacked several times for her work against political corruption.

Yet the woman who was known in Africa as the "tree woman" was later elected as a member of the Kenyan parliament. Now she worked within the system when possible. She served as assistant minister for environment, natural resources, and wildlife. She founded the Mazingira Green Party of Kenya and was the first president of the African Union's Economic, Social and Cultural Council.

For her progress toward "sustainable development, democracy and peace," Dr. Maathai was the first environmentalist to receive the Nobel Peace Prize. "At the time," Simon Robinson of *Time* magazine wrote, "some questioned the link between saving the environment and promoting peace. But millions of Kenyans understood the lesson that Maathai had taught them: that prosperity depends just

Wangari Maathai of Kenya's Green Belt Movement (The Green Belt Movement, Martin Rowe, photographer).

as much on caring for a fragile planet as on dousing human conflict."[4]

Three years later, former U.S. vice president Al Gore and the Intergovernmental Panel on Climate Change received the Nobel Peace Prize. Two awards in the decade solidified the bond between environmentalism and peace.

The Tipping Point

Malcolm Gladwell, in his book *The Tipping Point: How Little Things Can Make a Big Difference*, contends that great changes happen when conditions reach a critical mass. This threshold of change is a mysterious moment when ideas, technologies, and the actions of a few drive conditions to the boiling point and tip the scales toward an evolution of history.

Gladwell's "Law of the Few" points to people with the personality that lends a hand to change. He has a different take on the 80/20 rule in that 20 percent of people become the change agents for global evolution.

These people are described as "connectors" who link us with others.

"Mavens" are early adopters of technology and ideas. "Salesmen" have the charisma to persuade others and provide a great service in our society, using storytelling and computer technology to give context to what can be an overwhelming blast of information.

By the turn of the century context was definitely needed to clarify the issues related to global warming. The controversy was about whether or not humans were contributing to the heating of our planet with carbon pollution.

Many considered the science a foolproof explanation that humans were dramatically impacting the greenhouse effect, or the natural holding of heat by our atmosphere, thereby heating our environment. Others were unsure of the facts and pointed to the natural conditions and natural cycles in the cooling and warming of Earth.

In 2006, the world was on the verge of a tipping point regarding the issue. Former vice president and failed candidate for the presidency Al Gore became the focus of a documentary on global warming. The film and its star soon came to the forefront of the global debate. Months after the film's release the facts about the earth's warming were available for everyone to make a judgment.

Directed by Davis Guggenheim, *An Inconvenient Truth* showed Al Gore as connector, salesman, and maven, toting his suitcase with a slideshow about global warming and making it personal. Always a champion of the science of the earth's warming, Gore had convened the first congressional hearing in the 1980s and wrote a book, *Earth in the Balance*, yet nothing seemed to pierce the public's veil of unconcern.

When the film premiered at the Sundance Film Festival no one could have guessed the reaction. What was essentially a slideshow of facts, including the carbon dioxide measurements of Harvard University professor Roger Revelle, became an instant hit.

Awareness of global warming soon reached the public and the reaction of the conservative media was harsh. Yet the *Wall Street Journal* understood that the issue would not go away and began to use the nomenclature "climate change" instead of "global warming" for which humans were responsible.

The facts used in the film by global warming change agent Al Gore were familiar to long-term environmentalists. The ice glaciers of the two poles have been receding at an alarming rate. Antarctic ice core research at the Physics Institute at Bern showed current carbon dioxide concentrations higher than the last 650,000 years. The ten hottest years since 1980 had been mostly in the last decade.

And the Keeling Curve, measured at Mauna Loa Observatory in Hawaii, showed an increasing curve plotline for atmospheric carbon dioxide since 1958.

In a 2007 survey by the Nielsen Company, 66 percent of people who had seen the film said it had caused them to "change their minds" about global warming. *An Inconvenient Truth* has been widely credited for contributing, if not actually being the tipping point, for a serious movement toward reducing the impact of burning carbon fuels and other factors in the heating of our Earth.

Whether humans are a big factor in creating the change is still controversial, but most people acknowledge the change and are working to reduce the impact of carbon dioxide on the atmosphere. A collaboration of Laurie David, Guggenheim, and Lawrence Bender, among others, the film won two Academy Awards.

Walk Lightly on this Earth

There are thousands of creative and practical ways to reduce our ecological footprints. The 3R concept is a good place to start: reduce usage, reuse materials, and recycle into new products. Yet there are many things that can show environmental awareness.

- Keep your vehicles and appliances at peak efficiency
- Use fluorescent and diode light bulbs
- Caulk and weather-strip your home
- Use alternative mass transportation or walk and bike
- Limit unnecessary travel
- Use energy-efficient products such as appliances
- Use a tankless water heater or insulate your tank
- Monitor your thermostat for heating and air conditioning
- Purchase green electricity when options allow
- Check into purchasing carbon offset where applicable
- Turn off electronic devices when not in use
- Replace air filters and clean heating elements
- Choose low-flow plumbing devices and products
- Search second hand and recycled product stores
- Plant a garden or build a greenhouse
- Eat locally grown, organic, and in-season foods
- Frequent local farmer's markets and natural food stores
- Use green design features for houses and buildings
- Plant with indigenous plants and drought-tolerant plants

- Use biodegradable cleaning products
- Check cabinets for toxic chemical products and dispose of at a facility
- Use less water for showers and fix leaks
- Run household appliances only when necessary
- When washing cars, take them to a car wash that uses less water and prevents runoff
- Reduce consumption of unnecessary products
- Recycle degradable waste, including glass, plastic, paper, and aluminum
- Recycle electronic equipment
- Compost degradable food waste
- Purchase recycled products labeled post-consumer waste

Making a difference can entail using clean transport, adding energy-saving appliances to your home, adopting green habits, reducing your food and housing footprint, choosing sustainable home furnishings and building materials, saving water, and thinking about the impact of what you buy. The variety and scope of these ideas show we don't need to be a celebrity or scientist to be a change agent to reduce our ecological footprint and contribute to the energy of peace.

> We do not inherit the earth from our fathers. We borrow it from our children. — David Bower, American founder of Friends of the Earth

> We are not going to be able to operate our spaceship earth successfully nor for much longer unless we see it as a whole spaceship and our fate as common. — Buckminster Fuller, American inventor

18

Artistic Expression:
Imagine Peace Tower (2007)

The use of painting, writing, sculpture, music, humor, film, architecture, or other forms of artistic expression to produce an aesthetic result that inspires change.

In 1971, former Beatle John Lennon wrote the song "Imagine," which has become a recognized anthem of peace around the globe. It asks the listener to stop his or her preconceived notions for a moment and imagine a unified world, without countries or religions, without greed or hunger.

With its bold vision, the song was an instant success, though the lyrics have remained controversial due to their rejection of many long-held beliefs. Yet in the context of artistic expression and imagination, "Imagine" is one of the most played records in history.

Lennon knew the song would generate widespread criticism, but in the lyrics he foretells that many others would share his feelings. One of those others was his wife, Yoko Ono, an artist with international acclaim in her own right.

From the time of their marriage in 1969, John and Yoko began staging high-profile public "art for peace" exhibits. They used the notoriety of their honeymoon by staging a "bed-in" for peace at the Amsterdam Hilton Hotel.

The second bed-in was staged in Toronto with celebrities such as LSD advocate Timothy Leary and comedian Tommy Smothers. Lennon recorded the Roy Kerwood song "Give Peace a Chance," which has also become a standard in the peace movement.

Upon Lennon's death in 1980, Yoko Ono continued the work. In memorial to her husband and as a beacon for peace, Ono created the Imagine Peace Tower in Iceland. Located off the coast of Reykjavik on Videy Island, the

Peace Tower projects a "tower of light" from a huge stone well into the dark night sky.

The engraved stone in the Tower's well has "Imagine Peace" in twenty-four languages as well as 500,000 written peace wishes buried underneath the Tower. The Imagine Peace Tower projects a tower of light from October 9, Lennon's birthday, to December 8, the day the rock icon was killed in New York City.

The Virtue of Creativity

American existentialist author Rollo May said in *The Courage to Create*, "Creativity arises out of the tension between spontaneity and limitations, the latter (like the river banks) forcing the spontaneity into the various forms which are essential to the work of art or poem."[1]

The tension of the artists who see the world as it should be and the world as it is has created a body of work that continues to provoke thought and

Peace Poles with peace messages in multiple languages have been "planted" as artistic community expressions of peace in thousands of parks, homes, and institutions around the world.

action. Creativity in any medium or action requires the ability to transcend the status quo and make something new.

Peace art comes from this creative imagination. It depends on the artist's ideas, skill, and insight into the human condition. Art is often where we go to find new ways of looking at an issue. Art is a social action that is an important part of the envisioning process that creates our future.

Fostering creativity, especially as a means of working for peace, can be developed the same as other skills. Often art is seen as primarily a spontaneous effort, but the ability to act in and of ourselves, or spontaneously, has a great deal to do with being personally attuned to the methodology of creativity.

John Lennon and Yoko Ono were committed as partners to using music and public art as a nonviolent means of making progress. As part of a worldwide public art display commemorating Lennon and the urge to imagine peace, Ono also created a series of Peace Wish Trees. Based on a tradition in Japan, people can write their peace wish on small tags and affix them to the tree. The wishes are collected from time to time and burned so that the wishes might become part of the universe.

"As a child in Japan," Yoko Ono said, "I used to go to a temple and write out a wish on a piece of thin paper and tie it around the branch of a tree. Trees in temple courtyards were always filled with people's wish knots, which looked like white flowers blossoming from afar."[2]

Such art installations for peace are becoming commonplace everywhere and take imaginative forms. For instance, Peace Poles are a tradition that was started in 1955 by the World Peace Prayer Society in Japan. The square or hexagonal poles have "May Peace Prevail on Earth" carved or painted in different languages.

Peace Poles have been "planted" in thousands of places, including the Hiroshima Peace Memorial. Poles can be found in exotic places such as the North Magnetic Pole. They also can be found in thousands of neighborhood parks and faith-based centers.

Writing to Right the World

Art for peace does not necessarily mean painting or illustration. Art forms take many avenues, including the written word. Whether it's a tweet, or a blog, or a novel, or a column in a newspaper or Internet magazine, writing can be an act of personal liberation as well as social commentary.

Within the discipline and art of writing is political journalism. It refers to written commentary on governments, organizations, and people that wield political power. The writer analyzes political events and public reactions.

Often the political opinions of the author are overtly or subtly part of the narrative.

Investigative journalism is a type of political journalism that has a rich history of making a difference on a wide range of issues. The seasoned journalist sniffs out a story, often based on a contradiction or missing fact, that strikes their interest. The story can be about crime or corruption, governments or organizations, or even about celebrities and political leaders.

The tools of the trade are many and include reviewing documents such as tax records, corporate filings, government statistics and reports, and court cases. Records made available to the public as a result of the Freedom of Information Act have provided facts and discrepancies of some high level investigations.

Interviews with whistleblowers have brought down harmful business practices of corporations. Retired government and military officials often provide a different perspective on events that have led countries to war. Some high profile cases of investigative journalism follow:

• The Watergate affair, when Bob Woodward and Carl Bernstein of the *Washington Post* broke the story that led to the resignation of then-president Nixon. The two journalists won a Pulitzer.

• The Ford Pinto's record of causing fatalities, revealed by *Mother Jones* magazine. The car was discontinued as a result of the journalistic investigations of reporters Mark Dowie and Carolyn Marshall.

• The NSA warrantless search controversy, when *New York Times* reporters James Risen and Eric Lichtblau revealed the Bush administration's secret domestic eavesdropping program.

• *Novaya Gazeta* reporter Anna Politkovskaya's accounts of Russia's horrible treatment of the Chechen population, including a story about poisoning children.

The new media and computers have brought new technologies to bear on the investigations of journalists. WikiLeaks founder Julian Assange and colleagues set up various databases and websites with the mission to provide classified documents for all to see.

The documents are provided to groups like WikiLeaks by a variety of sources. Dissidents, whistleblowers, concerned citizens, and other providers have the common purpose to let secret, classified, and private correspondence that affect the public go public for all to review.

High profile cases of document releases include the video footage of a 2007 Baghdad air strike. Iraqi journalists were among those killed. Another controversy occurred when WikiLeaks distributed nearly 80,000 secret documents from the U.S. State Department regarding the War in Afghanistan.

The reporting of WikiLeaks has led to many changes in the world, including the release of information about the status of Arab leaders that played a part in the Arab Spring uprising. Other cables released by the group led to investigations by established newspapers and magazines into the actions of the U.S. and other foreign governments.

WikiLeaks won the *Economist's* New Media Award for 2008. Amnesty International gave the nonprofit organization the UK Media Award of 2009.

Creative Expressions for Human Rights

The activist approach to using art to work for peace often lands individual artists in trouble with their governments. Chinese political activist Ai Weiwei openly criticized his government's human rights policies and railed against the closed nature of communist rule.

One of the founders of the Chinese *avant garde* scene along with Huang Rui, Ma Desheng, and Wang Keping, among others, An Weiwei has mounted many controversial exhibitions considered immoral or anti-state by the government. In 1999, the artist founded the architectural school of FAKE Design and designed his studio to accommodate a teaching and learning center.

Understanding the importance of art to social stability, Chinese officials tried to convince the artist to design a cultural arts center that would not be so independent. When Ai Weiwei refused, authorities said his studio did not have the necessary permissions and threatened, according to the media, to knock the building down.

Ai Weiwei continued to gain worldwide fame during 2008 when he worked with Swiss architects from Herzog & du Meuron to create the Beijing National Stadium for the Olympics. Using his notoriety, the artist continued to inflame Chinese authorities with his decision to attend the Nobel Peace Prize ceremony for dissident Liu Xiaobo. He was prevented from leaving China and was soon under arrest. Ai Weiwei clamed it was in retaliation to his controversial artwork, especially the documentaries that featured dissidents, including one that highlighted the murder by police of Yang Jia.

In more protests against civil inefficiency and arbitrary government, the artist decided in 2010 to publicly demolish his studio. Before he could accomplish this public act of dissent, he was put under house arrest for what some believed was a trumped-up charge of tax evasion. In an attempt to stop Ai Weiwei from performing his high-profile display of opposition, his studio was demolished by authorities.

In April 2011, the artist was jailed for two months without the outside world knowing why. Supporters all over the world lobbied for his release. A

"Free Ai Weiwei" street art campaign drew international attention to his detainment. Another nonviolent protest, "1001 Chairs for Ai Weiwei," had the mission of bringing the world together to sit peacefully in support of the artist.

When authorities released the artist, Ai Weiwei said that he wasn't allowed to say much and he was prohibited from leaving Beijing for one year. World-wide supporters opened an Internet campaign to raise the money to pay his back taxes and so the struggle between the artist and the object of his protest continues in the light of open debate.

Poetry is an act of peace. Peace goes into the making of a poet as flour goes into the making of bread. — Pablo Neruda, Chilean writer

Art in its highest form is art that serves and instructs society and human development. — Harry Belafonte, American actor

19

Nonviolent Resistance: Burma's Buddhist Monk Vigils (2007)

Strategy for achieving socio-political or other goals without using violence; tactics such as nonviolent protests, civil disobedience, and economic or political non-cooperation.

In 1990, Aung San Suu Kyi's party, the National League for Democracy, won 59 percent of the vote in the general election in Burma. The newly elected members were arrested and Aung San Suu Kyi was denied the presidency. With their leader under house arrest all hope for democracy in the largest country in Indochina seemed, once again, doomed.

Nearly thirty years before, a military coup led by General Ne Win overthrew the democratic government of Burma. Aung Sang, father of Aung San Suu Kyi, was deposed by the new military rulers and for twenty-six years the dictatorship controlled the country by gunpoint, shooting and killing thousands of students and civilians. In 1989, the regime changed the name of the country from Burma to Myanmar, a reference to the majority ethnic group of the ruling regime.

After General Ne Win stepped down in 1988, there were mass protests calling for democratic elections. The military government reluctantly agreed in 1990. Yet when the opposition party won a majority, the military rulers failed to hand over power. The international community showed its condemnation by giving the Nobel Peace Prize to Aung San Suu Kyi.

The Virtue of Courage

In late 2007, Aung San Suu Kyi, who had encouraged her party to follow nonviolent principles, was still under house arrest. After forty-five years of

Aung San Suu Kyi, Nobel Peace Prize recipient and the democratic leader in Myanmar (Burma) (U.S. Campaign for Burma).

military rule, the opposition mounted another nonviolent resistance campaign against the government.

Over 20,000 Buddhist monks staged massive protests by clogging the streets of the capital.[1] The military responded by violently suppressing the revolt. As YouTube videos showed thousands of shaven-headed monks crowding the streets, new international awareness of the plight grew and widespread condemnation of the dictatorship gained energy.

Under increasingly intense pressure, the military government put forward a new constitution. They banned monks and protestors from voting and made campaigning against a government-backed referendum punishable with three years in prison.

Nonviolent resistance is a modern term for actions or refusals to comply with laws or demands in order to protest and eventually change the status quo. Evolved from the more inactive term "passive resistance," nonviolent resistance creates the inertia or energy needed to oppose powerful forces against change.

Mahatma Gandhi used nonviolent resistance strategies to drive the British colonial government out of India. Gandhi called it Satyagraha, or "truth force," by which the courage of conviction affects the hearts of the world as well as the actions of an opponent.

The courage to stand against a tyrant or bully or illegitimate government takes courage from the heart of a hero. From the Latin *coraticum*, or heart, courage is a quality of mind and spirit that enables the nonviolent activist to face danger and pain with bold action.

People with this virtue of conviction and bravery have used the tactics of nonviolent resistance to cause changes in many governments and laws. The peaceful transitions in India, the Philippines, Poland, and Serbia can all be directly linked to strategies that used nonviolence to overwhelm a dictatorship.

The protest movement in Myanmar employed many nonviolent tactics, including picketing, prayer vigils, protest art, community education, boycotts, sanctions, sabotage, and general strikes. Hunger strikes were staged by monks and supporters. Sixty helium balloons with "Butcher" and a swastika above a photo of General Than Shwe were released to cheering crowds. A banner at Insein Prison stated a plea to the late General and respected father of Aung San Suu Kyi: "They rape our country. Father General Aung San! Please come back and teach your army to be polite!"[2]

The government continued to dig in with repressive actions. When the cyclone of 2008 devastated the country and killed over 1,000 Burmese, the dictatorship refused international aid.

As of this printing, the nonviolent dissent in Myanmar has not resulted in a change in government. Yet international pressure is mounting and if the modern history of nonviolent resistance is any indication, the regime will eventually succumb to the "truth force" of a populace ready for freedom.

The Physics of Satyagraha

In addition to his influence on Aung San Suu Kyi, Mohandas Gandhi has been the inspiration for proponents of nonviolence since he stood on the banks of the sea, hand held high with salty sand, and called for the repeal of the oppressive salt tax. Gandhi was well aware of the philosophy of another icon of peace, Leo Tolstoy, calling him "the greatest apostle of non-violence that the present age has produced."[3]

Tolstoy built upon the Sermon on the Mount, a teaching by Jesus Christ, to advocate nonviolent resistance and anarcho-pacifism. Tolstoy wrote "A Letter to a Hindoo" to advocate the ways of nonviolence to achieve Indian independence from Great Britain. Gandhi and Tolstoy entered a correspondence, which in great part led to the Indian leader's dedication to nonviolence.

Satyagraha, or "Soul Force" or "Truth Force," was named by Gandhi as a reaction to the term "passive resistance," which was historically used to communicate the techniques of resistance without violence. Gandhi rejected the passive nature of the term in favor of one that communicated strength. "Truth (satya) implies love, and firmness (agraha) engenders and therefore serves as a synonym for force."[4]

When Gandhi became a firm adherent of nonviolence, the revolution begun by Albert Einstein in physics was nearly twenty-five years old. Though relativity and quantum mechanics were not identifiable sources of his conversion, Satyagraha used the word "force" as a central element in order to convey strength.

Agraha in Sanskrit means "with great enthusiasm" or "eagerness." It is an active term that conveys energy. Matched with Satya, or "truth" or "soul," this active element offers insight into how nonviolent resistance works and, more importantly, why it is necessary.

"The Satyagraha's object is to convert," Gandhi said, "not to coerce, the wrong-doer."[5] In the case of the British Raj or the military force of dictator Slobodan Milosevic, power is wielded by the central authority. In a fair fight, revolutionary groups will always be defeated by overwhelming force of arms.

In physics, force is an influence that causes something to undergo a change in direction, speed, or shape. Objects can be pushed and pulled. Newton's second law of motion (Force = mass $\times$ acceleration) tells us that something will keep going in proportion to the force acting upon it.

Power, according to physics, is the work performed or the energy converted. If you burn a chunk of coal, you convert the coal to energy, which can be used to act as a force.

In Satyagraha, the formulas of physics are in full force. When the oppressor uses an army to kill rebels, the revolution's energy is quelled. When the instruments of government are used to support the state, the force of dictatorship becomes far greater than the force for democracy.

However, the power of the people has the advantage of mass. In most cases, there is a tacit cooperation with the forces of oppression. The people pay taxes. They conform to rules. They obey curfews and speak of freedom only in the safety of their homes.

On the other hand, when cooperation and mass resistance is used against the forces of oppression, the energy begins to change from the oppressor to the oppressed. As rebellious citizens use methods of resistance, such as nonviolent protests and vigils, they change the dynamics of the energy that keeps them in chains.

What dictators often find, even when using violence to quell a protest, is that their power base begins to waver. Government officials begin to shirk their duties. The efficiency of fascism begins to bring chaos to civil systems. The military often goes over to the rebels when they realize that to fire upon the people means to fire on their families.

When news of protests begins to leak to the international press, public opinion becomes a force of energy to be reckoned with. First comes denunciation by human rights and justice organizations such as Amnesty International. Then comes public declarations by other governments. Then comes divestment and economic isolation.

The energy of dictatorship begins to change in the same way that the energy of a ball in motion begins to adapt to the forces upon it. Satyagraha moves the power of oppression from the oppressor to those that hold the "truth" or "soul" of freedom. It is no wonder that Albert Einstein became an icon of nonviolence. The formulas of physics apply to freedom the same as they apply to the rest of the universe.

By 1930, Gandhi's philosophy of nonviolence was well considered. He offered rules for satyagrahis to follow when entering a campaign of nonviolent resistance. These rules were intended to achieve a measure of discipline in adherents in order to strengthen the energy of the resistance.

The rules included harboring no anger and suffering the anger of the opponent. Gandhi told the satyagrahis to never retaliate and voluntarily submit to arrest. The Mahatma even cautioned against such personal behavior as cursing and insulting.

Even as prisoners, Gandhi said, satyagrahis must behave courteously and resist asking for special treatment. In all actions, the adherents display morality and common purpose. In this way, Gandhi believed, a nonviolent resistance can conquer the forces of power by bringing to bear the forces of truth.

Modern Strategies for Nonviolent Resistance

In Naypyidaw, Myanmar, when the monks took to the streets they not only took their long history of Buddhist nonviolence. Many were also well aware of the "book" on nonviolent revolution. When the protestors clogged Tahrir Square in Egypt during the Days of Rage, many had consulted the work of little-known Boston college professor Gene Sharp.

To chronicle and publicize the tactics of nonviolent struggle has been a life-long mission of Sharp. He is the founder of the Albert Einstein Institution, a nonprofit with the mission of defending democratic freedoms and institutions. The organization works to oppose dictatorship and oppression, stop genocide, and reduce the reliance on violence by governments and revolutionaries.

Professor Sharp literally wrote the book on nonviolent tactics in the 1990s. After studying the philosophies of Thoreau, Tolstoy, Gandhi, and other icons of nonviolence for his doctoral thesis, Sharp wrote in 1973 *The Politics of Nonviolence*. His central thesis is that power is not derived from a monolithic political state but rather from the citizens.

The systems that are set up to encourage and demand obedience by citizens consist of the courts and police, the culture and social norms, as well as the economic rewards and sanctions. All can be disrupted through the tactics of resistance. All can be brought down by nonviolent action.

His writings and philosophy have been inspirations to many individuals and organizations that decline the invitation of violence to meet their goals. The revolutionaries of Serbia's Otpor group wrote to Sharp about his book, *Dictatorship to Democracy*. The Einstein Institution provided 12,000 books for free. Some of Sharp's 198 ways of nonviolent resistance are summarized below:

- Formal statements such as public speeches and petitions
- Communications with a wider audience including banners, pamphlets and articles in newspapers
- Group representations such as mock awards and picketing
- Symbolic public acts such as public prayer and destruction of personally-owned property
- Pressure on individuals including taunting officials and vigils in front of an official's house

- Drama and music such as singing and performance of plays
- Processions such as parades and pilgrimages
- Honoring the dead with mock funerals and public mourning
- Public assemblies including teach-ins and meetings of protest
- Withdrawal and renunciations such as walk-outs and silences
- Ostracism of persons including social boycott and excommunication
- Non-cooperation with social events, customs, and institutions
- Withdrawal from social systems by staying at home or "flight"
- Action by consumers such as boycotts and withholding rent
- Action by workers and producers through boycott
- Action by middlemen by supplier boycotts
- Action by owners and management through lockouts and strikes
- Action by holders of financial resources by refusing to pay fees or provide funds
- Action by governments through trade embargos and blacklisting
- Economic non-cooperation through strikes and closures
- Rejection of authority by refusing public support
- Citizens' non-cooperation with government by boycotting elections and withdrawal from institutions
- Citizens' alternatives to obedience by slow compliance
- Actions by government personnel by blocking communication and mutiny
- Domestic government action through evasions and delays
- International government actions by closing embassies and refusal of membership in organizations
- Psychological intervention by hunger strikes and self-exposure
- Physical interventions by sit-ins and occupation
- Social interventions through guerrilla theater and creating alternative institutions
- Economic interventions such as land seizure and dumping
- Political interventions such as overloading administrative systems and creating parallel governments

The entire list of nonviolent methods was published in *The Politics of Nonviolent Actions, Vol. 2: The Methods of Nonviolent Action*, by Porter Sargent Publishers.[6] The list can be downloaded from the Albert Einstein Institution where Sharp is director (www.aeinstein.org).

It is not power that corrupts, but fear. Fear of losing power corrupts those who wield it and fear of the scourge of power corrupts those who are subject to it. — Aung San Suu Kyi, Burmese prime minister-elect

Nonviolence should never be used as a shield for cowardice. It is a weapon for the brave. — Mahatma Gandhi

The first principle of non-violent action is that of non-cooperation with everything that is humiliating. — César Chávez

20

Arms Reduction: Strategic Offensive Reduction Treaty (2003)

Negotiations and treaties for the purpose of reducing or eliminating arma-
ments, including nuclear, biological, chemical, and radiological weapons of
mass destruction as well as other weaponry of war.

At the height of the Cold War, the United States and the Soviet Union
had deployed an estimated 75,000 warheads more powerful than the bombs
dropped on Japan in 1945.[1] The world's two superpowers squared off with a
deadly mix of military coalitions, resource strategies, espionage, propaganda,
as well as a costly and dangerous arms race.

The two Cold War powers tried to impede the weapons race through
various arms reduction treaties, including the 1972 Anti-Ballistic Missile
(ABM) treaty. Yet after the Soviet Union collapsed in the late 1980s, the
nuclear club had grown to nine countries and was expanding. There was no
end in site to the expansion of new and more technologically sophisticated
arms.

At the turn of the century and with the administration of George W.
Bush, the forty-third president, dangerous nuclear posturing reached a new
level. The United States withdrew from the historic ABM treaty. One day
later, Russia withdrew from the Strategic Arms Reduction Talk (START II)
treaty, which was signed in 1993 by George H. W. Bush, the forty-first president, and the first president of the Russian Federation, Boris Yeltsin.

In 2002, George W. Bush traveled to meet with Russian president
Vladimir Putin to see whether a new arms treaty was possible. The resulting
Moscow Treaty, or Strategic Offensive Reduction Treaty (SORT), limited the
arsenals of Russia and the U.S. to 1700–2200 operationally deployed warheads.

Critics of the new treaty charged that there were no verification provisions or benchmarks. Most weapons limited were only to be disassembled, not destroyed. Also, the treaty could be ended with three months notice.

The SORT treaty, with all its hope and inadequacies, was an example and another step along the belabored process of disarmament. Written into the SORT agreement was a provision that the treaty would end after ten years. In 2011, a year before the deadline, SORT was replaced by the New START treaty, which was negotiated by U.S. president Obama and Russian Federation president Medvedev.

The name New START shows a telling lack of creativity that has plagued arms reduction. After START I expired, and the stillborn START II ended, and the START III talks were never concluded, a New START treaty seemed just another in a series of fall-short failures. One of the most important processes to the future of humankind simply continued in a familiar frame.

The Virtue of Logic

For over fifty years, the world's nuclear arsenal has been kept at the ready. One of the reasons those in charge do not pull the trigger is the remembrance of the horrific devastation from the first nuclear weapons. Photographs of burning bodies and dying children from Hiroshima and Nagasaki are still in our collective memory.

Even as the mushroom clouds dissipated over the two Japanese cities, death continued for decades to come. In addition to the 150,000 to 250,000 dead in the first four months, people experienced excruciating deaths from the effects of flash burns, radiation sickness, leukemia, and other related illnesses.

The reasoning or arguments against further use of nuclear weapons demanded the continuous use of logic by those in charge of the arsenal. Logic depends on sound reasoning or judgment. The devastation and human suffering of the nuclear bombing in 1945 provided the world with indisputable evidence of the insanity required for further use.

As the world's citizens looked on with a helpless mixture of fear and hope, the principle of "mutual assured destruction" provided the logic of common sense to prevent an incomprehensible disaster. Leaders of the nuclear powers found their way through this dangerous fifty-year period without resorting to atomic or nuclear weapons.

No More Nukes

Today, even amidst the uncreative treaties that still have a difficult time with ratification, there is a glimmer of hope for nuclear arms reduction and even for elimination. In 2007, several high-profile statesmen wrote an open letter that appeared in *The Wall Street Journal.*

Entitled "A World Free of Nuclear Weapons," the letter urged the world to galvanize in order to "reduce reliance on nuclear weapons, to prevent their spread into potentially dangerous hands, and ultimately to end them as a threat to the world."[2]

This high profile letter signed by national security experts and political leaders signaled a huge change. The idea of a nuclear-free world could no longer be ignored. The principals of the initiative were former U.S. secretaries of state George P. Shultz and Henry Kissinger, former secretary of defense William Perry, and former senator and CEO of the Nuclear Threat Initiative Sam Nunn.

All are respected leaders in foreign policy. Each hailed from different political traditions and joined regardless of party affiliation. These men were not who the world expected to advocate an end to nuclear weapons.

Yet their desire and intent was there in black and white on the pages of one of the most conservative newspapers in the world. Adding even more energy to the initiative was the recollection by Schultz of the 1986 Reagan-Gorbachev Reykjavik Summit in Iceland when the two came to the brink of eliminating all nuclear weapons. Reagan's insistence on keeping "Star Wars" research (Strategic Defense Initiative) was unacceptable to the Russian leader and the talks collapsed, yet the torch of full disarmament was lit.

The vision created that cold day in Iceland, of a world without nukes, stayed in the imaginations of policy wonks as well as concerned citizens of the world. When the letter written and signed by the principals of the Nuclear Security Project was published in *The Wall Street Journal*, millions took heart from the processes it expressed:

• Change the Cold War posture of deployed nuclear weapons to increase warning time and thereby reduce the danger of an accidental or unauthorized use of a nuclear weapon.

• Continue to reduce substantially the size of nuclear forces in all states that possess them.

• Eliminate short-range nuclear weapons designed to be forward-deployed.

• Initiate a bipartisan process with the Senate, including understandings to increase confidence and provide for periodic review, to achieve ratification of the Comprehensive Test Ban Treaty, taking advantage of recent technical advances, and working to secure ratification by other key states.

• Provide the highest possible standards of security for all stocks of weapons, weapons-usable plutonium, and highly enriched uranium everywhere in the world.

• Get control of the uranium enrichment process, combined with the guarantee that uranium for nuclear power reactors could be obtained at a reasonable price, first from the Nuclear Suppliers Group and then from the International Atomic Energy Agency (IAEA) or other controlled international reserves. It will also be necessary to deal with proliferation issues presented by spent fuel from reactors producing electricity.

• Halt the production of fissile material for weapons globally; phase out the use of highly enriched uranium in civil commerce and remove weapons-usable uranium from research facilities around the world and render the materials safe.

• Redouble our efforts to resolve regional confrontations and conflicts that give rise to new nuclear powers.

With these steps laid out by the Nuclear Security Project, the stage was set for a world debate on the elimination of nuclear weapons. Now all that was needed was for a new generation of leaders to embrace the vision of these respected and stalwart policy experts and begin the hard work necessary for implementation.

A Controversial Peace Prize

"My Administration," President Barack Obama said in 2010 in a letter that continued a series of writings and speeches advocating radical arms control, "is dedicated to seeking the peace and security of a world without nuclear weapons, and we are taking concrete steps toward that goal."[3]

With the stops and starts that plagued arms reduction in the twentieth century, a new vision of nuclear negotiations is beginning to evolve. Building on the momentum that the Nuclear Security Project was building, Obama began to promote the idea that a nuclear weapon-free world was possible. His campaign promise of "Yes, we can" had resounded among idealists and pragmatists alike.

After he negotiated the New Start treaty, he promised it "will set the stage for further cuts, and we will seek to include all nuclear weapons states in this endeavor."[4] He also promised to ratify the Comprehensive Test Ban Treaty and secure nuclear materials around the globe.

Much progress has been made. Steps have been taken to secure the world's nuclear materials, which after the fall of the Soviet Union were dangerously

United States president Obama and president of the Russian Federation Medvedev signing a nuclear reduction treaty, 2010 (The White House, Chuck Kennedy).

undocumented and stored. The military has endeavored to limit the cold-war thinking in its consideration of a military strike. The U.S. also promised not to threaten non-nuclear nations with nuclear weapons.

Politics, election cycles, and fear have combined to bring Obama's initial enthusiasm to a halt. Yet the celebratory spirit of his election regarding militarism is not without a remembrance. In a surprise move, the Nobel Committee awarded the 2009 Nobel Peace Prize to Barack Obama, citing the new president "for his extraordinary efforts to strengthen international diplomacy and cooperation between peoples."[5]

In addition, the Committee lauded him for his commitment to nuclear nonproliferation and his efforts to open dialogue and understanding with the Muslim world. Indeed in 2009 as the world celebrated the election of the first African American to the presidency, the world seemed a more hopeful place.

Yet words are not actions, so many were critical of the Committee's decision. In his acceptance speech in Oslo, Obama admitted that the work had only begun and promised an "effort to prevent the spread of nuclear weapons, and to seek a world without them."[6]

Putting aside the fear that would have to be overcome in order to achieve real arms reduction, the arms trade industry is an extremely powerful lobby. It consists of a symbiotic web of arms manufacturers, sellers, politicians, and hundreds of national, international, and private militaries. The arms lobby supplies the world with missiles and guns, ammunition and electronics, drones and surveillance equipment, ships and aircraft, as well as thousands of miscellaneous small arms and munitions.

The worldwide total for military expenditures each year is estimated to be over $1.5 trillion. This is nearly 3 percent of World Gross Product (WGP). This does not account for the legitimate secondary arms trade or the extensive black market. The military-industrial complex, as former President Dwight D. Eisenhower called it, weaves a powerful network of arms hawkers between the governments and businesses throughout the world.

In addition to nuclear weapons proliferation and large arms sales, the race to deploy weapons in space began in the 1960s with the potential deployment of the Soviet Union's Polyot-Kosmos anti-satellite system (ASAT). The ABM treaty stopped that program at that time but both superpowers continue to flirt with space-based weapons.

Regarding other armaments, several treaties have been introduced to limit the use of dangerous weapons during and after a conflict where the horrors of their use became real. Chemical weapons treaties have been in effect since 1925 after the torturous use of mustard gas in World War I. In 1975, to prevent another horrible test of weapons technology, the Biological Weapons Convention went into force.

Today, many nations have also signed the Ottawa Treaty, or Mine Ban Treaty, which bans all anti-personnel landmines. In addition, efforts are also being mounted to ban the use of cluster bombs, which endanger children who later find unexploded bombs.

Jody Williams, Nobel Peace Prize recipient for her untiring and successful work on the historic land mine treaty (The Nobel Foundation, Eriend Aas).

The drive to reduce the flow of smaller weapons has had little success but there are signs of promise. The Nairobi Protocol for the Prevention, Control and Reduction of Small Arms and Light Weapons, was signed in 2004. Until the international community gets behind such agreements, the arms industry will continue to arm the world.

Let us not deceive ourself: we must elect world peace or world destruction.— Bernard Mannes Baruch, American financier

Our future on this planet, exposed as it is to nuclear annihilation, depends on one single factor: humanity must make a moral about-face. — Pope John Paul II

The way to win an atomic war is to make sure it never starts. — Omar Bradley, American general

21

Humanitarianism: Rescue of the Hungarian Jews (1944–1945)

Active compassion toward other human beings through kindness, benevolent treatment, and assistance; the doctrine that a person's duty is to promote universal human welfare.

During World War II, when the horrors of the Holocaust became apparent, Swedish diplomat Raoul Wallenberg was serving at the embassy in Budapest, Hungary, where he saw Nazi invaders take Jewish property and ban Jewish publications. He watched helplessly while soldiers gathered and forced entire families into concentration camps.

Wallenberg had a deep, heartfelt reaction and decided to act against what he saw as an abomination against humanity. Inspired by the *Scarlet Pimpernel*, an adventure novel set during the French Revolution, he gave diplomatic protection to several thousand Jews. Wallenberg housed them and gave them false embassy passports to identify them as Swedish nationals.

It is estimated that Wallenberg's program saved 15,000 people from the Nazi "final solution."[1] Yet it was not just the Swedish diplomat who risked his life. Over 300 people were involved in the successful effort to save Hungarian Jews. Indeed, during that disgraceful time, there were untold thousands in many countries, including industrialist Oskar Schindler, who put their own lives at risk to save their fellow human beings.

The Virtue of Empathy

To have such courage takes a potent combination of sensitivity to others, combined with an intense need to alleviate others' misfortunes. To be empathic means having the capacity to deeply experience the feelings or thoughts of another person. Empathy was derived from the late eighteenth century translation by German philosopher Rudolf Lotze of the Greek term *empatheia,* which he found helpful in conveying the idea of *pathos,* or suffering.

A person with empathy has the power to be in communion with the emotions of others, which leads to understanding, compassion, and action. Those who possess the virtue of empathy find it difficult to stand by and watch injustices. They suffer with those who are the victims. These individuals are the heroes of history, yet because of their pure intentions to act for the benefit of others, these heroes most often go unnoticed and unrecognized, or even distrusted and punished for their efforts.

In Wallenberg's case, his legacy is a poignant postscript of such an injustice. After the Nazis were defeated in 1945, the Soviet Union occupied the Western front, including Hungary. Apparently on orders from the paranoid dictator Joseph Stalin, Raoul Wallenberg was arrested on suspicion of being an American spy.

The man who saved so many lives from the Holocaust ended his life in Moscow's Lubyanka prison in 1947. The circumstances of his death are shrouded in mystery.

Humanitarianism is often associated with individuals but it is also at the core belief of many service organizations. In 1859, Henri Dunant wrote a book that inspired the creation of the International Committee of the Red Cross (ICRC). Today, the Red Cross and Red Crescent are international organizations with an estimated 97 million volunteers working to protect human life. In 1901, Dunant received one of the first Nobel Peace Prizes.

In his commentary, *The Fundamental Principles of the Red Cross,* former ICRC Director Jean Pictet pointed out the universal characteristics of humanitarianism. "The wellspring of the principle of humanity," he said in *The Fundamental Principles of the Red Cross,* "is in the essence of social morality which can be summed up in a single sentence, Whatsoever ye would that men should do to you, do ye even so to them."[2]

This fundamental precept of humanitarianism can be found in almost identical form in all the great religions. Its principle can also be found in secular aid organizations that mount regional and global responses to humanitarian crises such as natural disasters and famine. For instance, the United Nations Office for the Coordination of Humanitarian Affairs was formed in 1991 to coordinate the U.N.'s response to disasters and humanitarian crises.

Another example of organized humanitarianism was the response to the 2004 earthquake in the Indian Ocean, which sent a wave of destruction across Indonesia, Sri Lanka, and Thailand. Over 200,000 people were killed and millions lost their homes. The profound health crisis caused by the tsunami saw large populations in the Indian Ocean region plagued with dysentery, cholera, and typhoid. Millions lacked clean water, food, and health care. The international community responded to images of the mass destruction in the Indian Ocean with an unprecedented humanitarianism: $14 billion in humanitarian aid.[3]

Universal Declaration of Human Rights

Humanitarians are inspired to act in ways that preserve the full range of human rights. From freedom from hunger to protection from arbitrary government, the basic rights and freedoms that prevent abuse and oppression and preserve the dignity and health of all people are the basis for our authority to act on behalf of others.

Throughout history the great documents of humankind have given direction and the basis for action to those who would act for their human brothers and sisters. In ancient times, the Edict of Cyrus the Great was a testament to toleration of other religions and forms of worship. The Magna Carta of 1215 limited the power of petty lords and set out the need for agreement between political powers. The Twelve Articles of 1526 recorded human rights of peasants against the backdrop of war against the Swabian League.

In America, the Declaration of Independence and the Constitution encoded the civil rights and freedoms espoused by European Enlightenment philosophy. The Emancipation Proclamation of Lincoln opened the first door to many required for an end to slavery.

The culmination of the effort to fully document the rights of humanity was adopted in 1948 at the Palais de Chaillot in Paris by the United Nations. The progressive articles of the document, outlining hard-won rights of all humans, now have the force of international law.

In the Preamble of the Declaration, the rights and freedoms of all humans are expressed in both general and specific tenants. "All human beings are born free and equal in dignity and rights. They are endowed with reason and conscience and should act towards one another in a spirit of brotherhood."

According to the Universal Declaration of Human Rights, everyone, all peoples and individuals from all nations, have the following rights:

- Right to life, liberty and security
- Right to freedom from slavery or servitude
- Right to freedom from torture or from cruel, inhuman or degrading treatment or punishment
- Right to equality and protection before and of the law

UNICEF is one of the United Nations humanitarian efforts funded by government and private donations (UNICEF/NYHQ2008-0255, Susan Markisz).

- Right to freedom from arbitrary arrest, detention, or exile
- Right to a fair and public hearing by an independent and impartial tribunal
- Right to the presumption of innocence
- Right to freedom from harsh penalties
- Right to freedom from attacks or arbitrary interference with privacy
- Right to freedom of movement and residence within the borders of each state
- Right to seek asylum from persecution
- Right to a nationality
- Right to freely enter into marriage and found a family
- Right to own property
- Right to freedom of thought, conscience, and religion

- Right to freedom of opinion and expression
- Right to peaceful assembly and association
- Right to take part in government, directly or through freely chosen representatives
- Right to the will of the people as the basis of the authority of government
- Right to work and equal pay
- Right to form and to join trade unions
- Right to rest and leisure
- Right to an adequate standard of living
- Right to special care, protection, and assistance for mothers and children
- Right to education directed to the full development of the human personality and to the strengthening of respect for human rights and fundamental freedoms
- Right to freely participate in the cultural life of the community, to enjoy the arts, and to share in scientific advancement and its benefits

The World House

For the rights and freedoms of humanity to truly be expressed, they must be of the greatest concern to everyone on the planet. The Rev. Dr. Martin Luther King, Jr., held a grand vision of what the world will look like when its citizens embrace the idea that everyone can be invited under the great tent of freedom.

In King's "World House Essay," which was a chapter in his 1967 book, *Where Do We Go from Here: Chaos or Community*, King urges us to live together in harmony. It is a call to humanitarians everywhere to fight what he considers the three great challenges, racism, poverty, and war.

Racism leads to economic exploitation. Poverty shows a lacking of the human will to eradicate hunger, disease, and lack of the basic necessities for life. War is the scourge of humanity, often the first choice when alternatives are available. Peace is having the wisdom to make these obsolete.

"We have inherited a big house," King said in a speech at the University of Oslo, "a great 'world house' in which we have to live together — black and white, Easterners and Westerners, Gentiles and Jews, Catholics and Protestants, Moslem and Hindu, a family unduly separated in ideas, culture, and interests who, because we can never again live without each other, must learn, somehow, in this one big world, to live with each other."[4]

We must live together, King says, or we will "perish as fools." Humanitarians must realize that we are connected, rich and poor, and that we are our brother's keeper, especially when circumstances prevent human dignity.

"This call for a world-wide fellowship that lifts neighborly concern beyond one's tribe, race, class and nation is in reality a call for an all-embracing and unconditional love for all men."

In this essay and his other great works and speeches, King called for a strategy of nonviolence that would be taught in schools and be the subject of experimentation. We must move from a materialistic culture, King believed, to a people-focused society, then the world will no longer be subject to the devastation and indignities of racism, poverty, and war.

"We still have a choice today," he set out our choice, "nonviolent coexistence or violent coannihilation. This may well be mankind's last chance to choose between chaos and community."

Teach this triple truth to all: A generous heart, kind speech, and a life of service are the things which renew humanity.—Siddhartha Guatama, *the Buddha*

Humanitarianism consists in never sacrificing a human being to a purpose.—Albert Schweitzer, Franco-German theologian and physician

22

Distributive Justice: Jubilee 2000 Drop the Debt Campaign (2000)

An egalitarian philosophy of working for the just or right distribution of goods in the world; ensuring that unequal, unjust standards of living do not create the conditions for violence.

Average citizens in many developing countries live what is essentially a ball-and-chain existence due to their country's exorbitant interest payments on a national debt. Hundreds of billions of dollars in what are essentially "unpayable loans" have been issued to debtor nations by global development organizations such as the World Bank and the International Monetary Fund (IMF).[1]

The idea of using the wealth of rich nations to fund development in poorer nations through international loans goes back to the global development strategies of the 1970s. With the rapid rise in oil prices, Oil Producing Exporting Countries (OPEC) began to amass huge reserves in Western banks. The availability of this capital was seen as a way to help developing nations fund prosperity and decrease political instability in the world.

However, payments of interest on these huge debts soon became overwhelming for many struggling countries. And the results from many funded projects did not necessarily lead to increased economic growth or political stability. In many cases, corrupt dictators and their cronies siphoned off much of the money while the populace was left to pay the mounting interest.

This unsustainable situation led many debtor nations to default. Countries were forced to renegotiate new loans to support the old debt. The loans were now hindering development in the very countries they were meant to help. The global wealth redistribution programs of the IMF and the World Bank seemed to have accomplished the opposite of their intent.

As the situation became more untenable, many who believe in distributive justice began calling for Western banks to forgive the loans. Sparse capital, which was being used for interest payments, was desperately needed for sustainable development. The issue of fairness was at the core of the debate: fairness to the banks who issued the loans, and fairness for the citizens of debtor nations who were now paying for a legacy of bad debt.

Through the 1980s, debt reduction debates gained little international concern until celebrities focused the world's attention on the problem. In the 1990s, musicians Bob Geldof of the band Boomtown Rats and Bruce Springsteen of the E Street Band began staging humanitarian concerts in high-profile venues in many countries.

The Virtue of Fairness

Just as there is a sense of righteousness in justice, there is a deep sense of beauty in fairness. Indeed, fairness is derived from the Old English word *fægernyss*, which means beauty. Fair treatment is unbiased and free of injustice. To give a fair shake requires more than a superficial view of conditions. It demands full consideration of the circumstances along with evenhandedness in the application of justice.

The association of fairness and justice was not lost on the celebrities that brought focus to the plight of debtor nations. Geldof and Bono of the Irish band U2 had displayed a commitment to justice in their private and public lives, as well as in their song lyrics.

It was a boost to the debt forgiveness campaign when Bono signed on with the Jubilee 2000 campaign, the name of which recalls the Jewish and Christian tradition of forgiving loans on a person's fiftieth birthday. Under the banner of the U.N. initiative NetAid, Bono and others began staging live concerts.

In 2000, the Irish rocker paid a highly publicized visit to the Pope as part of the Church's Jubilee celebration in Rome. Soon other famous politicians and artists, such as Bill Clinton, Nelson Mandela, David Bowie, and Quincy Jones, lent their support for the mounting global effort.

High-profile publicity put intense international pressure on Western governments and banks to forgive the loans of nations on the verge of bankruptcy. For many people, the "Drop the Debt" campaign was a moral and economic issue, not a political issue. In a world of increasing globalization, the restraints on development for the few, said activists, hold back the entire world.

Bono and other campaigners traveled to meet with many country leaders, including then-president George W. Bush of the United States. Bono was invited to speak at the G7 economic forum in 2005. The nations in attendance had begun to understand the extent of the threat to world prosperity and peace.

In a victory for distributive justice, the loaning countries, the banks, and international organizations negotiated an agreement. To the surprise of many, they announced the cancellation of around $40 billion of unpayable loans.[2]

Injustices in Society

The accomplishment of the debt relief campaign was a great boon to those who work for justice. Yet the world is in far greater need of fair shakes than one victory can repair.

The national and individual distribution of burdens and rewards globally is the subject of much study and debate. The disparity, or gap, in the distribution of rewards and burdens of global economic income and assets has risen to alarming proportions.

It is not just country-to-country disparity, which has been the case for thousands of years. With increased communication, especially through the Internet, the gap between the rich and poor is not only more apparent to everyone but also more destructive to good feelings between humans. According to the International Monetary Fund, the richest 1 percent of people receive nearly 14 percent of global income, while the bottom 20 percent receive only 1.27 percent of the total.[3] By 2012, due to the global turndown, growth was nearly flat.

North America, with just 5 percent of the world's population, has over 34 percent of the world's riches. Asia, with over 50 percent of the population has less than 26 percent. The statistics go on to prove that the gap between rich people and poor people, rich countries and poor, is increasing due to many factors.

No matter how the statistics are framed, the disparity in income and assets is causing resentment and animosity. The call for a more just global society has risen in tempo until the incidence of citizens taking to the streets and terrorism occurring around the world can be, at least partially, attributed to the growing awareness of social injustice.

Restoring the Balance of Justice

Social injustice is felt in many ways, including the imbalance of goods and services, or freedoms and equality, or access to rule of law. Injustices occur when people are treated differently because of gender or race, or caste or creed.

It might be measured in the inability to find health care, education, and quality housing, or in the ability to afford food or have access to life-saving drugs. Barriers to a balanced society can be as subtle as stereotyping or as overt as disenfranchisement due to lack of property and voting rights or simply being female.

When economic disparity increases between nations and among individuals within nations, it limits opportunity. Oppressive laws, racism, and other barriers to employment are many times tilted against the least powerful in society. Low wages, unequal pay, and burdensome taxation often lead to below subsistence outcomes.

The effects on the victims of economic disparity are expressed in emotional depression, dangerous health problems, shorter life expectancy, and a life lived in the violence wrought by slum-like conditions. No matter what the cause, the subtle ravages of injustice affect our basic rights.

In many parts of the world, the indicators of income and economic justice fluctuate dramatically. During the early decades of the twentieth century, for instance, American prosperity increased at a rapid rate. Yet in the latter decades, with the need for workers with news skills to meet technological changes as well as the competition caused by globalization, income disparity between the haves and have-nots indicated economic stagnation.

As the gap between the rich and poor becomes so wide as to cause potential violent upheaval, the debate about corrective measures is more intense. When new knowledge and awareness about racial injustices and economic exploitation surfaces, the idea of restorative justice enters the debate.

Theories of redistributive justice are concerned mainly with the restoration of justice. To right the wrong, or at least make amends, is the intention. Many times, the simple acknowledgment of an injustice done is enough to settle a dispute. As in the case of a public apology, such as the speech U.S. president Bill Clinton gave to address the historical injustices on the American Indian population, the lack of denial for historic injustice is often more important than compensation.

For injustices that are egregious or long-suffering, a transfer of physical assets is often required to redress the grievance. Recompense can be land transferred, or fair value paid for property, or an apology for an injustice that led to lack of opportunity. It also can be a change in a law or in the settlement of a court case where the victim is vindicated by the judgment of a judge or jury.

The measure of how much action needs to be taken depends on the availability of resources and the distribution methods available. In considering how to correct social injustice, three questions must be considered.

1. What is the basis for the injustice?
2. Who should be restored?
3. What should be restored?

In the case of the Native American population of the United States, the basis for injustice was the historical overrunning of land and the massacre of populations. The restorative action, per Clinton's apology, was meant to restore dignity to the heirs of the tribes that still survive and express remorse for actions done by ancestors long dead. To many of the American indigenous populations, the apology was a weak attempt at recompense, yet the action is now on the record.

The overall purpose of distributive justice is to maximize justice across the vast differences and circumstances of the human condition. Restorative justice moves beyond the idea of punishment of the perpetrators, which is often inadequate compensation with no real benefit to the victim. To un-do the wrong, as far as possible, through monetary reparations or service to a community goes much further in creating the conditions of present peace.

There are many tangible and intangible benefits to acknowledging an injury. Restorative justice encourages better actions and behavior in the future and increases current security and the potential for prosperity. Actions of restorative and distributive justice foster a culture of peace by increasing dialogue between victim and victimizer. Dealing with injustices, rather than sweeping them under the carpet, inevitably leads to accountability and diminishes the compounding effects of suspicion, hate, and long-standing tensions.

> *The progress of freedom depends more upon the maintenance of peace, the spread of commerce, and the diffusion of education, than upon the labours of cabinets and foreign offices.* — Richard Cobden, English statesman

> *Justice is the first virtue of social institutions, as truth is of systems of thought.* — John Rawls, American philosopher

23

Witnessing Violence: Human Shield Action in Iraq (2003)

To observe and document acts of violence, inhumanity, and war; to keep violent acts in the public eye in order to increase pressure on the perpetrators.

Violence is traumatizing, whether it's a child in an abusive home or refugees fleeing the ravages of war. Those who experience violence, or observe it firsthand, can't help but internalize its negative effects. The result is often a profound and self-defeating silence.

When people look the other way, persons or groups committing acts of violence have free rein to act with little regard to humanity. Bullies and abusers depend on the fearful as well as the complicit silence of victims and bystanders. This is why vocal witnesses to violence are ultimately important in our hope to limit violence in families, neighborhoods, and throughout our global community.

Today, witnessing violence has new tools. Advances in media technology such as the Internet have made it increasingly difficult for the purveyors of violence to be hidden from the public eye. Those tools are being utilized by many organizations, such as Amnesty International and Christian Peacemaker Teams (CPT), which have the specific mission of witnessing violence in hotbeds of conflict.

CPT is a program of Brethren, Quaker, and Mennonite churches that sends teams to troubled spots such as Palestine, Colombia, and the Congo. These courageous witnesses believe their unarmed, nonviolent intervention into conflict zones, where team members are often exposed to injury and death, can transform the situation or at least reduce the potential for violence.

In April of 2003, as the world debated whether the use of violence in Iraq was justified, the United States launched operation "Shock and Awe" to depose the dictatorship of Saddam Hussein. For those who did not believe in the reasoning for the impending war, preparations began to oppose the invasion by various means, including being on the ground as human shields when the bombing began.

As early as October of 2002, delegations from Christian Peacemakers had gathered in Baghdad. Soon the sixty-two members were visiting with church leaders and U.N. representatives. They held vigils across the mainly Muslim country, focusing on Baghdad, Basra, and Mosul. They visited hospitals, schools, orphanages, and markets, and met with ordinary Iraqis.

The Virtue of Mindfulness

Witnesses to violence see their role in the world not as passive bystanders, but as activists for nonviolence. Christian Peacemaker Teams and other groups and individuals are in some ways the opposite of the Japanese maxim of the "wise" monkeys. To "see no evil, hear no evil, and speak no evil" is to stand by and let the violence continue.

A fourth "wise" monkey is sometimes added to cultural representations of the proverb. To "do no evil" becomes the active, moral imperative. It is the opposite of standing on the sidelines, being silent, or putting the violence wrought on our brothers and sisters out of our minds.

The only way to "do" no evil is to be active in witnessing it, to be mindful of its conditions. Witnesses are aware of the violence. They are present to it. The concept of mindfulness is to be attentive or aware of one's responsibility in life.

On the night of the "Shock and Awe" campaign, the CPT teams stood as witnesses of the impending war. Together with the Chicago-based Voices in the Wilderness, the teams held around-the-clock vigils at a water treatment plant near a hospital in Baghdad. Despite being vilified as traitors in the media, the group held to their ideals.

In a few short days, the bombing devastated many Iraqi cities. As far as the invasion goes, the war was deemed successful. Yet the Iraqi army simply folded seamlessly into the populace. As the U.S.–led coalition settled in for what was intended to be a short and transitional occupation, the fighting simply took on other forms. A guerrilla war began in the cities where sectarian violence, which had been held at bay by the dominant Sunni party of Saddam Hussein, soon erupted.

Thousands of innocents as well as the parties to violence lost their lives in a long and bloody occupation. The Christian Peacemaker Teams continued to document, photograph, videotape, and send interviews to the world. In November of 2005, tragedy struck as the world looked on. Four members of a team were kidnapped. Veteran CPTer Tom Fox, a Quaker activist from Clear Brook, Virginia, was murdered.

James W. Booth writes in *Communities of Memory*: "I will then consider bearing witness as a matter of doing justice, in the sense of seeing that the victims of injustice have their day before the law, even if they themselves were no longer present."[1]

It takes courage to be against the drumbeat of war and especially to become a "shield" against violence. Theories in response-based therapy show that when people are treated inhumanely, they will rise up and resist. When people give accounts of violence, the world is more likely to find a determined resistance.

The Activists of Amnesty International

"Open your newspaper any day of the week," wrote British lawyer Peter Benenson in his 1961 article "The Forgotten Prisoners," "and you will find a report from somewhere in the world of someone being imprisoned, tortured or executed because his opinions or religion are unacceptable to his government. There are several million such people in prison — by no means all of them behind the Iron and Bamboo Curtains — and their numbers are growing."[2]

Amnesty International was founded that same year by Benenson and six others committed to witnessing on behalf of the untold abused and abandoned. It is Amnesty's mission to conduct research and generate action to "prevent and end grave abuses of human rights." They extend their action to a demand for justice to those whose rights have been violated.

Around the world, thousands and thousands of people are in prison for their beliefs, lifestyles, and actions in defense of freedom. In Myanmar, where Aung San Suu Kyi has spent decades under house arrest, it is estimated that over 2,000 political prisoners are held. And that's just one country.

The extent of the carnage of imprisonment, killings, kidnappings, and torture can never be known. Yet those individuals who work and support Amnesty International make it their duty to find examples and situations where witnessing the violence can make a difference.

Amnesty's teams get information from many sources, including prisoners and survivors, journalists and lawyers, and refugees and diplomats. Many workers for Nongovernmental Organizations forward documents, videos, photos, and word-of-mouth stories about what they've seen and heard. The information is checked out and verified, then passed along to their global army of witnessing human rights workers who write letters and get the word out on past crimes and current abuse.

The Internet and all forms of digital media help mobilize public opinion and put pressure on the abusers. Standard media such as newspapers and television help with in-depth stories and background. Websites, blogs, and social networking all contribute to the distribution of information and the uncovering of concerns about new imprisonments and intimidation.

The results are impressive. The group brought the term "prisoner of consciousness" into the public dialogue. Adding the right to fair trial and the horrible effects of "disappearances" to their list of concerns, Amnesty International expanded their attention to beyond the prison walls. The list of abuses included struggling countries like Rwanda, the Congo, and the former Yugoslavia as well as powerful nations such as the United States and China.

The constant attention of groups like Amnesty International has kept in the public light the abuses at the U.S. government's detention facility at Guantanamo Bay. In Iraq and Afghanistan, Amnesty has charged both sides, Coalition forces as well as the Taliban, with grave human rights abuses and killing of civilians.

Recently, the work of Amnesty's members have bore witness to the constantly changing environments of abuse in the wake of the Arab Spring. In Libya and Syria, Bahrain and the occupied territories of Palestine, to name a few, nonviolent protestors were jailed and killed.

In the East, the work continues. In North Korea, Amnesty has called for the release of all prisoners of consciousness being held in the country's six known prisons. The camp at Yodok holds men, women, and children forced to do hard labor. Antigovernment activity can be as little as listening to television from the South or poor performance in their jobs. Witnesses have told stories of beatings and hunger, and of confessions by torture. Estimates hold that around 50,000 people are held in Yudok alone.

Letter writing campaigns and petitions for the prisoners at Yodok are just one of the actions members of Amnesty International can take. Other options for actions include protests, taking photos, doing artwork, social networking, texting and blogging, uploading videos, holding press conferences, writing articles and books, appearing on television shows, holding lectures and classes, creating musical and poetry venues, and wearing activist clothing and jewelry.

Visiting the country or location and viewing the abuse firsthand is also an option but care must be taken to avoid the same danger the action is taken to alleviate. Developing countries with the overt brutality of dictatorial governments is where Amnesty achieves the most impact yet subtle abuse is rampant across the world.

Success is hard to pinpoint but with over three million members in over 150 countries, the energy put against the forces of violence is profound. Among the honors witnessing Amnesty International's work are the Nobel Peace Prize in 1977 and the United Nations human rights prize in 1996.

An act of love, a voluntary taking on oneself of some of the pain of the world, increases the courage of love and hope of all. — Dorothy Day, American journalist

Injustice anywhere is a threat to justice everywhere. We are caught in an inescapable network of mutuality, tied in a single garment of destiny. — The Rev. Dr. Martin Luther King, Jr.

If you see injustice and say nothing, you have taken the side of the oppressor. — Desmond Tutu, South African Anglican bishop

24

Rule of Law: International Tribunal for the Former Yugoslavia (2003)

The legal philosophy that no one is above the law, which helps prevent arbitrary government and the illegal use of power; the rules that govern the actions of people and nations.

In 2003, nearly ten years after over 100,000 people had died in the Bosnian War, the United Nations established the International Tribunal for the former Yugoslavia. Investigating alleged murder and genocide during the wars in the Balkans during the 1990s, the Tribunal has indicted over a hundred individuals, including soldiers and politicians.

Perhaps the most notorious was Slobodan Milosevic, former president of Serbia and the first head of state indicted for war crimes. Though his role in the Balkan War is undeniable, his exact role was hard to determine. According to Madeline Albright, former U.S. secretary of state, "Slobodan Milosevic initiated four wars during the 1990s, including a devastating campaign of ethnic cleansing in Kosovo which killed thousands and drove almost a million people from their homes."[1]

The Virtue of Equality

The basis for "rule of law" is that the rules and guidelines of law apply to everyone, regardless of position or status. This concept of supremacy of law ensures that equality is first and foremost among the principles of justice.

From Greek and Islamic writings to British jurisprudence, the philosophy of law has sought to understand how laws relate to human rights. The

154

concept of natural law, based on unchangeable moral principles, is often considered the basis to which all laws should align.

The basic intention of rule of law differs little in cultures around the world, but there are some variations. In Anglo-American tradition, "rule of law" is considered a safeguard against legal despotism and too much power in the state. On the other hand, in China, where many consider law as an enhancement of the state, the government has adopted the term "rule by law."

With each nation and culture having its own legal tradition and system, the need has grown for new structures to deal with crimes on a global scale. The International Criminal Court was established in 2002 as part of what is generally termed the World Court. It investigates heinous crimes by individuals referred to the international court by the United Nations Security Council.

Located in the Tribunal Building at The Hague, the International Criminal Court considers crimes of humanity, war, aggression, and genocide. The Court takes cases where existing national judicial systems will not, or cannot, investigate the alleged crime because it is beyond their power or jurisdiction. The International Criminal Court has investigated crimes in the Congo, the Central African Republic, Uganda, and in the Sudanese region of Darfur.

International Court of Justice, The Hague (International Court of Justice, The Hague).

Results from the International Criminal Court are mixed. In Slobodan Milosevic's case, the defendant contended that the Court had no jurisdiction and that it was biased against him. He became ill during the trial and died before he received a final sentence.

Another high-profile case for the Court is Radovan Karadzic, who allegedly ordered the Srebrenica massacre and for ten years eluded authorities in a test of power. Since the Court itself has no arresting authority, it must rely on international and national police and military to bring indicted criminals to the Court's prison. Karadzic was recently arrested and, at this writing, is now facing trial.

Because of the high profile and deliberative nature of such cases, it takes an enormous amount of time to reach a ruling. Several individuals are now in custody awaiting trial. Two accused have died while their cases were being tried. Others indicted have managed to elude capture all together.

Another international judicial body often referred to under the umbrella of World Court is the U.N. International Court of Justice, which settles disputes between nations. In addition, there are other special courts created to prosecute people responsible for violations of international humanitarian law.

With appeals and continuing proceedings, the accomplishments of these courts are debatable. Yet the very act of indicting perpetrators of violence sends a clear message to those who contemplate genocide.

Name, Rank, and Serial Number

Due to globalization, increased trade, the rise of multinational corporations, and other global trends, international rule of law is constantly being written, adjudicated, and tested. One important global rule is the Geneva Convention, which is the international law for treatment of victims of war.

Based on four treaties established between 1864 and 1949, the Geneva Convention is a humanitarian law that defined basic rights of prisoners, the wounded, and civilians near a war zone. After World War II, 194 countries ratified the treaty but it is still subject to questions and controversy.

The roots of the Convention go back to a Nobel Peace Prize winner, Henry Dunant, who established the Red Cross. Due to the needs of those helping with medical situations on the battlefield, Dunant wrote *Memoir of Solferino* about the horrors of war. He called not only for a permanent humanitarian relief agency but also for a treaty that recognized the neutrality of those providing aid for wounded soldiers.

Dunant's proposed treaty resulted in the first Geneva Convention between twelve nations. Succeeding treaties have extended protections and humane treatment for prisoners of war, civilians, and non-combatant service personnel.

The term "grave breaches" was devised to include crimes of war. Signatories for the Convention are obligated to find those guilty of war crimes and bring them to justice.[2] The following are considered grave breaches:

- Willful killing, torture, or inhumane treatment
- Willful causing of great suffering or serious injury
- Compelling a person to fight for a hostile force
- Depriving a person from a fair trial
- Hostage taking
- Extreme destruction of property with military necessity
- Unlawful deportation or confinement

At the end of the day, the Geneva Convention is followed only by those individuals and societies that hold a high ethical standard. Many remember the movies from World War II when a captured soldier was only responsible for his "name, rank, and serial number." Yet many despotic countries, as well as democratic nations with secret programs, still torture as well as bomb civilian populations.

Controversy recently arose in the United States over the treatment of combatants who did not wear military uniforms. These "non-combatants" were considered by some in the administration of then-president George W. Bush as not protected under the Geneva Convention.

The global realities of war without national boundaries have tested the Geneva Convention's applicability to modern conflicts. Yet the fact that our world has such a rule of law has given international tribunals and courts the basis for criminalizing genocide and brutal repression. The Convention may need updating but its precedent is important in the evolution of human rights.

A Legal Basis for International Progress

"The rule of law is the foundation for communities of opportunity and equity," according to World Justice Project founder William H. Neukom. "It is the predicate for the eradication of poverty, violence, corruption, pandemics, and other threats to civil society."[3]

Without a strong system of international law, it is more difficult to get food and medicine to areas of famine. Journalists are kept from investigating abuse. Women are prevented from participating in elections and commerce.

Children suffer from diseases that can be eradicated with health care that is now being hindered by corruption and nationalistic policies.

The World Justice Project has developed the trademarked WJP Rule of Law Index in order to give us a snapshot of how areas of our global community are faring. Taking into consideration such factors as corruption, security, government powers, fundamental rights, and access to the justice system, the Index shows the impact of rule of law on ordinary lives.

The data for Western Europe show a different story than the nations of Africa or South America. Some areas have a more developed and sophisticated law structure. Some areas are struggling to emerge out of total lack of documentation and a reliance on tribal structures or dictatorial systems of good-old-boy corruption.

The following four questions are important for evaluating how rule of law contributes to the overall peace in a society:

- Are government officials accountable under the law?
- Are laws clear, fair, and open in protecting rights?
- Is the process of enacting laws efficient and enforcement fair?
- Is the judiciary accessible, competent, independent, and ethical?

It is a paradox that being subject to the limitations of law is one of the ways we achieve freedom and peace in our lives. The Roman Cicero said, "We are all servants of the law in order that we may be free."[4] Perhaps there will come a time when fewer laws are needed, but until that time we use the most just, reasonable, and long-lasting of our legal precedents to find the way forward.

> *Treat the people equally in your court and give them equal attention, so that the noble shall not aspire to your partiality, not the humble despair of your justice.* — Umar bin a-Khattab, the second khalifa of Islam

> *That which is not just is not law.* — William Lloyd Garrison, American abolitionist

> *There can be no peace without law.* — Dwight D. Eisenhower, American president

25

Alternative Resources Acquisition: Non-Conflict Diamond Certification (2003)

Acquiring materials and services from alternate sources in order to avoid potential conflict; sourcing resources or developing technologies that do not require the use of violence and war to meet a current or future need.

Due to the distinctive beauty of diamonds, as well as an extremely successful marketing campaign by producers, worldwide demand for the gemstones has been consistently strong. Though the diamond industry has always been subject to criticism for the use of slave labor and monopolistic practices, in the 1990s there was a new and terrible development of their international trade.

With Africa being the largest source of raw diamonds, this coveted resource was bound to become a part of the civil wars that ravaged the continent. Such resource-rich countries as Sierra Leone and the Ivory Coast were quickly becoming failed states. The world began to acknowledge, especially with the 1996 U.N. Machel Report, that an estimated 250,000 child soldiers were actively under forced conscription and encouraged to murder and rape.[1]

A vast majority of the conflicts throughout history can be mapped to the quest for resources unavailable in one country or another. From diamonds and fertile land to slave labor and reserves of oil, the needs and desires thought to ensure the survival or prosperity of one people have driven many nations and cultures to war with another.

Yet the simple solution, often heard, of "send in the troops" is most often destructive to both parties in the dispute. The extraordinary effort needed to gain one resource can often deplete another, including the youth sent to die on distant battlefields.

The strategies for alternative resource acquisition include finding other sources or finding another way to satisfy a need. According to time-tested economic principles, when alternative sources or resources are found, demand for those items goes down. When there is a drop in demand, there is a drop in price. Resistance to trade at a reasonable price is, thereby, reduced.

Yet beyond sound economic principles, another consideration is even more important. How much is a young person's life worth? When our children come home wounded in body and mind, can the loss be balanced by wealth obtained?

The Virtue of Resourcefulness

We have a moral imperative to be resourceful in satisfying needs and desires without violence. The ability to deal with a situation or difficulty in a skillful and creative way is the virtue of resourcefulness.

Sourcing alternatives is, indeed, more challenging, so outside influences are often essential. Whether the attempt is a moral imperative, or citizen demands, or government legislation, or an industry association's guidelines, a directive to be resourceful in acquiring alternative resources is a practical view, especially when it comes to personal desires.

In the 1990s, the diamond industry and the United Nations attempted to address the diamond war problem. They placed an embargo on "conflict diamonds" from areas where revenue was being used to fuel the wars. Yet like the arms trade, smugglers simply took the "blood diamonds" to neighboring countries and traded them for deadly arms.

Several investigative reporters and the popular movie *Blood Diamond* brought worldwide attention to the murderous trade situation in Africa. Calls for a more workable alternative resource acquisition plan soon gained strength. The United Nations responded with Resolution 55/56, which created the Kimberley Process Certification Scheme.

Diamonds certified as "conflict-free" diamonds are now made from rough diamonds mined in areas where profits are not used for funneling arms and financing child soldiers. Consumers who buy diamonds with a Kimberley Process certificate can be relatively sure that their money will not be used to murder and rape.

Energy is another area where finding resource alternatives can work to stop violence and war. Military and political might have often been used to ensure low prices and open supply channels for oil. As the energy needs of both developed and developing nations rise, the need for fossil fuels continues at an ever-alarming rate.

As reserves dwindle, oil prices will naturally rise and competition for supplies will be intense. Today there is a growing movement to find alternatives to fossil fuels in new technologies such as wind and solar.

Decreasing Scarcity through Ideas and Creativity

Our planet is our only source of raw materials, short of planetary expansion or extraordinary technological advances. The unsustainable practices of the past have come to haunt us in today's conflicts and wars. Our dependence on oil is the most obvious. Many of the wars between nations have been caused, at least in large part, from the perceived competition between economic progress and the acquisition of oil.

To prevent such conflicts in the future, nations and societies need to look ahead to what might be the next need or scarcity. For instance, as the world's sources of the "blue water," or potable water, required for sustaining life becomes rarer and subject to pollution, the potential for conflict over water availability and access rights is coming to the fore.

Deforestation, overpopulation, over-consumption, and pollution put our global freshwater table at risk. The sustainability of the world's water footprint, or impact, changes over time, but the statistics of freshwater show its fragility.

With saltwater oceans and estuaries covering most of the earth, freshwater accounts for just 3 percent of the world's water resource. Most of this blue water is contained in the glacial reserves or underground reservoirs.

With consumption statistics providing a jarring view, such as the fact that Americans alone use nearly 100 gallons of water per day, protection of our freshwater sources is becoming a global concern. According to the WHO/UNICEF Joint Monitoring Program for Water Supply and Sanitation, safe drinking water is unavailable for nearly 900 million people. Access to sanitation and waste disposal is inadequate for over 2.5 billion.

The world has been slow in responding to water scarcity. There are so many global sustainability concerns that water gets short shrift. Yet scientists and biotechnologists from global companies and organizations are coming up with new ideas and technologies that will provide needed alternatives for the future.

For instance, new desalination technologies have dramatically reduced the cost of removing salt from ocean water. International organizations such as the United Nations are establishing global water standards while nations are implementing water protection laws. More secure and efficient water septic systems and farm nutrient runoff policies are also protecting our freshwater resources.

Providing sustainable water supplies means providing enough fresh water for the basic water requirements that maintain the health of all human beings on Earth. It means using water in a manner that allows the planet to restore freshwater and groundwater stocks and flows. It also means establishing and ensuring that minimum water quality standards be maintained. Finally, it means providing laws and dispute resolution for water conflicts and ensuring that water allocation is determined with a democratic and open system of governance.

The watery planet as viewed from space (NASA).

Peace Is a Cool Drink of Water

We all use water for drinking and cooking, for showering and washing clothes. Businesses use water for manufacturing products and getting food to market. The sustainability of our water consumption lifestyle depends on the individual choices we make in our personal work and lives.

Our water "footprint" is the total consumption of water, both direct and indirect. Direct water consumption is the amount we use to drink, prepare our food, shower, and use in our swimming pools and for our gardens.

Indirect consumption also contributes to our overall water footprint. Factors include the manufacture of synthetic fibers and the maintenance and pollution removal in our community water and septic systems. The supply chain for businesses also reveals the need for vast amounts of water to bring goods and services to market. Indirect water consumption includes how much water it takes to bring the cows, chickens, pigs, and other sources of meat to our table. For instance, it takes 15,000 liters of water to produce one kilogram of beef.

A sustainable water footprint, according to the Water Footprint Network, is when "the total remains below your equal share of the freshwater resources in the world."[2] There is a huge difference between water consumption in one country and another. For instance, U.S. consumers have a water footprint of 2,840 cubic meters. Chinese consumers have only 1,070 cubic meters and in developing countries the meter runs far less.

The following are considerations for lowering our individual water footprint, or the impact we make on the environment. Becoming aware of our consumption is the first step. The second is taking action to find alternatives to intensive water usage:

• Plant indigenous species to reduce need for watering
• Water gardens only when needed
• Install a water-saving toilet and low-flow showerhead
• Turn off the tap when brushing teeth
• Do not dispose of pollutants or medicines in sinks
• Eat less meat
• Drink plain water instead of coffee
• Buy cotton instead of artificial fiber clothing
• Reduce waste by recycling plastic, paper, and glass

There are websites and books that give us a baseline for our individual or organizational water footprint. Once understood, we can establish a target for reducing our consumption, both direct and indirect.

Until the overall world consumption of blue water, or fresh surface or groundwater, is brought under control, the potential of future conflict rises. One country experiencing scarcity will surely look toward alternative resource acquisition in the supply of another country. The long-term solution for future conflicts lies in finding alternatives to scarce resources and how we use new technologies to conserve those we have and expand our options.

History teaches that wars begin when governments believe the price of aggression is cheap. — Ronald Reagan, American president

Is life so dear or peace so sweet as to be purchased at the price of chains and slavery? Forbid it, Almighty God! — Patrick Henry, American revolutionary

26

The Golden Rule: Mayor "Golden Rule" Jones (1897)

The moral principle or active philosophy that people should behave toward others as they want others to behave toward them; a maxim in various forms: "Do unto others as you would have them do unto you."

Tradition has it that the "Golden Rule" was first expressed by Confucius and put down on paper in *The Analytics*. The Chinese sage (551–479 B.C.E.) offered the word "consideration" as its underlying principle. "Do not impose on others what you do not desire others to impose upon you."[1]

Fundamental to the Golden Rule are the values of justice and benevolence. It answers with clarity the questions: "How should you treat others?" and "How do you want to be treated?"

The "positive" form of the Golden Rule is to treat others as you would like them to treat you. The "negative" form, or Silver Rule, is just as direct in its wisdom: do not treat others as you would like them to not treat you. Whether practiced out of positive benevolence or considered self-interest, the Rule allows us to build peace through mutual respect, toleration, understanding of differences, and active compassion expressed in the random acts of kindness that happen every moment of the day.

The Virtue of Reciprocity

Known as the "ethic of reciprocity," the Golden Rule's combination of fair-mindedness and compassion sets the practitioner on a moral path toward respect for human rights. Reciprocity dates from the eighteenth century French word for reciprocal. It is an interchange, a mutuality, a cooperation.

In mathematics, reciprocal is also called the "multiplicative inverse." The reciprocal ratio is the quantity that, once multiplied, results in unity. The reciprocal of x is 1/x, which, when multiplied by x, equals one, which is referred to, simply, as unity.

Many individuals have embraced the philosophy of striving for this kind of unity. Yet only one person seems to have taken it on as a name. Welshman Samuel Jones immigrated to America in the mid–1800s and found work in the Pennsylvania oil fields. Later he moved to Ohio and helped start the Ohio Oil Company, which was eventually bought out by the larger Standard Oil Company.

With money from the sale, Jones started the S.M. Jones Company, making tools for the oil industry. A man of deep conviction and respect for the common man, he vowed to use the Golden Rule as the guiding principle in his business. He treated employees with a fairness that was rare at the time. He paid high wages and provided good working conditions, then asked his workers for an honest day's work.

Jones' reputation as a just and benevolent employer began to grow. In the last decade of the 1800s, with the rise of the progressive Republican Party, he decided to put the Golden Rule into public service and was elected mayor of Toledo, Ohio.

Immediately, "Golden Rule Jones" began directing public policy for the good of the people. He set up free kindergartens and built parks across the city. He tried to reform city government and gave city workers an eight-hour day so they could spend more time with their families.

The mayor's generosity with the city's income was soon at odds with the forces of the status quo. "You boast of spending a tenth part of your income in charity," he told them, "may be you should spend the nine tenths so, and be done with it...."[2] Jones' progressive actions caused many businessmen and the Republican Party to oppose him in the next election, but he was reelected by the common people who liked his policies. He served as Toledo's mayor until he died in office in 1904.

Many examples of the use of the Golden Rule are hidden in the simple actions of individuals, yet its practice also has an institutional history. The 1993 "Declaration Toward a Global Ethic," for instance, had 143 signatories from a wide variety of faiths and religious traditions. This Parliament of the World's Religions deemed the Golden Rule a common principle for spiritual faith.

Indeed, the Golden Rule is fundamental to all the great religions of the world. Expressed in ways that show individuality and cultural difference, the virtue of reciprocity provides a common teaching that demands of our reason and heart the open toleration of other faiths and persuasions:

Blessed is he who preferreth his brother before himself. — Baha'i: Tablets of Baha'ullah, 71

Hurt not others in ways that you yourself would find hurtful. — Buddhism: Udana-Varga, 5:18

All things whatsoever ye would that men should do to you, do ye even so to them. — Christianity: Jesus, Matthew 7:12

This is the sum of duty: do naught unto others which would cause you pain if done to you. — Hinduism: Mahabharata 5:1517

No one of you is a believer until he desires for his brother that which he desires for himself. — Islam: Sunnah

In happiness and suffering, in joy and grief, we should regard all creatures as we regard our own self. — Jainism: Lord Mahavira, 24th Tirthankara

What is hateful to you, do not to your fellowman. That is the law: all the rest is commentary. — Judaism: Talmud, Shabbat 31a

Respect for all life is the foundation. — Native-American: The Great Law of Peace

Don't create enmity with anyone as God is within everyone. — Sikhism: Guru Arjan Devji 259, Guru Granth Sahib

That nature only is good when it shall not do unto another whatever is not good for its own self. — Zoroastrianism: Dadistan-i-Dinik, 94:5

Quantum Updates

It doesn't take a huge leap to go from "do unto others what you would like done unto you" to the subtle and intentional power of positive thinking. An understanding of the benefits of the Golden Rule has long philosophical roots, dating back thousands of years beyond Confucius to Zoroaster. Yet the actual physical power of delivering practical, intentional benefits from doing good actions has always been steeped in mysticism and controversy, especially with several modern variations.

In the mid-twentieth century, quantum mechanics began to enter the language of physicists and non-physicists alike. Some in the scientific community saw in the universe an implicit order beyond the laws of mechanics and thermodynamics. This order entailed a connectivity that has piqued the imaginations of scientists and metaphysicians ever since.

Respected British-American physicist David Bohm was an early proponent of the implicit universe. He saw that "In the enfolded order, space and time are no longer the dominant factors determining the relationships of dependence or independence of different elements."[3]

Rather, he said, there is a deeper order that connects all things. Bohm's "undivided whole" attested to the far more pervasive connectivity that we, in our relative world, simply misunderstand as distinct and independent parts. The universe, the physicist postulated, can be seen as a flowing stream in constant flux.

To David Bohm, events in one area of the world can affect other areas of the world without regard to the limitations of speed of light. These non-local phenomena have yet to be proven definitively in the laboratory. If they do occur, they would show an entanglement that would necessitate the interrelatedness — indeed the reciprocity — of all actions and thoughts.

With this background of quantum mechanics as well as Einstein's quixotic search for the Unified Field Theory, the connectivity of thought and action pervaded the popular media. In the 1950s, the Christian Methodist minister Dr. Norman Vincent Peale popularized the idea that our thoughts can determine our world. The author of *The Power of Positive Thinking*, Peale was a huge cultural phenomenon with books, television appearances, and a radio show that lasted fifty-four years.

With an intriguing compilation of inspiring stories and axioms about living, and positive titles of his books, such as *You Can If You Think You Can*, Peale updated the virtue of reciprocity in everyday life. "Joy increases as you give it," he wrote, "and diminishes as you try to keep it for yourself."[4]

Peale, along with many other self-made philosophers, foreshadowed a movement toward directly linking physical goods and benefits with the power of thought and action. "In giving, you will accumulate a deposit of joy," Peale said, "greater than you ever believed possible."

There are many current spin-offs of reciprocity. The "law of attraction" is loosely associated with the metaphysical New Age movement, which has morphed into hundreds of different variations, some claiming to be science, others comfortable in the spiritual realm. At the core of these connectivity beliefs is the idea that "like attracts like" and that thoughts can do work on the part of individuals and societies.

In the 2006 sensation *The Secret*, a popular book and film espoused the ancient value of reciprocity. The law of attraction contends that if thoughts and actions are fully intended, we can create our future. In effect, the vibratory frequency of our wants, needs, and desires will necessarily match the frequency of a result that can change our lives and bring abundance of wealth, health, and happiness.

For peacemakers, reciprocity, quantum connectivity, and modern derivatives such as the law of attraction and subtle activism have spawned a flurry of experiments and actions. In Washington, D.C., a meditation group intentionally tried to lower the rate of criminal activity during a particularly hot week of summer that always delivered high crime statistics.

"We predicted a 20 percent drop in crime, and we achieved a 25 percent drop," said physicist John Hagelin of the International Center for Invincible Defense.[5] The group of around 4,000 meditation practitioners provided what organizers called a "spillover effect" where a reduction in stress apparently caused a reduction in stress-related behaviors. The study was published in the December 1988 edition of the *Journal of Conflict Resolution* and has been repeated in several stressed areas, including the Middle East during the Lebanon-Israel War.

Correlations from these studies seem to favor the result that the meditation practice worked. As with other non-local experiments and hypotheses, the jury is still out on the measurement of thought affecting our lives. Yet the self-fulfilling prophecy in the power of doing good for the sake of all concerned, or reciprocity, is an ancient form of action that is fundamental to creating peace.

> *Desire nothing for yourself which you do not desire for others.* — Baruch Spinoza, Portuguese philosopher

> *The anti-war movement creates more war. The anti-drug movement has actually created more drugs. Because we're focusing on what we don't want— drugs!* — Jack Canfield, from *The Secret*

27

Peace Education: Nobel Peace Prize (1901–present)

Educating about the advantages, methods, skills, and practices of working, living, and endeavoring toward peace; celebrating the heroes and history of peace.

Swedish industrialist Alfred Nobel was an unlikely hero of peace. The inventor of dynamite was accused in a French newspaper of being the "merchant of death." Yet upon his death in 1896, Alfred Nobel surprised his peers by establishing a trust for the most famous peace prize in history.

For over 100 years, the Nobel Peace Prize has been given for "the best work for fraternity between nations, for the abolition or reduction of standing armies and for the holding and promotion of peace congresses."[1]

The Peace Prize was added to other Nobel prizes for chemistry, physics, medicine, literature and, later, economics. Some say Alfred Nobel was trying to make amends for his invention of dynamite and its potential for destruction against humans. Others say it was because of his respect for Baroness von Suttner, his secretary and a peace advocate whose book *Lay Down Your Arms* helped her win the Nobel Peace Prize in 1905.

The cherished Nobel Peace Prize is given annually by a committee of five members of the Norwegian Parliament in Oslo. The announcement focuses the world's attention not only on the specific work for peace but also on areas and situations in the world that continue to struggle for peace and justice.

Most Nobel Peace Prize winners are people who have spent a lifetime working for peace, such as missionary surgeon Albert Schweitzer (1952). Others won for an act of courage, such as Cordell Hull (1945) for helping start the United Nations. Still others are organizations such as Amnesty International (1977), which work to protect human rights.

The Virtue of Wisdom

The story of each Nobel Peace Prize winner instructs us and educates us in the ways of peace. Their lives and work give us constructive understanding of a way to make a difference in the world. They show us how they used their individual virtues of peace, the power of reasoning, judgment, empathy, forgiveness, and other values deeply held.

When we learn about the work of Nobel Peace Prize winners we become apprentices to the very wise among us. Wisdom means knowing a way of proceeding, a course of action. We look to the winners of this esteemed prize for the way forward out of our history of violent struggle.

The winners of the Nobel Peace Prize have put their wisdom to work for a wide variety of public interests and come from many nations and cultures. They include such peace icons as anti-nuclear advocate and biologist Linus Pauling (1962), poverty campaigner Mother Teresa (1979), anti–apartheid leader Nelson Mandela (1993), U.S. civil rights leader Martin Luther King, Jr. (1964), climate change activist and former U.S. vice president Al Gore (2007), and Burmese democracy leader Aung San Suu Kyi (1991).

The Nobel for peace is not without controversy. Many individuals have been overlooked, such as nonviolence archetype Mahatma Gandhi. Other Prizes have been controversial, such as Palestinian militant turned statesman Yasser Arafat, who in 1994 shared the prize with Israeli leaders Shimon Peres and Yitzhak Rabin.

Yet even with and perhaps because of the controversy, the very act of celebrating the heroes of peace has had a profound effect on the world. It has provided a rich history and curriculum for studying peace. The Nobel Peace Prize has also provided a platform for defining what working for peace is. For instance, the selection of Wangari Maathai (1994) forever linked environmentalism and peace.

There are many other prizes, groups, and organizations specializing in peace education. High schools throughout the world have peace clubs. Colleges and Universities have peace studies curricula. Private groups, such as faith-based communities, are also dedicated to teaching peace. The Dalai Lama Center for Peace and Education was founded in 2005 in Vancouver, Canada. The Center, which has no religious affiliation, teaches how to "develop the heart, be compassionate, work for peace in your heart and the world."[2]

Peace education is an expansive field that acknowledges the plurality of ways to achieve peace. Teaching the values and attitudes and the ways in how to develop the skills and behaviors that will lead to peace are essential to achieving peace in ourselves and in the world.

UNESCO Prize for Peace Education

The United Nations Educational, Scientific, and Cultural Organization (UNESCO) was established to contribute to the peace and security of the world. By promoting international collaboration in the areas of education, science, and culture, UNESCO's many programs promote human rights, freedom, and rule of law.

Each year, the agency awards a person or group the UNESCO Prize for Peace. The winners of the $60,000 prize have included many educational and justice organizations that are largely unheralded but do extraordinary and important work:

- The Institute for Justice and Reconciliation (South Africa, 2008)
- The City Montessori School in Lucknow (India, 2003)
- The Arab Center for Peace Education in Givat Haviva (Israel, 2001)
- Educators for Peace and Mutual Understanding (Ukraine, 1998)
- The Study Center for Peace and Conflict Resolution (Austria, 1995)
- The Graduate Institute of Peace Studies at Kyung Hee University (South Korea, 1993)
- Stockholm International Peace Research Institute (Sweden, 1982)

UNESCO is also the main driver for the International Day of Peace observance that is celebrated globally on September 21 each year. A growing movement since its inception in 1981, International Day of Peace was created to increase dialogue and encourage people to build a culture of peace in their communities and the world.

Self-Defining Ourselves as People of Peace

To encourage citizens of every nation to contemplate the state of peace in their community,

Nobel Peace Prize recipient Mother Teresa, a Roman Catholic nun of Albanian ethnicity, put her spiritual calling into practice in the slums of Calcutta, India (www.ageorg.ca, Sonia Georg).

UNESCO has defined a culture of peace. In several resolutions, the United Nations organization established the necessity of educating and taking actions on the most basic rights and opportunities for our globe.

"The Culture of Peace," UNESCO Resolution A/RES/52/13 states, "is a set of values, attitudes, modes of behavior and ways of life that reject violence and prevent conflicts...." The definition doesn't stop at the vision, but also calls us to action.

We can achieve a culture of peace "by tackling their root causes to solve problems through dialogue and negotiations among individuals, groups and nations." More specifically, the resolutions lay down eight basic areas for work:

- Foster a culture of peace through education
- Promote sustainable economic and social development
- Promote respect for all human rights
- Ensure equality between women and men
- Foster democratic participation
- Advance understanding, tolerance, and solidarity
- Support participatory communication and the free flow of information and knowledge
- Promote international peace and security

The Constitution of UNESCO emphasizes the role of education in creating a culture that can support a peaceful future. "Since wars begin in the minds of men," the document states, "it is in the minds of men than defences of peace must be constructed." Creating a culture of peace in our neighborhoods, villages, and nations is an essential grassroots endeavor that gives hope to finally creating peace in the world.

When we have inner peace, we can be at peace with those around us.
— Dalai Lama, Tibetan Buddhist leader

We must inoculate our children against militarism, by educating them in the spirit of pacifism.... Our schoolbooks glorify war and conceal its horrors. They indoctrinate children with hatred. I would teach peace rather than war, love rather than hate. — Albert Einstein

28

Global Wellness: Doctors
Without Borders (1971)

*A healthy, sustainable balance of safety, prosperity, and quality of life for all
people on earth; the state of well-being for our planet and its inhabitants.*

From 1967 to 1971, the Nigerian army blockaded and fought a major civil
war with Biafra, a breakaway country on the African nation's Atlantic coast. From
the brutalities of war, disease, and famine, an estimated one million people died.

A group of dedicated French doctors tried to provide medical support
for civilians caught in the deadly mix of bombs and devastation. Frustrated
by corrupt politicians, bureaucracy, and brutal military strategies, the French
doctors came away from the experience with the resolve to find a way to provide medical care without regard to national borders. In 1971, those same
French doctors formed Médecins Sans Frontières, or Doctors Without Borders.
The group determined to create an organization that ignored national and religious boundaries and concentrated simply on the health of the people.

Today, Doctors Without Borders is a highly respected and effective worldwide organization. It now sends field mission teams of doctors and support
staff to some of the most needy of developing countries and regions ravaged
by war. They gather data on malnutrition and observe mortality rates. They
map disease occurrences and document violence. They set up food and medical centers to combat starvation, infectious diseases, and diarrhea.

The Virtue of Balance

Health is a major part of global wellness, but it is only a part of what it
will take to create a less violent and more humane world. In "A Theory of

173

Human Motivation," Abraham Maslow proposed a hierarchy of needs in order to reach each individual's potential. From a base of physiological needs such as food and water, Maslow saw higher-level needs for safety, love/belonging, esteem, and self-actualization.

Each individual certainly deserves basic physiological needs. The seeds of the world's conflicts sprout in the suffering and discontent of people without these necessities. Global wellness goes to the core of Maslow's hierarchy in creating a vision of balance for the world. With images of the ancient scale where two pans in equilibrium show equality, balance between individuals as well as within each individual is a worthy goal.

The term "wellness" was devised in the 1950s by Halbert Dunn, a medical doctor writing about a healthy life beyond a focus on curing and illness. In *High Level Wellness for Man and Society*, Dunn defined it as "an integrated method of functioning which is oriented toward maximizing the potential of which the individual is capable."[1]

The term wellness now encompasses much more than health. It addresses the fact that humans and our planet are part of a living matrix of life. Indicators of global wellness are many, including disease outbreak, life expectancy, literacy, standard of living, and sustainable development. Once we meet the basic physiological needs of those who inhabit this planet, perhaps the higher level needs can be addressed — love and belonging, high self-esteem, and self-actualization.

Many individuals and organizations have found creative ways to work for global wellness. The U.N. World Food Program is supplying sustenance to nearly 100 million people, half of which are children.[2] Many Nongovernmental Organizations struggle to build pumping wells and ensure the clean water that builds immune systems, decreases child mortality, and prevents the spread of AIDS.

Doctors Without Borders has expanded the scope of their humanitarian efforts. The group now lobbies governments and organizations to address abuses, expose genocide, and combat the heath effects of famine and war. They set up vaccination centers for measles, meningitis, polio, cholera, and other infectious diseases. They do surgeries and set up recovery centers for the wounded in wars. They have also been a source of education and anti-retroviral drugs for HIV/AIDS.

Doctors Without Borders is at the cutting edge of global wellness and peacebuilding. Now working in over sixty countries, the group has called for military intervention only once, during the bloody Rwandan genocide where the massacre on the ground was happening too fast for a measured response. In 1999, the group received the Nobel Peace Prize.

A Vision of Global Wellness

In 2000, the United Nations established eight international development goals that address global wellness. The intent was to put programs in place so that by 2015 true progress could be made on poverty and hunger, child mortality, and diseases such as AIDS and malaria.

The goals included twenty-one targets in order to provide specific objectives and visions of how measurable progress could be reached. For instance, one target in Goal 6 strove to provide universal access to HIV/AIDS drugs for "all" who need them. It was a lofty goal but one where much progress has been made due to the world beginning to focus resources on the problem. The Millennium Development Goals include:

Goal 1: Eradicate extreme poverty and hunger

Goal 2: Achieve universal primary education

Goal 3: Promote gender equality and empower women

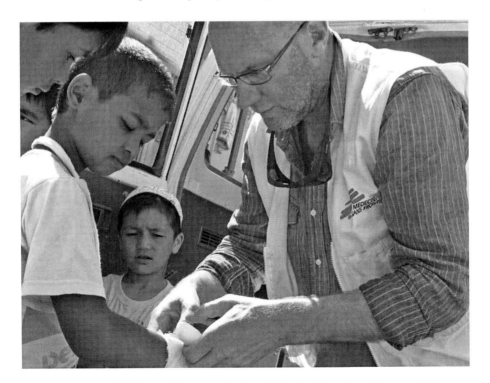

A team from Nobel Peace Prize organization Médecins Sans Frontières providing medical relief in Kyrgyzstan, 2010 (Médicine San Frontiéres, François Dumont).

Goal 4: Reduce child mortality rates

Goal 5: Improve maternal health

Goal 6: Combat HIV/AIDS, malaria, and other diseases

Goal 7: Ensure environmental sustainability

Goal 8: Develop a global partnership for development

These U.N.–established Goals address some of the world's most intractable problems. There are millions living on less than one dollar a day. The gap between the rich and the poor is ever increasing. According to UNESCO, one in six adults is illiterate and over sixty-seven million children are not attending school. Worldwide educational access for girls is very troubling and extremely important in terms of reducing the disparity in women finding employment with good wages.

The challenges are sobering: reduction of the mortality rate of children, access to reproductive options, distribution of condoms and medicines, and insecticide-treated bed nets to lower the escalating rate of malaria. The targeted objectives of the Millennium Development Goals include making our political and economic systems align with efficiency and participation. Questions of global trade and the accountability of financial systems as well as debt restructuring of nations is a matter of the long-term sustainability of our interconnected world. We must continue to evolve to rule-based, predictable, open, non-discriminatory, and empathic systems.

In the Millennium Development Goals Report for 2011, U.N. Secretary-General Ban Ki-moon said, "The MDGs have helped lift millions of people out of poverty, save countless children's lives and ensure that they attend school." Yet he acknowledged more work is needed. "At the same time, we still have a long way to go in empowering women and girls, promoting sustainable development, and protecting the most vulnerable."[3]

Goal number seven of the U.N. Goals envisions a future where environmental stewardship is linked to health. Reducing biodiversity loss, promoting sustainable development, protecting the rain forests, reducing pollution and emissions, stabilizing fish stocks, protecting marine environments, and ensuring freshwater sources are all part of the global health picture.

The Earth as a Living Planet

At the end of his life, Abraham Maslow was working on an even higher level of need than his initial hierarchy suggested. The professor of psychology imagined a state even beyond self-actualization of self-transcendence where we yearn for serenity and peace.

We can all relate to that urge for transformation, yet we know the world is still working on ensuring that billions have the basic necessities. Indeed when we fully embrace our challenges, we begin to comprehend the complexity and pervasiveness of that quest. Fulfilling the needs of the human condition may be more intimately connected than we previously thought to the wider needs of the earth.

In Gaia Theory, the health of humans is only one component of a much larger scope of global wellness. All of the animals and plants, the plethora of life under the sea, the air we breathe, the inorganic material of rock and stone beneath our feet, everything that makes up planet Earth forms a single, self-regulating, living ecosystem.

Tightly coupled and simultaneously evolving, these systems strive for the optimal conditions. We now understand that factors such as ocean salinity and atmospheric carbon dioxide are too important to our future to ignore. Global warming, loss of species, and depletion of the ocean's stock will directly affect the health of human beings. The evolving condition of all life forms under the sun depends on the health of each factor.

To really consider global wellness, we must understand that the health of the entire system depends on the decisions we make and the lifestyles we choose. Just as our single lives are integrated into our families and neighborhoods, our human societies are part of the biosphere, atmosphere, hydrosphere, and pedosphere that compose our environment.

The Gaia hypothesis was first developed in the 1970s by chemist James Lovelock and, later, microbiologist Lynn Margulis. Named after the Greek goddess that is interpreted as Mother Earth, the theory was devised upon contemplation of whether life could be sustained on another planet such as Mars. Looking at it in this holistic manner provided Lovelock a means of considering the chemical, and Margulis the biological, implications of all the systems on a planet working together for a healthy homeostasis, or balance.

Today, the Gaia Theory or Principle provides an important basis, if metaphorical in origin, for studies of our self-regulating systems. To devise international policy as well as make decisions in our lives requires a grasp of the living, breathing connectivity of all the components of planet Earth.

In the "weak Gaia" scenario, life forms have minimal influence over larger systems and the evolving, non-homeostasis state is the very reason some species survive and others do not. In the "strong Gaia" scenario, the biological species on Earth manipulate the environment to create conditions favorable to their own health, thereby changing the planet as part of a self-sustaining evolution.

Whether weak or strong, metaphorical or scientific, the idea that our planet is a living, breathing, "conscious" part of our lives allows us to consider the reciprocal effects of our actions. The Gaia "movement" has spawned many committed individuals and organizations that propose "self-sustaining" actions to achieve healthier living systems, thereby increasing health and lessening violence and conflict.

> *Peace, to have meaning for many who have only known suffering in both peace and war, must be translated into bread or rice, shelter, health and education, as well as freedom and human dignity.* — Ralph Johnson Bunche, American diplomat

> *When we heal the earth, we heal ourselves.* — David Orr, environmentalist

29

Two-Party Conflict Resolution: Schoolyard Swing Dispute (every day)

The process of identifying common ground and solving differences to the satisfaction of each party; engagement for the purpose of alleviating or eliminating discord.

Conflict resolution is the process of positive engagement. In the world of violence, however, engagement is negative. The focus is on the opposing sides in a dispute. If one person or group wins, the other loses. In the dynamics of violence, there is a culprit and a victim.

On the other hand, in the world of positive engagement the emphasis is on the dispute itself. The focus changes from the struggle between two parties to a common struggle against the differences that created the conflict in the first place. In the dynamics of nonviolence, there are no culprits and victims, only two sets of opinions on how the world should be.

When people engage in the process of conflict resolution, the rush to judgment is deferred so that the underlying facts can come to light. Both parties must have an understanding that to fully resolve a dispute, there can be no winners and losers. History shows that a win/loss result based on who has the power to dominate usually leads to increased resentment and, eventually, to the resurgence of more violence.

When the techniques of conflict resolution are used properly, even the most complex situations can be restructured for the advantage of both parties. Conflict resolution involves finding a solution that ensures one side's power does not abuse the other. It involves listening and sharing, empathizing and understanding, negotiating, and compromising. It also involves giving and receiving in order to achieve shared goals.

The essential skills in conflict resolution are analysis and negotiation rather than domination and control. Success of the process depends on both parties being committed to a resolution, either by disposition, desire, or need.

In the Thomas-Kilmann grid, developed in 1976, people respond to conflict in five different ways. First, we can accommodate the other parties wishes or demands. Second, we can avoid the situation by ignoring it. Third, we can react in a competitive way, asserting viewpoints and forwarding demands.

Sometimes these three ways, accommodation, avoidance, or taking a competitive stance, can buy time or prevent a more dangerous situation from developing. On the negative side, the stakes are sometimes too high for accommodation, avoidance will often let a situation fester, and competition sometimes works to elevate the violence.

The next two ways to respond to violence, according to Thomas-Kilmann, are actions that seek a resolution. The fourth way, compromise, entails reaching an agreement that is less than the wants or needs originally conceived. The fifth way, collaboration, means working together to find a solution to a conflict not only agreeable to the parties but that has the potential for adding value to all sides.

Conflict resolution is when the processes and techniques of nonviolent engagement guide our responses to violence. The steps involved in conflict resolution bring our five basic reactions to violence into the light of day so we can consider their effects on all parties concerned.

Sometimes the term "conflict resolution" is used interchangeably with other alternative dispute resolution methods such as mediation, litigation, and arbitration. These methods involve a third party in the process but the steps of engagement are, indeed, fundamental. Third-party mediation and arbitration use the principles of conflict resolution as well as diplomacy, statecraft, reconciliation, and more.

Vice versa, two-party conflict resolution uses a range of peacemaking methods during the process. Diplomacy, mediation, negotiation, and arbitration are sometimes needed during the process in order to reduce tension, increase trust, or reveal to the parties a path forward. Whether the conflict is in a playground or on the global stage, the fundamental steps involved in the process of resolving the conflict remain the same.

Two Boys and a Swing...

One morning at recess, a young boy grabs a swing from another boy. The second objects and raises his arms to fight, but he realizes the other is far bigger.

"You took my swing!" the smaller one bellows.

"It's mine!" blasts the other.

"I'll tell the teacher," the smaller one threatens.

"If you do, I'll beat you up!"

The bigger one holds the swing away from the other as if to mark his position. The two boys square off. Neither gives ground.

"It's not fair," the smaller one begins to negotiate.

"Go away."

"I won't. I was here first. I'll tell the teacher."

The bigger boy considers. He could certainly beat the boy up, but then the debate would be between him and a more powerful party, the teacher who has spent many class hours extolling the virtues of sharing and empathy.

"You were taking too long," the bigger boy tries.

The methods and processes of conflict resolution are mainstays in the peaceful social interactions of everyday life.

"What's too long?" asks the smaller one.

"Five minutes."

"Then I still have three minutes."

The bigger boy is unsure of the facts, but there seems to be a compromise proposed and the teacher's intervention might be avoided. Besides, the smaller boy was not that bad. He was even pretty good at baseball.

"If I give you the swing, will you play on my team?"

The smaller one nods. It was actually something he wanted. The proposal has changed the dynamic of the conflict. Suddenly, there is a value-added proposition.

"Okay, three minutes." The bigger boy holds the swing beyond the smaller one's reach. "You promise?"

"I do."

The bigger one slowly gives the smaller the swing, then he stands clear as the other swings for far less than three minutes then relinquishes.

As the bigger boy begins his turn, the smaller one stays to watch. As the sun rises a little farther in the sky, their differences are forgotten. They switch back and forth and both can't help but share the pendulum lightness of morning recess.

Somewhere in the world, every second of the day, a scenario such as this is begging for a solution. No matter what the situation, conflict generates strong emotions, yet it can be an opportunity for growth and transformation.

The principles of conflict resolution are as practical on the playground as they are in the realm of international affairs. At the basis of many great historical peacemaking episodes is the commitment of key individuals, including parties to the dispute as well as third-party facilitators, to the timeworn principles of conflict resolution:

• President Carter's brokering of the Camp David Agreement between Egypt and Israel (1978)

• U.N. Secretary General de Cuellar's mediation of a ceasefire in the Iran-Iraq War in the 1980s

• Oscar Arias' negotiated plan for the Central American Peace Agreement (1987) between El Salvador, Honduras, Guatemala, and Nicaragua

• Chester Croker's bringing together disputants from Angola, Cuba, and South Africa for the Namibian independence settlement (1991)

The Virtue of Attentiveness

Whether at the negotiation table between Palestine and Israel, the living room couch in your home, or on a swing set, the art of listening is essential in creating a nonviolent world. To be attentive, or alert to the conditions that create the potential for violence, is a necessity for resolving the divisions that create conflict. The steps are tried-and-true:

1. Define the problem in terms of both parties' interests
2. Identify all possible options for solution
3. Evaluate those options for solution
4. Add additional value to the options, if necessary
5. Decide on a solution acceptable to all parties
6. Develop an implementation plan
7. Develop a process for evaluating the results
8. Talk about the experience and learn for the future

Since conflict will always be with us, it is how we handle natural disputes that determine the kind of world in which we live. The conflict resolution process is simply a natural way to alleviate or eliminate the polarization of conflict. After a satisfactory solution is attained, observers and historians will label the method used as any one of the many nonviolent methods outlined in this book, such as negotiation, diplomacy, mediation, or arbitration. Fundamental to all of these diverse tools are the basic tenets in the engagement process.

Yet beyond the basic conflict resolution process, where restructuring of current tensions provides a win-win situation in present time, is another evolution of nonviolence. Conflict transformation is the process of changing the patterns that create the future endemic, or repetitive, dynamics of conflict.

For long lasting peace to reign, we must learn from past experiences. There must be an evolution from conflict resolution to conflict transformation, where the structures, beliefs, and interests of the parties are altered to address the underlying roots of future tensions.

Speaking and Listening for Peace

One of the most important means of transforming potential violent tensions into healthy communication is to talk openly, honestly, and in a nonviolent manner. One of the groundbreaking methods in communicating compassionately is the Nonviolent Communication (NVC) technique developed by psychologist Marshall Rosenberg.

In the NVC process, nonviolent communication focuses on honest self-expression and empathy. Rather than the dominating or manipulating language that perpetuates conflicts, Nonviolent Communication seeks to calm the waters with compassionate, two-way interchange. Rather than words that foster fear or humiliation in the other, NVC seeks to bring the attention back to human needs.

At the base of Rosenberg's method is the idea that conflicts arise from misunderstanding. When human needs arise and clash with the strategies that others have chosen to meet their needs, conflict naturally occurs. In Nonviolent Communication, needs are not necessarily at the root of the problem. Rather it is how people seek to meet their wants and needs, or the strategies for fulfillment, that creates the basis for conflict.

The way to resolve conflict through the use of Nonviolent Communication is to identify with the needs of others and empathize with their feelings. NVC is taught as a process of conflict resolution. Through the use of these techniques, a person can develop a compassionate connection with others as well as embody a compassionate life mode, or in Rosenberg's language manifest a compassionate spirit.

Practitioners of nonviolent communication follow four steps when developing a deeper understanding of the needs of others:

1. Make neutral or objective observations without judgment
2. Express honest feelings about the observations
3. Make clear requests of the other party
4. Verify what others are saying to avoid misinterpretation

The purpose of Rosenberg's Nonviolent Communication technique is twofold. First, as practitioners embrace and put into practice the technique, they begin to create habits. They change their way of interacting with others toward a mode where conflict is reduced by a lifestyle that embodies compassion.

Second, the purpose of nonviolent communication in the conflict resolution process is to move a conflict away from the zero-sum strategies toward a discussion of needs. NVC differs from approaches such as negotiation and arbitration where a balanced agreement is usually based on a compromise of competing needs. By facilitating mutual understanding and empathic responses, the parties in a dispute can find a solution without anyone winning or losing. Only through compassion and attention to everyone's needs is the potential of conflict resolution realized.

To make peace with an enemy one must work with the enemy, and that enemy becomes one's partner. — Nelson Mandela, South African president

We have two ears and one mouth so that we can listen twice as much as we speak. — Epictetus, Stoic philosopher

30

Personal Transformation: Sadako Sasaki's Peace Cranes (1955)

A shift in individual consciousness from isolation toward empathy, connection, and community; a qualitative change in defining oneself as peace.

Sadako Sasaki lived in Hiroshima, Japan, just a mile from where the atomic bomb exploded on August 6, 1945. Unlike nearly 100,000 of her neighbors, two-year-old Sadako survived the destruction. Ten years later, purple spots began to appear on her neck and she was hospitalized for leukemia, the "atom bomb disease."

One day as Sadako lay in a hospital bed, a friend brought a piece of paper to her room and folded a traditional origami crane. A creative and beautiful Japanese tradition foretells that one who folds 1,000 cranes can make their wish come true. Even in her weakened condition, Sadako was inspired. She had an epiphany, a vision. Lying in that bed, she found the mission for which she will be always remembered.

Sadako began folding the paper birds with her heartfelt wish for each one of them to fly and spread peace throughout the world. The twelve-year-old managed to find enough paper in that war-torn and depleted country to fold 644 peace cranes before she was lost to cancer. Her friends found more paper and folded the rest of the cranes, then buried them with their friend's delicate, cancer-ridden body.

Today, Sadako's deathbed transformation from victim to prophet is told throughout the world. The young girl's life, with all its challenges and tenderness, has become an inspiration to all those who love peace.

Yet this true story begs a question. How did this weakened, Japanese teenager have the courage to transition to a state of peace even amidst a world reeling from violence and war?

Traditional origami peace cranes as folded by Sadako Sasaki.

We may never have a sufficient answer. Our journeys are as varied and individual as there are human beings. Indeed, there is a strange debate within the peace community. Must there be peace in the world before we can be at peace within ourselves?

This chicken-or-egg conundrum is unsolvable, but it highlights a great need and desire for personal transformation. Such transcendent states of consciousness are often associated with experiences that are highly creative in nature. The nineteenth century poet William Wordsworth is credited with linking creativity with imagination, which gave rise in the artist to transcendent poetry.

The imaginative or creative urge often transforms our traditional patterns, modes, and ideas into new and meaningful forms and interpretations. In a new state of consciousness, our lives change and we often add our individual expressions to the betterment of the world.

Sadako's use of creativity to attain a state of inner peace may be within reach of us all. Spiritual, mystical, and experiential transformations are highly creative in nature. They can occur through epiphanies, religious rebirth, profound realizations, or even near-death experiences where day-to-day worries are replaced by a transcendent state of living. Our brains respond to such states with peaceful patterns of harmony. We find balance, fulfillment, understanding, and contentment.

An epiphany is a sudden realization about the larger order of things. It can come as a new comprehension, an idea, or in putting together the last "piece in a puzzle" that has been on our minds. The root of the word epiphany comes from the Greek for "manifestation or striking appearance." It is the comprehension of the deeper meaning or depth of something that has previously eluded us.

Such eureka moments can have great significance in our lives. Inventors of new technologies often remember a time of discovery. Prophets attribute their prescience to a Divine revelation. Each of us has moments that illuminate and alter the way the world appears and our place in the larger purpose.

Epiphany has many metaphysical and religious connotations. In Middle English the word was associated with apparitions or the manifestation of a deity. The sudden appearance of a vision comes with amazement and astonishment. We are stuck by a "thunderbolt" and witness the moment as miraculous.

In most cases, an epiphany entails an insight into what before was a common experience that suddenly becomes a wonder. We put ourselves in the position of having an epiphany or transcendent experience by being conscious of ourselves and the world around us. Creating the conditions that lead to such insights and creativity entail living in a mode of awareness and seeking where wonders are revealed:

- Be honest with yourself
- Approach life with humor and interest
- Be willing to take risks
- Look at the world with new eyes
- Find your passion
- Go deep and seek understanding
- Face new territory with courage
- Seek education and new experiences
- Conquer your fears
- Embody the change you wish to come

A transformative experience is one where we go beyond our normal confines, where we climb higher in our understanding of the world than we've ever gone before. At the base of the transformative nature of an epiphany is the formation of a unity that brings two or more isolated facts or feelings together into a single, higher level thought.

The Virtue of Unity

Today, neuroscience is being used to study the conditions and expression of these creative, transcendent experiences. The term neurotheology was first used by Aldous Huxley in a nineteenth century novel. Today Andrew Newberg, a neuroscientist from the University of Pennsylvania, is using a single proton emission computed tomography (SPECT) to scan the brains of people in a transcendent state in order to see what we can learn.

The scans of a Catholic nun in prayer and a Buddhist monk in meditation reveal common neurological activity. Blood flow which correlates with the level of activity, in the brain, in the posterior superior parietal lobe had noticeably decreased. This photo from Newberg's work shows the monk's brain in a normal state (left) and in a state of meditation (right). Note the decrease in activity at the bottom of the brain, which denotes reduced interference from the outside world.

The monk and nun and others involved in one of the many forms of meditation and prayer were experiencing, according to this researcher, a feeling of unity that is beyond our confines of normal space and time.[1] Unity hails from the Latin *unitatem*, or oneness, sameness, or agreement. The state of being one part of a totality or whole contributes to a feeling of harmony or concord.

During the neurotheology experiments, comparable scans with other subjects in various states of worship show a remarkable similarity. Whether

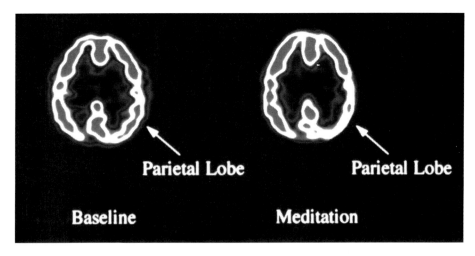

Images of meditative brain activity showing decreased activity in the parietal lobe during meditation (Dr. Andrew Newberg).

monk or nun, the individual goes beyond their confines to achieve a sense of the interconnectedness of the universe and humanity.

Not only does this feeling of unity make the case for toleration of differing forms of worship, but it also shows a physiological basis for personal transformation. Whether or not we can create a state of transformation by induced neurological means, as Newberg contends, the brain scans of people in prayer and meditation show that altered states of consciousness are, indeed, possible.

How we decide to create our personal transformation is a highly individual choice. Yet transformation is also a choice for our larger world, our families and groups, our neighborhoods and communities, our cities and nations. If we are to define ourselves as people of peace, we must evolve our notions of how we see the world, what we say, the way we act, and how we value ourselves as transformative and transcendent beings.

> *Peace Crane, I will write peace on your wings and you will fly all over the world.* — Sadako Sasaki, Japanese peace icon

> *We must be the peace we wish to see in the world.* — Mahatma Gandhi

31

Summary of Methods

On a cold September morning in 2004, an elementary school in Beslan, Russia, became host to a parasitic gang of global bullies. Faces masked, dressed in boots and military fatigues, these terrorists were armed with semiautomatic weapons, grenades, and an array of improvised explosive devices.

They believed they were assaulting that school for a greater purpose: Chechen nationalism, retribution for alleged ethnic cleansing of the Ingush people, perhaps to stop persecution of Muslims. Whatever was in the minds of these violent men and women, it was clear that the innocent children of Beslan School would be their sacrifice.

Over 1,200 people were captured that morning and held frightened in a small, ill-equipped gymnasium. Local police and military combat troops from the Russian Federation immediately surrounded the facility and set up a command post. The prisoners had little food and water, and for nearly three days they suffered under extreme conditions of fear and degradation.

Negotiators entered into talks with the leaders of the militants, yet after the second day the situation rapidly deteriorated. The noise and chaos of failure began in earnest. Tanks and helicopters, bullets and rockets, flamethrowers and grenades exploded in a dance of hyper-violence.

At the end of the siege, over 300 people were killed. Murdered were 186 elementary school students who knew little of the causes they were furthering or the points their deaths were making.

Why did these innocent children have to die? Was it because of a disagreement over land? Over Chechen independence? Was it the result of religious differences, or retribution for a cultural genocide that dated back nearly sixty years to 1944?

Or was it, in the final analysis, the failure of humanity, of inspiration, of creativity to solve the tensions that will always arise? The march to war and violence is certainly the easiest response to conditions of suffering and

Boys walk near a mural promoting peace at the Eastern Peace Centre in a violence-ridden area of Jamaica. The Centre provides recreational activities, life skills, and conflict resolution training (UNICEF/NYHQ2008-0255, Susan Markisz).

pain. Yet where is our reason, our patience and understanding, our faith, our deep commitment to the tried-and-true practices and methods of nonviolence?

Each day the seeds of new tensions blow with the winds of poverty and discontent. Normal conflicts grow to irreconcilable differences in a culture that seems to accept the inevitability of oppression, abuse, and the zero-sum games of greed and power. Bullying, domestic abuse, cyber targeting, nuclear proliferation, dictatorship, torture, environmental plundering, trade wars, genocide, human trafficking — the methods and means of violence seem endless.

The Power of Nonviolence

Indeed, high profile violence such as that in Littleton, Colorado, or Beslan, Russia, can be devastating to our spirit. The amount of violence on the evening news can cause us to conclude that faith and hope are idealistic, and that the power of nonviolence is weak.

Such conclusions are simply wrong. The power of violence may be mesmerizing, but it is the verifiable statistics of nonviolence that give us a glimpse of truth.

As the respected theologian Walter Wink has profoundly noted: if we consider all the nonviolent revolutions of the twentieth century — from India and the Philippines to Poland and South Africa — the lives of nearly 3.5 billion people were changed through nonviolent means.[1]

That statistic is astonishing and growing, yet it barely covers the surface of nonviolent change. Negotiations go on every moment of the day, among families and schools, in neighborhoods and cities, between cultures and nations. Conflict resolution, mediation, diplomacy, and humanitarian efforts are a huge part of the human condition. The statistics of peace are little tabulated and sorely under-documented, yet peace is apparent in every part of our lives.

Even in the face of such facts, and with the common understanding that acts of violence plant the seeds of new violence, people still doggedly hold onto the illusion that violence is the most effective way to peace.

How do we end this illusory dynamic? How do we gain confidence in the history of nonviolence? Where is the best place to put our efforts toward achieving greater peace?

Four Strategies to Reduce Violence

From the first glimmer of tension to the grudging memory that violence leaves behind, nonviolent methods have proven to stop the cycle of violence. For clarity, these diverse methods historically have been categorized into four major strategies that can be utilized to reduce conflict.

Each of these general strategies of action holds the power of nonviolence at its core. Each has a time and place when it is most effective. Many conflicts progress or evolve through more than one strategy before the right way to peace is found.

What history has proven time and again — from the playground to international negotiations — is that we can solve the challenges of violence by engaging in the strategies of prevention, resolution, management, and transformation.

1. PREVENT CONFLICTS

To prevent normal tensions from building into violent conflict, we can identify the triggers and eliminate the roots of injustice and misunderstanding before they cause violence. A potential school bully will often show signs of aggression, withdrawal, or low self-esteem. An imbalance of power between nations is often preceded by a build-up of arms.

The tools of prevention that are used on schoolyards and in neighborhoods to prevent violence include creating safe environments, talking through differences, community building, and peace education. On the global stage, we see the use of economic aid, fair trade, cultural exchange, distributive justice, rule of law, alternative resources acquisition, and enhancing global wellness. On a personal level, we choose humanitarianism, pacifism, nonviolent disobedience, and environmental action.

Prevention is usually unheralded and forgotten in the chaos of political gamesmanship. A violent act prevented is one that becomes hypothetical or the circumstances quickly forgotten in the face of new fears. Yet to identify and correct the root causes of violence is a worthy and highly productive endeavor that ultimately saves treasure and lives.

2. RESOLVE CONFLICTS

If a conflict has already devolved into violence, we must work to find a solution before it follows its natural path to more destructive results. To resolve a conflict, we first identify the differences between the parties in a dispute. Then we try to remove the underlying conditions that are causing the tension.

In our Newtonian cause-and-effect world, each action requires a reaction. Once a conflict arises, the resulting violence is subject to the same laws as any other form of energy. As the laws of physics tell us, unless the energy of tension is addressed, the cycle of violence will continue until one party wins and the other gives way.

Indeed, the negative dynamics of win/loss solutions ensure that a violent situation will only get worse. History shows us that the repercussions and side effects, even if stilled at the moment, will inevitably come back to haunt us.

To actually resolve a conflict, whether it's an incidence of bullying at school or the oppression of a dictatorship, the conditions of the dispute must be brought into the light of day. Tools for politicians and statesmen, with parallels for children and schools, include diplomacy, statecraft, utilizing alternate channels of communication, and the sophisticated processes of third-party and two-person conflict resolution.

Resolving a condition of violence means that the sources of tensions that caused the problems are no longer active. To limit the potential for future outbreaks, a resolution must alter the structural mechanisms that caused the conflict in the first place.

3. MANAGE CONFLICTS

When a conflict seems intractable, it may become necessary to form a long-term strategy to alleviate or contain the violence. Managing a conflict, or negotiating a stalemate, in order to keep a situation from getting worse is preferred to letting unrestrained violence wreak havoc on innocents.

The repetition of negative actions within an imbalance of power is a good working definition of what makes a bully. When an intractable imbalance of power seems fixed, the best plan of action may be to keep the conditions that created that imbalance from elevating while watching for avenues of resolution.

Tools of violence management are the same for school administrators, political activists, envoys from nations, or anyone else that is working on a seemingly immovable situation. These tools include third-party maintenance of an uncertain peace by a peacekeeping force or authority, or entering into a diplomatic negotiation.

Tools for maintenance also include actions that might do nothing to make the situation worse but, instead, put pressure on the perpetuators to end their violence. These include boycotts, united action, witnessing the violence, civil disobedience, conscientious objection, nonviolent resistance, and reduction of weapons or means of intimidation.

Multinational negotiations, roundtable discussions, treaty agreements, and conflict resolution processes are striving to lessen tensions in an increasingly globalized world, as evident in this Nuclear Security Summit, 2010 (The White House).

4. TRANSFORM CONFLICTS

Since tensions and conflicts will always be with us, we can endeavor to deal with the energy of violence in new, more constructive ways. The parties to violence can shift a situation from isolation and polarization to the unifying actions of empathy, connection, and community.

To transform violence into a new, more positive dynamic requires that we change our responses to violence. It means that we find within ourselves the virtues that open doors rather than close them. Once we find this ability to view a violent situation as an opportunity to grow and expand, we can move beyond our fixed positions and begin to restructure the underlying cause of tension. Only then can the energy of violence be used to not only make a better life for ourselves but also to achieve a more equitable and empowering world.

Skills for people who find the will to transform conflict are toleration, understanding, listening, taking responsibility, and reflecting on their participation in the violence. Skills for victims who wish to transform their conditions of violence include forming community, having trust, asking for help, building self-respect, and avoiding feelings of rejection and humiliation.

Tools for conflict transformation in homes and nations include the nonviolent methods of reconciliation, spirituality, artistic expression, application of the Golden Rule, enhancing global wellness, and personal transformation.

Beyond Cause-and-Effect

Whether we prevent, resolve, manage, or transform our conflicts, the act of engaging in nonviolent methods makes the world less violent. Using the strategies of nonviolence with the goal of working for a better world acknowledges that we're all in this together. Our actions have consequences for ourselves and for others.

Yet just as the Golden Rule tells us that good deeds are reciprocated in kind, the do-unto-others rule, unfortunately, has a parallel in violence. The dynamics of conflict are enervated by the violent energy of reciprocity. It takes more than a perpetrator, or bad guy, or "evil-doer" to exchange the Newtonian energy of brutality and abuse. It takes a victim that responds in kind with more violence or one that takes no action at all.

Nonviolence is as active as violence. As differentiated from the old term "passive resistance," nonviolence is engagement. It requires us to take action. According to physical laws of motion, actions can be of two types. Our responses can be cause-and-effect, as in a reaction to others. Or our approach to violence can be spontaneous, an action that comes from inside us, from our hearts and minds.

Cause-and-effect reactions to violence are responses that are primarily influenced by outside factors. Meeting violence with violence is the negative action. It is often our first response, our knee-jerk reaction, an unthinking comeback.

On the other hand, spontaneous actions come from within us as thoughtful, considered responses. Spontaneous actions are made by self-actualization of our best character traits, our internalization of the many virtues of peace. When fully instilled, the virtues of peace alter our knee-jerk, cause-and-effect reactions toward the self-expression of our peaceful nature. This is the evolution of our society. It can be a collective effort by a society that values peace or it can be a personal effort, a hero's journey.

To truly shift from the primitive dance of violence toward the evolved walk of peace requires a movement away from a reliance on negative cause-and-effect responses to more positive, spontaneous actions that arise from a peaceful nature. To act spontaneously requires a deep seating of the character traits and skills, the values, and virtues that make us evolved humans.

As we have seen through the many real-world examples in this book, only through rational, nonviolent action can the energy of violence be dissipated. To respond with more violence, or even to ignore it, gives more energy to the conflict. By engaging with love and nonviolence, we repel the negative energy and capture the positive energy in our endeavors toward peace.

The nonviolent icon Nelson Mandela had this same awareness in a small cell on Robben Island off the coast of South Africa:

> It was during those long and lonely years that my hunger for the freedom of my own people became a hunger for the freedom of all people, white and black. I knew as I knew anything that the oppressor must be liberated just as surely as the oppressed, for all had been robbed of humanity. When I walked out of prison, that was my mission, to liberate the oppressed and the oppressor both.[2]

The language and methods of nonviolence, as our societal icons of peacemaking have found, are simply tools in the hands of our virtues. Our day-to-day experience and an inspired study of the history of peace give us the confidence that nonviolence can truly stop the cycle of violence. As we foster inside us the virtues of peace, especially the profound virtue of compassionate love, we become fully equipped to engage in nonviolence as the natural tensions of life arise.

> *Peace is the only battle worth waging.* — Albert Camus, French-Algerian writer

> *The essence of nonviolence is love. Out of love and the willingness to act selflessly, strategies, tactics, and techniques for a nonviolent struggle arise naturally. Nonviolence is not a dogma; it is a process.* — Thich Nhat Hanh

> *There is no way to peace. Peace is the way.* — A.J. Muste, Dutch-American Protestant minister

Conclusion: The Virtuoso of Peace

What would a perfect person be like? Surely they would help others. Their interactions with everyone would be compassionate and cooperative. They would certainly be forgiving and fair, empathic and wise, generous and calm. The perfect human being would manifest internal purity and beauty in all their external actions to the mutual benefit of themselves and the world around them.

How exhausting. To always be good and right in every situation, every moment of our lives is neither possible nor a requirement for peacemaking. We realize there is no such thing as a perfect person, so most of us endeavor to become the best we can be. That is what we call individual human progress.

With the gifts we're born with and the character we develop throughout our lives, most of us strive to leave for our children a more peaceful society than the one we found. Whether our urge to contribute arises from our communal instinct to survive as a species or from a Divine challenge with a Heavenly boon, we open our ears and minds to listen and learn. We act with as much decency as we can muster then hope our lives will be good and beneficial to all.

We fail in some ways. Succeed in others. Just as the athlete who trains for a contest, we work hard and struggle. We seek information along with affirmation. We try one thing then another in a constant effort to diminish the role that violence plays in our lives.

Our quest as peacemakers is to evolve our innate and acquired abilities to make positive changes in an imperfect world. We embody the character and values that give us internal peace and allow us to contribute in a positive way. Those of us who reject violence as a means to approach conflict try to strengthen the virtues we must have in order to be authentic when we use the nonviolent tools at our disposal. We journey beyond all odds to hone our individual characters, to successfully practice nonviolent methods, to become virtuosos of peace.

Fundamental to this journey are thirty specific virtues that are core to practicing nonviolence and manifesting peace in our lives. A virtuoso is one who is expert. No longer a student of peacemaking but a master in the art of peace, the virtuoso exhibits expertise and cultivates an appreciation of the methods of peacemaking. The virtuoso is a collector of friendships, a connoisseur of justice, a skillful and imaginative artist for peace.

And for all of our efforts what do we reap? A world less violent than the one that might have been.

Kong Qiu, or Confucius as his name was later Latinized, has manifested peace for over 2,500 years. Born in Qufu on the southwestern province of Shandong in China, Confucius imagined the perfect "gentleman" who exhibited a correctness of behavior and morality as well as acted with justice and sincerity.

The sage's philosophy, as compiled by later disciples in the book *Analytics,* believed in self-cultivation. Acquiring the skills of good judgment is more important to Confucius, his followers tell us, than knowing all the rules of society. Rules are intended to be our guide when we lack necessary judgment. The gentleman, or gentleperson in modern usage, is engaged in learning and living life to its fullest. To be given a fish for dinner, as one of his Chinese contemporaries noted, was less valuable than being taught to fish for a lifetime.

Confucius is believed to have been the first to enunciate the Golden Rule, proposing the maxim: "Do not do to others what you do not want done to yourself." The term Yï conveys the idea of reciprocity, not from self-interest necessarily, but from a sense of righteousness.

The sage also used the term Janzu, which assigns to us a duty. To have the character of a Confucian gentleperson is to fulfill one's responsibility. Perfectly fulfilling our duty entails having a benevolent character and embracing the idea of humanness with all its potential.

To combine the "qualities of the saint, scholar, and gentleman" may seem too much to ask, but a cavalcade of philosophers and theologians have contributed insight into the matter since at least the beginning of written history. Inevitably, the path to which they have pointed is bejeweled with the shining stones of virtue.

How do we acquire a virtue? A character trait is a personal quality or skill that allows us to exhibit what we value. A value is a principle that indicates to us a good moral character. To possess a virtue, which is a condition of moral excellence, is to embody these values. "Wisdom is knowing what to do next;" said educator and director of the World Peace Foundation David Starr, "virtue is doing it."

The reason we work to evolve our virtues is simply described. We seek peace. Our objective is to find a life of harmony, without violence in ourselves or with others, barring no culture or nation, being respectful of the land, water, and sky.

To that end, what does it take to develop the traits and skills that build our virtuous character? Genetically and behaviorally, we form our character from birth or even before we emerge from the womb. Our parents, caregivers, and mentors teach us how to use our traits and develop our skills. It is up to us to make these skills the habits that express our virtues without fail.

There are several models that lay out the process of developing virtues. We internalize a particular virtue by learning about it, by increasing our understanding of its expression. Then we act on the virtues we acquire and reflect on the outcome. In effect, we practice to make a virtue part of our fundamental character.

Yet the full embodiment of a virtue requires deep commitment. We continue throughout our lives to learn from the stories we hear and the examples of our mentors. Deeper understanding of the virtues of peace comes with holding the space for them within our character. What does it feel like to be friendly or determined? What actions by resistance or rule of law result in less violence? If our actions are not successful, we alter our thinking and modify our behavior.

The last steps to instilling a virtue are consideration, contemplation, and reflection. Did my intention result in a good outcome? How can I do better next time? The examined life, as Socrates is to have said, is a life worth living.

As we begin to understand the virtues that are foremost in our character, we learn which methods of nonviolence are the surest way, as individuals, to find peace. What traits and skills do we possess? What values do we hold in esteem? Which virtues do we embody in our character? Each of us finds different and unique answers.

In fully embracing our individual virtues of peace we find that the ways of nonviolence are fundamental to our lives. In doing so, we step out of the daily struggle into the light of human meaning and purpose, ready to manifest a better world.

The Virtue of Tactfulness (Diplomacy)

To be a master of diplomatic negotiations does not involve lying but rather discretion. "Tact is the art of making a point without making an enemy," is a quip attributed to author Howard W. Newton. To be tactful is to know when to speak or stay silent. It means listening to others and understanding their circumstances. Having tact entails considering the effect your words have on other people then choosing them wisely and well.

In the early twentieth century, when President Theodore Roosevelt agreed to be a mediator and helped end the Japanese-Russo War, he was seen as an objective and discreet third party. His tactfulness earned him a Nobel Peace Prize. Later, when Roosevelt sided with the Russians in their decision against paying war reparations, the president's impartial position was abandoned in favor of geopolitical positioning, which laid the seeds for distrust and future war.

The tactful diplomat is witty without being cynical, arrogant, or inappropriate. "We are masters of the unsaid words, but slaves of those we let slip out," said Winston Churchill, who not only led his nation to victory in World War II but also through the difficult negotiations at Malta.

Being careful, thoughtful, and discriminating about what we say allows a deeper intention from the experienced negotiator. Being tactful often leaves the meaning of words open for interpretation. The ambiguity allows us to be honest without causing undue fear or offense, which can be expressed in a negative outcome.

The tactful skills entail the ability to listen, to think about what others feel, to be considerate about what others need. The tactful put themselves in the other person's shoes and understand conflict from their perspective.

The negotiator who embodies the virtue of tact accomplishes the desired goals by lowering resistance and illuminating the real differences. A tactful response provides breathing space that we all need to move from aggression and impasse to trust and solution. "Without tact you can learn nothing," said one of Britain's most successful negotiators, Benjamin Disraeli. "Tact teaches you when to be silent. Inquirers who are always questioning never learn anything."

Synonyms: finesse and subtlety

Skills: considerate, thoughtful, and discreet

The Virtue of Foresight (Statecraft)

Foresight does not require a soothsayer's skill. A person with the ability to look into the future for a practical solution, especially the true statesman, does not need to have extrasensory perception. Rather, foresight is the ability to perceive conditions that are significant and, with that understanding, to develop insight into the nature of events in order to act before the future occurs.

"There is not any present moment that is unconnected with some future one," said English essayist Joseph Addison. "The life of every man is a continued chain of incidents, each link of which hangs upon the former."

Foresight gives leaders the ability to see connections and predict the future based on present conditions. It takes a considered review and thoughtful analysis of the chain of incidents. To see clearly, to discern what is important from what is less important provides us with a measure of prudence to act with judgment and wisdom. Those with foresight synthesize the past and calculate what one action or another will do to create the future.

In his book on American foreign policy, Middle East negotiator Dennis Ross emphasized the need for foresight as a strategic advantage.[2] Good policy decisions, he said, have implications far into the future. Face-to-face discussions, sustained efforts, constant reassessment of realities on the ground are the hard work of peacemaking. The statesperson, Ross said, is like a general on the battlefield, wielding all the tools available, assessing present conditions, then imagining what will happen if one or the other strategies are taken.[1]

However, the ability to understand and evaluate entails intuition and hunch as much as it does observation and reasoning. "The foresight that awaits is the same Genius that creates," Ralph Waldo Emerson noted in his poem *Fate*.

Successful cases of statecraft, such as the transfer of Hong Kong in 1999 from British to Chinese rule, required leaders who may have seemed to use a crystal ball but relied instead on their well-considered imaginations. Yet when it comes to the visionary, foresight can seem a mystical quality. In a 1968 presidential campaign speech Robert Kennedy paraphrased George Bernard Shaw when he expressed the process of creative foresight, "Some people see things as they are and say: why? I dream things that never were and say: why not?"

Synonyms: mental preparedness and insight

Skills: anticipation, circumspection, and discernment

The Virtue of Forgiveness (Reconciliation)

To hold resentment and indignation might be the easy way to handle offenses, but it is a difficult way to move beyond them. To be unforgiving means carrying forward an offense which, as many studies show, is an unhealthy condition that can ruin lives and even destroy the balance of society.[1]

To those on the receiving end of violence, the forgiving and reconciliation process can take a lifetime or can fail to happen at all. The typical definition of forgiveness is to grant pardon or give up claim to resentment and restitution, which takes a healthy amount of courage for victims of both minor offenses and heinous crimes.

"The weak can never forgive," said Gandhi. "Forgiveness is the attribute of the strong." The leadership of Mandela and Bishop Tutu enabled the entire South African society to move beyond the crimes of apartheid. Reconciliation gave victims voice and criminals the opportunity to feel remorse.

Forgiveness is, perhaps, most beneficial when it involves public or private acknowledgement of the act of forgiving. Engaging in reconciliation and restitution provides that medium. In these cases the simple act of pardoning is supplemented with restorative justice either in monetary transactions or acts of contrition.

Yet forgiveness has a much deeper dimension that goes beyond pardoning and restitution. It entails healing. In study after study, those who relieve stress by forgiving instead of holding anger and resentment find ways to benefit from the original violence in ways both concrete and miraculous.

In the popular *A Course on Miracles*, published by the Foundation for Inner Peace, forgiveness is an awakening of the understanding that difficulties and those who act against us are here solely for helping us find our way to peace.

Forgiveness provides a means of spiritual attainment and personal health. "Forgiveness is the greatest preventive maintenance," said Marianne Williamson, "as well as the greatest healer."

Synonym: pardon, release

Skills: compassion, objectivity, and grace

The Virtue of Integrity (Mediation)

Architect and futurist R. Buckminster Fuller said on personal integrity "hangs humanity's fate." As the inventor of the extremely stable geodesic dome, Fuller was particularly aware of the causal and structural reasons for success and failure.

In the scientific method, perfect integrity is when the observed results of an experiment match expectations. Indeed, in the science of electronics, the integrity of a circuit is strong when there is little difference in the electrical signal no matter where measured along the route.

The origin of integrity is in the Latin roots for whole or complete. Integrity on a personal level involves consistency of values. A person who has integrity shows honesty in thought and action. "Integrity simply means not violating one's own identity," said German social philosopher Erich Fromm.

Such soundness of character becomes a measure of a person's moral and ethical principles. In a mediation, the mediator must have the confidence of those in the conflict. As in the case of the negotiations over Northern Ireland during the 1990s, George Mitchell's integrity provided the structural soundness for that country's historic achievement.

Ayn Rand, the philosopher of Objectivism, put it in the context of virtues: "Happiness, not pain or mindless self-indulgence," she believed, "is the proof of your moral integrity, since it is the proof and the result of your loyalty to the achievement of your values."

Synonyms: upright and honorable
Skills: honest, objective, and incorruptible

The Virtue of Decisiveness (Arbitration)

For most, seeing a stray animal, especially one that is hurt and in pain, involves a decision. Do you ignore it, help it to a shelter, or take it home as your own? In such situations, do you act by your mind or your heart?

Most decisions certainly involve both. To act through the processes of your mind involves reason. To act by the processes we associate with the heart involves emotion, gut feelings, empathy, or perhaps the most controversial: intuition.

Decisions made by reason are based on cause and effect. They take into consideration your experience and knowledge. They are based on real or imagined facts. With your mental powers, you weigh the consequences.

Decisions based on intuition are based on direct perception of what you absorb through your senses. You feel apprehension or anticipation. You balance the conditions and consequences then weigh your emotional levels and go with your "gut."

A case in point of the use of both processes is the arbitration effort that eventually resulted in low cost HIV/AIDS drugs to developing nations. The World Court necessarily combined the more structured, rational decision-making model with the more subjective intuitive model. They objectively analyzed facts and measured patterns but considered the moral alternatives before they decided in their subjective judgment that the poor needed lower-cost access to life-saving drugs.

To be personally decisive is much the same. It does not mean making quick or unconsidered decisions. "The direction of a man's thought," wrote German theologian Erich Sauer, "is always the decisive factor in his personality. His whole outer life will be determined by the inward inclination of his mind."

In peacemaking, decisiveness, like all virtues, has its positive and negative. "The world is now aware," said former Gabonese president Omar Bongo, "that the most unavoidable and most dangerous weapon that exists is the blind decisiveness of a man ready to sacrifice his life for an obscure cause."

Yet to act decisively upon contemplation is to find a reasoned path to the future. The wise man understands that no matter what decision is made, it was the right decision at the time. There is no looking back, for in the next moment the conditions and the development of the virtues that brought you there will have evolved into new circumstances requiring another thoughtful decision.

Synonyms: strength of mind and purpose
Skills: will, certainty, and resolve

The Virtue of Calmness (Peacekeeping)

In the science of mechanics, stress is the amount of force exerted on an object, which has several modes. Compressive stress is the ability to keep from being crushed. Yield stress, on the other hand, is how much an object will take before it deforms. Tension stress is the ability to expand until an object snaps.

The stress of war and violence is a physical force as well as a mental condition. This is experienced most vividly in manifestations of "shell shock" or Posttraumatic Stress Disorder. An inordinate amount of psychological stress affects our ability to keep things in perspective and think rationally.

Unfortunately, the science of calm is less expressive. The state of calm implies being in control of oneself, in command of our actions. To be unruffled, to be cool, calm, and collected is a dignified state of being, a condition of self-possession.

"The cyclone derives its powers from a calm center," said Norman Vincent Peale. "So does a person." Clarity of judgment and absence of the strong feelings that blur decisions are the skills of a leader in crisis. To be calm is to be free from agitation. It provides the alertness and awareness essential to wisdom.

Nowhere is calm more important than in areas of war and conflict. When peacekeepers from the African Union landed under threat of fire in Sudan or when Australian forces under the U.N. banner separated warring parties in Timor, calm was the objective and intention. In many areas of the world, peacekeepers have brought relative calm to war-torn Sudan, Chad, and Sierra Leone, to the tent cities of refugee camps in Ethiopia and Burundi, and the opportunity for peace in many other conflict-ridden regions.

To restore calm in conditions of great stress gives the parties time to consider the effects of stress on children and mothers who have little to gain from the ravages of war. "The more tranquil a man becomes, the greater is his success, his influence, his power for good," said British philosopher James Allen.

Some people train themselves to be calm by practices such as meditation, relaxation training, or breathing exercises. Others turn a steely eye on the decisions at hand, focusing on spurning emotional disturbances or the complexity of passions.

The character and ability to be calm in a storm is necessary in order to the foster peace of mind as well as peace in the world. "Power is so characteristically calm," said nineteenth century Viceroy of India Robert Bulwer-Lytton, "that calmness in itself has the aspect of strength."

Synonyms: composure and self-possession

Skills: patience, serenity, and restraint

The Virtue of Generosity (Economic Aid)

In the parable of the "widow's mite," generosity comes from the heart and not from the purse. The poor widow, as the Christian prophet Jesus taught his disciples, had sacrificed to give two hard-earned coins, or mites, to do the good work of the Church.

Though others contributed much more than the widow, it was the heartfelt act of giving that made the simple gift so worthy. Pure generosity is giving without expecting anything in return. It can be an offer of money, or time, or a talent that provides comfort or aid of others in need.

Yet an act of generosity or charity or economic aid has a reciprocal value. "Be happy with what you have and are," said British prime minister William Gladstone, "be generous with both, and you won't have to hunt for happiness."

Nowhere is the reciprocal value of generosity more apparent than in the poor, famine-prone villages of Africa, which receive precious food and medicine from aid programs for developed countries. Nongovernmental Organizations generously provide educational opportunities, water wells, forest plantings, and other peacebuilding efforts that eventually return the investment by providing stable societies and profitable markets.

In addition to physical gifts of generosity, giving can be openness of spirit. We can endeavor to be free of meanness and small-mindedness. To release others from our judgments, biases, and racisms can be acts of kindness and understanding that, inevitably, will return a bounty to the giver.

"The way you get meaning into your life is to devote yourself to loving others," contends author Mitch Albom, "devote yourself to your community around you, and devote yourself to creating something that gives you purpose and meaning."

When one looks at the world, with all the war and natural disasters, with the ill effects of disease and hunger, it can be overwhelming to think of where to start. Yet generosity is not measured in quantity but rather intent. "If you can't feed a hundred people," Mother Teresa advised, "then just feed one."

Synonyms: benevolence and giving
Skills: charity, kindness, and hospitable

The Virtue of Justice (Fair Trade)

To be just is to value and act upon the principles of equity and fairness. To uphold justice in a cause is to associate that purpose with an ethical position, through reason or belief.

Justice can be given or it can be exacted. "Justice that love gives is a surrender," noted Gandhi, "justice that law gives is a punishment." The moral principle of justice can be embodied by way of personal ethics or delivered through the acceptance of law.

The concept of justice as fairness is a fairly new association. In previous centuries justice was associated with fate or Divine intervention, where a just reward or punishment would find those hearts that were good or evil.

Yet the modern context of justice as fairness presents us with a workable process by which to see progress. "Justice and power must be brought together," said French philosopher Blaise Pascal, "so that whatever is just may be powerful, and whatever is powerful may be just."

A just society is a well-ordered society. The consequences of our actions determine our future. Criminals get their due and crime is reduced. Those who contribute their labors get fair wages. Fair trade for a coffee farmer in South America is seen as mutually beneficial for the coffee consumer in New York.

On the other hand, when the world is not well-ordered, there are calls for rebuke and retribution. Justice is the antithesis of oppressive laws and wars of aggression. If someone has suffered, justice through monetary or social measures can potentially restore the natural balance.

"If you want peace," said Pope Paul VI in his 1972 Day of Peace message, "work for justice." The worldwide movement toward fair trade is an example of restoring balance through justice. Returning fair wages for the labor to create a product is a just solution that lessens the potential for resentment and conflict.

Peace and justice, said American President Dwight D. Eisenhower, "are two sides of the same coin." Since the beginning of human history, through our philosophies, religions, actions, and institutions, we have endeavored to uphold the right of people to find both.

Synonyms: fairness and equity
Skills: judicious, even-handed, and reasonable

The Virtue of Discretion (Boycott)

Discretion is the quality of showing good judgment and making responsible decisions. A person with discretion will act with an understanding of what they consider right, moral, lawful, and wise. "Discretion is the perfection of reason," said Sir Walter Scott, "and a guide to us in all the duties of life."

The virtue of discretion, especially in the case of boycott, entails examining the facts, weighing intuitions, and forming opinions after considerate deliberation. English judge Lord Scarman elevated discretion to the art "of suiting actions to particular circumstances."

Having a choice is inherent in the opportunity to invoke discretion. It is separating or distinguishing the unusable chaff from the wheat, the harmful from the healthy, the unjust from the just. In this way the peacemaker can be deliberate about actions to seek justice. People chose to boycott grapes, for example, when César Chávez pointed out the migrant workers' plight. Many businesses pulled their operations from South Africa and contributed to the collapse of apartheid.

Discretion said German sociologist Georg Simmel, "is nothing other than the sense of justice with respect to the sphere of the intimate contents of life."

On a personal level, the skill of having discretion, or being cautious with our words and actions, provides a way to prevent corrupting relationships with domination. "Mutual respect implies discretion and reserve," affirmed Swiss philosopher Henri-Frédéric Amiel, "even in love itself; it means preserving as much liberty as possible to those whose life we share."

Synonyms: judgment and consideration
Skills: acumen, discriminate, and measuring

The Virtue of Cooperation (United Action)

"Now join your hands," William Shakespeare invoked from *Henry VI*, "and with your hands your hearts." Such calls for humans to work together for the common good is thought by anthropologists to date to the early stages of evolution. Working side-by-side, participating in unified action, using our brains and labor for a purpose that is mutually beneficial, has allowed our species to survive.

Competition is many times touted as the strongest motivation for progress. Yet what seems like selfish and independent parts of a system are working together in overt and subtle ways to create a whole that is greater-than-the-sum-of-the-parts. From multi-cellular bacteria to complex governments, evolution has favored those systems that work in conjunction to survive and flourish.

"A tribe," Darwin concluded in his evolutionary description, "including many members who, from possessing in a high degree the spirit of patriotism, fidelity, obedience, courage, and sympathy, were always ready to aid one another, and to sacrifice for the common good, would be victorious over most other tribes; and this would be natural selection."

Even in coercive environments, punishment for not working together provides a negative incentive for cooperation. Whether looked at as survival of the tribe or personal self-interest, cooperation is a necessity.

"Every great movement in the history of Western civilization," said historian Christopher Dawson, "from the Carolingian age to the nineteenth century has been an international movement which owed its existence and its development to the cooperation of many different peoples."

Humans who cooperate see mutual desires for future outcomes. To date, the height of modern state cooperation is the United Nations. Most of the countries on Earth hold sovereignty and self-interest as their heralds but combine in the United Nations out of need for mutual cooperation in the struggle against natural or manmade challenges.

Through cooperation, we find unity and develop a special relationship with our closest companions. With total strangers, we adapt to new situations and cooperate in spite of the uncertainty. "In the last analysis, every kind of peaceful cooperation among men is primarily based on mutual trust," said Albert Einstein.

We see unity of language and symbols, culture and institutions, as well as technology and incentives to encourage cooperation. Nothing in nature shows the evolution of cooperation better than the synchronicity of nature. Who is not in awe of the darting schools of fish that seem to act together, or the contingent of birds that fly as if in concert? For humans equipped with a powerful will, cooperation is the choice by which our future is won.

Synonyms: collaboration and association
Skills: helpful, communing, and synergistic

The Virtue of Dissent (Civil Disobedience)

The need for civil disobedience, as well as the reason oppressive governments must repress those who protest, has been obvious to many throughout history, including some of the more infamous. Noted Hitler's Nazi propaganda minister Joseph Goebbels: "If you tell a lie big enough and keep repeating it, people will eventually come to believe it. The lie can be maintained only for such time as the State can shield the people from the political, economic and/or military consequences of the lie. It thus becomes vitally important for the

State to use all of its powers to repress dissent, for the truth is the mortal enemy of the lie, and thus by extension, the truth is the greatest enemy of the State."

To dissent is to take an opposing viewpoint. It expresses our individuality and preserves our natural right to our own opinion. Dissent entails a questioning of power. When differing from a majority, especially with a government or political party, the dissenter transforms passive disagreement into active expression.

The institutionalized forms of dissent include participating in out-of-power political parties or mounting a legislative campaign to change a law. The methods of dissent that fall outside institutionalized methods are many, some nonviolent, others violent.

During the Arab Spring, protestors took to the streets in nonviolent acts of civil disobedience that brought down several oppressive regimes. It is noteworthy that in this post–Enlightenment age the natural right to protest was never questioned. To counter the nonviolent protests, dictators could only characterize the participants as terrorists or gangs, a lie that further isolated their regimes.

In the relationship of humans to their form of government, historian and activist Howard Zinn established the order when he said, "Dissent is the highest form of patriotism." Only when actions devolve into violence does the virtue of dissent as a force for good lose power.

"Here in America," said former general and later president Dwight D. Eisenhower, "we are descended in blood and in spirit from revolutionists and rebels — men and women who dare to dissent from accepted doctrine. As their heirs, may we never confuse honest dissent with disloyal subversion."

Dissidents in countries with oppressive regimes often choose a role outside a party politic that has achieved illegitimate dominance by coercion and dishonesty. These dissidents are often spied on, harassed, kidnapped, persecuted, jailed, and even killed. Writer George Bernard Shaw made the dissenter essential to evolutionary history when he wrote, "All progress depends on the unreasonable man."

Synonyms: disapproval and disagreement
Skills: refusing, discordant, and contentiousness

The Virtue of Conscience (Conscientious Objection)

That we seem to have a sense of what is right and wrong is not as debatable as to the source from which it comes. The Dutch artist Vincent Van Gogh determined that "conscience is a man's compass." It is the virtue that determines our judgments on the actions of others as well as our own.

A moral sense of consciousness is different from simply being conscious, but both words have the same root. To be aware of something, to be awake comes from the term *conscientia*, which is a type of knowledge, either intuitive or learned.

Consciousness is the inner faculty of our intellect that allows us to make judgments and determines our actions. When we follow our conscience, we are at the end of a complex process of weighing our ethical and moral principles and rules of behavior.

Conscientious objectors, for instance, make the decision based on a thorough analysis of their innermost thoughts. Henry David Thoreau, one of the most famous conscientious objectors, expressed his inner thoughts about conscience in the great American pacifist essay originally entitled "Resistance to Civil Government." "The only obligation which I have a right to assume," he said, "is to do at any time what I think right...."

When we feel remorse over our actions, that is our inner voice cajoling us to right action. The debate that goes on inside our head informs our decisions and determines what kind of person we wish to be. Some who are deaf to the subtle sounds of their conscience choose violence. Those who hear the inner voice loud and clear choose peace.

Scientific definitions of consciousness focus on the structure of DNA. The ability to determine right from wrong becomes an imprint as part of our history and culture. Conscience can also be a capacity to learn to the degree that our genetic makeup allows for the skills of judgment and reason. To use our conscience is to employ a considerable mental analysis to the process of determining and acting on the neural structures that make up our convictions.

Most religions, on the other hand, focus on defining the conscience as coming from a spiritual source of moral sense. Through our religious practices, rituals, prayers, and meditations many believe we can tap into the Divine or universal conscience. Said the Buddha, "When the mind is face to face with the Truth, a self-luminous spark of thought is revealed at the inner core of ourselves and, by analogy, all reality."

The individual as well as the societal search for this "spark of thought" is no less than the history of the quest for peace. To have ever more evolved judgment and decisions is the elusive goal to which people of good conscience strive.

"Peace demands the most heroic labor and the most difficult sacrifice," said Trappist monk Thomas Merton. "It demands greater heroism than war. It demands greater fidelity to the truth and a much more perfect purity of conscience."

To be a part of an evolved "world conscience" is to share a sense of the ethics of our evolutionary human experience. "Nothing is more powerful than an individual acting out of his conscience," prophesized essayist Norman Cousins, "thus helping to bring the collective conscience to life."

This global consciousness is not limited by individual fears and circumstances but rises toward a collective moral sense of humanity. Whether natural law or spiritual gift, whether individual or collective, that we have an inner light to help us negotiate this life is a profound gift. "Two things fill the mind with ever new and increasing wonder and awe," waxed German philosopher Immanuel Kant, "the starry heavens above me and the moral law within me."

Synonyms: moral sense and inner voice
Skills: qualms, principles, and scruples

The Virtue of Compassion (Spiritual Practices)

The ability to suffer from seeing the misfortunes of others is the first step for many who choose spiritual practices as their most important work for peace. Lord Byron said, "The dew of compassion is a tear." Yet the power in compassion seems to come from the accompanying and deeply held desire to alleviate that misfortune.

Such a tender feeling and call to action is considered one of the most important virtues of peace. "Compassion is the basis of all morality," insisted German philosopher Arthur Schopenhauer. This underlying function of compassion is evident in its etymology. The word is fixed firmly in the Latin *pati* and Greek *sympatheia*, or to suffer. The communal emphasis comes from the Latin prefix *com*, or together with or in combination. In essence, compassion is to share in the suffering of others.

The true passion of religions, spiritual traditions, and philosophies comes from the universal concept of compassion. Indeed at the time the Romans embraced Christianity, the *Passion of Christ*— a twelfth century derivative of the original Greek — succinctly conveyed the suffering that Christ endured on the Cross. In Islam, during the month of Ramadan, one of the purposes of fasting is to empathize with the suffering of others, or to feel compassion for the poor and destitute.

Said seventh century author Thomas Browne, Jr., "By compassion we make others' misery our own, and so, by relieving them, we relieve ourselves also."

The *pathos* in compassion has come to be understood as the communication of suffering. It is often invoked by victim accounts, or through epic storytelling, or by the sublime emotions expressed by the theater or paintings. Pathos makes the observer identify with the victims of abuse, difficult circumstances, or injustices.

"Compassion is sometimes the fatal capacity for feeling what it is like to live inside somebody else's skin," said author Frederick Buechner. "It is the knowledge that there can never really be any peace and joy for me until there is peace and joy finally for you too."

More active than empathy, compassion has a quantitative aspect that demands altruistic or unselfish works. Thomas Merton put it in the spiritual context of connectivity between the suffering of others and the suffering of our self. "The whole idea of compassion," the Catholic social activist said, "is based on a keen awareness of the interdependence of all these living beings, which are all part of one another, and all involved in one another."

Synonyms: tender feelings and empathy
Skills: commiserate, kind, and conscientious

The Virtue of Morality (Pacifism)

When people say someone has ethics, they really mean that the person has morals. Ethics is the study of morality and, as the normative basis for appropriate behavior, morality deserves lifelong study by all of us who love peace.

"A man does what he must," said John F. Kennedy, "in spite of personal consequences, in spite of obstacles and dangers and pressures — and that is the basis of all human morality."

In the modern sense, morality has come to mean conduct that distinguishes between right and wrong. To have morality is to conform to the rules of right conduct. In that context, the hardest part may be to decide what the rules are. So we have help from our internal moral "barometer," from our family and tribe, and from our nations and cultural groups.

A moral code is a set of beliefs that has achieved consensus with a group. A moral is any practice within that moral code. There are some, however, who believe that there is no such thing as a definitive right and wrong. For these moral nihilists, there is no such thing as truth in morality. Even for the less extreme moral subjectivists, opinion is individual, or it can be a "normative" view as consensus within a group.

The morality that has allowed the human race to survive and flourish is a selective and evolving set of beliefs. We seek a sense of our societal code of morality in our leaders and give political and social power to those of our selective moral character. Yet the gift is tentative, especially when a breach is detected.

"The relationship of morality and power is a very subtle one," said author James Baldwin. "Because ultimately power without morality is no longer power."

To understand what is "right and wrong" may not necessarily be the only process for becoming a moral person. The roots of the word are derived from the phrase "pertaining to character or temperament" or "one's disposition." Therefore, having morality is a deeper part of character than having the last word on right and wrong.

Morality, then, becomes an intention for behavior that shows good character. Intention becomes important to the attainment of peace as we move toward a more just and nonviolent world. Pacifism to some is the ultimate morality, a choice for living within a personal code of nonkilling. To others, pacifism is an ideal of a distant future.

As Ethiopian emperor Haile Selassie described an international ethic: "Until the basic human rights are equally guaranteed to all without regard to race, there is war. And until that day, the dream of lasting peace, world citizenship, rule of international morality, will remain but a fleeting illusion to be pursued, but never attained ... now everywhere is war."

Synonyms: principled and incorruptible
Skills: decent, righteous, and ethical

The Virtue of Friendship (Cultural Exchange)

To love or to favor, to possess the ability to make friends in this world provides us great hope and solace. "We are all travelers in the wilderness of this world," said Robert Louis Stevenson, "and the best we can find in our travels is an honest friend."

A friend attached to another by feeling or regard wants the best for the other. There is honesty and truth in the relationship, as well as compassion and understanding. Aristotle defined friendship as "a single soul dwelling in two bodies."

When one friend is having trouble, the other has empathy. They give assistance and support. They provide companionship and an ear to hear. "Listening is a magnetic and strange thing," said Karl Menninger, "a creative force. The friends who listen to us are the ones we move toward. When we are listened to, it creates us, makes us unfold and expand."

The relationship between friends gains strength when there is give and take. We learn to trust the other. We have a sense of equality. "There is an energy field between humans," said psychologist Rollo May. "And, when we reach out in passion, it is met with an answering passion and changes the relationship forever."

Friendship between individuals has parallels to the relationship between nations and cultures. Cultural exchange is the surest way to foster understanding, tolerance, and reduced conflict. The "stranger" may be hard-wired into our primitive consciousness as the subject of fear, but the friend wrought from an exchange between cultures is to be trusted and given respect.

"People can only live fully by helping others to live," said the leader of Soka Gakkai International, Daisaku Ikeda. "When you give life to friends you truly live. Cultures can only realize their further richness by honoring other traditions. And only by respecting natural life can humanity continue to exist."

Friendship between peoples is an indication that peace and harmony can, indeed, be achieved. Whether it's trade rights or territorial ambitions, the intransigent nature of enemies prevents both sides from achieving their goals.

The Holy Roman Emperor Sigismund, according to the 1846 *Sociable Story-teller*, provided characteristic insight into the wisdom of friendship. "Do I not most effectively destroy my enemies, in making them my friends?"

Synonyms: companionship and association
Skills: affection, affinity, and goodwill

The Virtue of Initiative (Citizen Diplomacy)

Initiative is the first step, the introductory action. "What we think or what we know or what we believe is, in the end, of little consequence," said John Ruskin. "The only consequence is what we do."

After we make the decision about what we believe, we need to act by our own initiative. That takes readiness and the ability to follow through. It's not easy to walk the talk, or put our money where our mouth is. To take the lead is an act of great courage.

"Thinking is easy, acting is difficult," said Johann Wolfgang von Goethe, "and to put one's thoughts into action is the most difficult thing in the world."

Recognizing what needs to be done and taking the initiative has nothing to do with aggressive or obnoxious behavior. Taking the lead can be done in subtle ways and in the background with little awareness or accolades from others. Initiative involves doing something before being asked. It takes seeing what is necessary and possible. For those with initiative, the barriers and problems of taking action become less important than the result.

"Twenty years from now you will be more disappointed by the things that you didn't do than by the ones you did do," wrote humorist of the mighty Mississippi, Mark Twain. "So throw off the bowlines. Sail away from the safe harbor. Catch the trade winds in your sails. Explore. Dream. Discover."

In the political arena, an initiative is a way that citizens can change laws.

When a petition is signed by a prescribed number of people, a public vote is forced and changes can be made. This direct form of democracy has resulted in greater public response of government and enhances our feeling that change can happen even when "fighting city hall" can seem impossible.

Inside us all is an eagerness to do something, to make a difference, to effect positive change. When our leaders are ineffective or reach a stalemate, we have a strong urge to put our energy to work. In many cases, as in the citizen diplomacy of Jimmy Carter's election monitoring, or the intervention of a celebrity in cases of political kidnapping, those taking the initiative have shown positive results. Initiative is valued by the world and always trumps the energy of intransigence or inaction.

Steve Jobs, one of the founders of Apple Computer, set the challenge of initiative high enough to matter and low enough to succeed: "Let's make a dent in the universe."

Synonyms: enterprise and enthusiasm
Skills: eager, active, and enterprising

The Virtue of Sustainability (Environmentalism)

The present and the future are intimately connected in the Native American proverb, "We do not inherit the earth from our ancestors, we borrow it from our children." The consequences of how we treat the earth today are linked directly to the availability of its beauty and bounty tomorrow.

Sustainability, then, is a concept of time. It predicts the outcome of present practices with the availability of resources in the future. Derived from the Latin *sustinere*, or to hold, sustainability means to bear under the weight of something important. It can be used in context of a cautionary tale to encourage mitigating our desires or requiring a change in our current lifestyle. Or it can be a celebration of our thoughtful stewardship of the environment as we continue to reap the bounty of the earth.

"Sustainability is a condition of existence," said author Guy Dauncey, "which enables the present generation of humans and other species to enjoy social wellbeing, a vibrant economy, and a healthy environment, and to experience fulfillment, beauty and joy, without compromising the ability of future generations of humans and other species to enjoy the same."

Sustainability is about societal and personal choices. The implications of how we use resources are undeniable. As the capacity of humans to impact the planet and have negative long-term effects grows exponentially, the inefficiencies of war and violence become a measurable part of an unsustainable future.

Local conflicts over resources have always been part of the human story, yet today they are becoming global in reach. The current wars for oil and natural gas can only get worse as developing nations industrialize to compete in the global economy. The intensity and unsustainability of wars for resources, such as water and raw materials, is sure to increase. According to the World Bank, military expenditures, which do not include the cost in blood and lost economic potential, are already nearly $1.8 trillion.

The term sustainability is a relatively recent concept in the evolving way we look at our world. The older term ecology simply concerns the biology of our ecosystem. Environmentalism includes an active element in its concern for the protection and conservation of our natural resources.

The phrase deep ecology expanded the concept to include the philosophical underpinnings of sustainability. Eclipsing the narrow view that our planet is simply our host and that the resources are ours to exploit, deep ecology speaks to the interconnectedness of humans to our environment. In some ways it puts every other living creature, indeed inorganic as well as organic matter, on a level field. The human experience is seen as only a part of the holistic ecosystem that gives life and substance to our universe.

"However fragmented the world, however intense the national rivalries," said Jacques Cousteau, "it is an inexorable fact that we become more interdependent every day. I believe that national sovereignties will shrink in the face of universal interdependence. The sea, the great unifier, is man's only hope. Now, as never before, the old phrase has a literal meaning: We are all in the same boat."

The virtue of sustainability entails positioning ourselves with the values and skills to face the challenges of the future. We embrace sustainability by improving education and decreasing the triggers for conflict such as the growing gap between rich and poor. On a personal basis, sustainability means doing our part to keep our lakes and rivers clean, our rain forests healthy, our seas free of contaminants. "The first rule of sustainability is to align with natural forces," said author Paul Hawken, "or at least not try to defy them."

Internationally, sustainability means creating and keeping global agreements on our shared resources, including water, land, and air. It means dealing with the implications of climate change before the ice caps melt and drastic changes in local economies require tumultuous shifts that our social structures will be unable to bear.

Ethical consumerism is an area of sustainability where individuals can make a positive impact. Green design, new energy technologies, and individual choices such as recycling and voting with our money for sustainable products have the capability of meeting our obligations for future generations.

"Designing for sustainability," said furniture maker Steelcase Inc. vice president Allan Smith, "requires a dedication to evaluating a product's long-term effects and lowering the environmental impact at every stage of a product's life — from materials extraction to end-of-use."

Synonyms: ecology and preservation

Skills: circumspect, defensive, and reasonable

The Virtue of Creativity (Artistic Expression)

Imagination, spontaneity, and originality — the highest aspirations of human industry are the result of human creativity. The artistry of creating something that did not exist before gives us power and pleasure.

"I saw the angel in the marble," Michelangelo told us, "and carved until I set him free." Creativity is having the power to create something new. It comes from a source of spontaneity and originality that confounds definitions.

Neither great intelligence nor high education is necessary to be creative. It transcends personality types and resists formal training. Yet creativity is one of the identifiers of the human species and the virtue that has given us the ability to eclipse our companion species.

"The significant problems we face cannot be solved by the same level of thinking that created them," said Albert Einstein. At first the source of our need for creativity was survival. Fire, language, and culture, these and other fundamental innovations are examples of the creativity that enable us to survive and prosper.

From its roots in survival, creativity is now not only a useful avocation but the mother of all invention. Santa Fe peace activist Mary Lou Cook said, "Creativity is inventing, experimenting, growing, taking risks, breaking rules, making mistakes, and having fun."

In Greek mythology, creativity was the domain of the muses who provided the inspirational mediary between humans and the gods. In some non–Western cultures, creativity is seen as a form of mimicry, where innovations from the circle of life are simply rediscovered. To those in religious circles, the creation of the world was the original innovation, the result of a Divine spark.

Common, everyday creativity is seen as less dependent on the mysterious and more on neural functions. Research shows heightened activity in many parts of the brain. "Creativity is the ability to see relationships where none exist," gleaned novelist Thomas Disch.

With technology advancing to the beat of Moore's Law, the artistry of creativity has never been more important. Humans are adapting and finding new and better ways to deal with constant and evolutionary change. Education emphasizing problem solving and imagination has become a necessity for survival.

For each of us creativity is the action that makes us individual. The ability to see and create something inspiring is also what makes our greatest contribution to society. "A rock pile ceases to be a rock pile the moment a single man contemplates it," wrote Antoine de Saint-Exupéry, "bearing within him the image of a cathedral."

Synonyms: artistry and imagination
Skills: clever, inventive, and original

The Virtue of Courage (Nonviolent Resistance)

To face difficulty despite the danger and pain, to have bravery in the face of fear, to have the quality of mind and spirit to act according to your beliefs is to be courageous. "Courage is not simply one of the virtues," said C.S. Lewis, "but the form of every virtue at the testing point."

Having the fortitude to face uncertainty, intimidation, even threat of death is a necessity when resisting situations that require you to participate in violence and war. "Courage is the most important of all the virtues," the poet Maya Angelou echoes Lewis, "because without courage you can't practice any other virtue consistently."

The word courage is derived from the Old French *corage*, from *cuer*, or heart. Yet those who express courage show heightened brain activity in the cingulate cortex, meaning that courage like any other brain activity can be learned and developed.

"Courage is not the absence of fear," wrote the Beat Generation's James Neil Hollingworth, "but rather the judgment that something else is more important than fear." To do the right thing without promise of reward is the highest moral courage. It is the realm of the hero who slays the dragon or saves a damsel from distress. It is choosing peace over violence, nonviolence over war.

Yet courage does not require a knight's attributes. To be bold is not the exclusive domain of the powerful and pure. "Courage doesn't always roar," said writer and artist Mary Anne Radmacher. "Sometimes courage is the little voice at the end of the day that says I'll try again tomorrow."

Synonyms: bravery and fortitude
Skills: valor, strength, and fearless

The Virtue of Logic (Arms Reduction)

How do we make our decisions? On what basis do we pose arguments and arrive at opinions? How do we think what we think? "Logic takes care of itself," said Ludwig Wittgenstein, "all we have to do is to look and see how it does it."

Logic comes from the Greek word for technique. Aristotle said it is the science and method of reasoning. The methodical process of reasoning allows us to progress from one idea to another. It gives us the ability to learn and modify our beliefs and attitudes. It gives us freedom of choice.

It is difficult to follow some logic, for instance the stockpiling of nuclear weapons and arming the world with everything from small arms to biological and chemical cocktails. Yet logic is called upon to justify proliferation, whether it's the mutually assured destruction strategy or the hyperbolic logical imperative: "If you take away our guns, only the criminals will have weapons."

It seems logic can be used to make any risk supportable, but the ancient science of logic is not to blame. Logic simply explores how we make inferences about the correct state of the world. Logic can be used in any discipline, from mathematics to philosophy. "Logic is not a body of doctrine," added Wittgenstein, "but a mirror-image of the world. Logic is transcendental."

The methods we use to perform logic are highly personal. We have individual ways of reasoning or arguing a point. "Logic is the technique," noted French moralist Jean de la Bruyère, "by which we add conviction to truth."

Yet we consider logic to be distinct from opinion. The skills of logic include knowing the soundness of an argument or assertion that is consistent and free from contradictions. We find a statement valid if it is free from false premise. A logical argument is complete if it can be proven with either inductive or deductive reasoning.

Inductive logic, as established by the Greeks, allows us to make generalizations from individual and particular instances. We go from seeing a dog several times at a person's house to thinking that person has a dog, whether or not it's true.

Deductive logic allows us to come to conclusions based on a set of assertions or arguments. From these premises or hypotheses we deduce our truth. Aristotle's law of syllogism takes two conditions and arrives at a third conclusion. The dog is at the house. The man owns the house. Therefore, the man owns the dog, true or not.

Beyond the scope of rules and principles of logic are the intuitive senses. "There is a certain logic to events that pushes you along a certain path," said songwriter Michael Nesmith. "You go along the path that feels the most true, and most according to the principles that are guiding you, and that's the way the decisions are made."

When logic is used in its negative connotation, we speak of its short-comings in terms of knowing all of the conditions that make an argument true. According to Ambrose Bierce, logic is "the art of thinking and reasoning in strict accordance with the limitations and incapacities of the human mis-understanding."

The history of arms reduction talks seems to tell a tale of illogic and mis-understanding posing as logic. Lewis Carroll's characters Tweedledum and Twee-dledee in *Through the Looking Glass* is constructive: "Contrariwise, if it was so, it might be; and if it were so, it would be; but as it isn't, it ain't. That's logic."

Synonyms: reasoning and synthesis

Skills: argumentative, deductive, and inductive

The Virtue of Empathy (Humanitarianism)

To recognize and share the feelings of others is a prerequisite to com-passionate action. To feel the pain and heartache, the need for food by the hungry, or the desire for freedom by the oppressed, is to feel those same emo-tions as our own. It creates the necessity for the humanitarianism that saved many Jews from the Holocaust and fed the hungry during the dust-bowl droughts in Somalia.

Empathy offers us a mirror to see the deepest part of our being. "It's sur-prising how many persons go through life," said journalist Sydney Harris, "without ever recognizing that their feelings toward other people are largely determined by their feelings toward themselves, and if you're not comfortable within yourself, you can't be comfortable with others."

Hailing from the Greek word for affection, empathy was first used in its present form by E.B. Titchener. The psychologist believed the mind had struc-tures and component parts for our thoughts and actions. Empathy, with its root *pathos*, was the component that allows us to have deep feelings for great artwork or to suffer with the pain of others.

While sympathy is a general feeling, empathy denotes a projection into the other's state of mind. Empathy allows us to step into the other's shoes, to experience the hardships, understand the conditions that cause unrest and violence.

"When we focus on ourselves, our world contracts as our problems and preoccupations loom large," said psychologist Daniel Goleman. "But when we focus on others, our world expands. Our own problems drift to the periph-ery of the mind and so seem smaller, and we increase our capacity for con-nection — or compassionate action."

Empathy dissolves the separation we feel for other humans and expands our feelings of connection. "Everything we do is in service of our needs," said Center for Nonviolent Communication founder Marshall Rosenberg. "When this one concept is applied to our view of others, we'll see that we have no real enemies, that what others do to us is the best possible thing they know to do to get their needs met."

Synonyms: deep understanding and affinity

Skills: appreciation, compassion, and caring

The Virtue of Fairness (Distributive Justice)

Cervantes seemed to imagine that all is fair in love and war when he put into the mouth of *Don Quixote*: "Love and War are the same thing, and stratagems and polity are as allowable in the one as in the other." It seems, in some ways, that fairness is up for grabs. "All some folks want," quipped humorist Arnold H. Glasgow, "is their fair share and yours."

The classic example of fairness comes from the art of cake cutting. One cake. Two children. How do you cut the cake so that both children feel the result is fair?

The solution might be to let one child cut the cake with the understanding that the second child can pick the first piece. In this scenario, self-interest is the great motivator for fairness. The first child, knowing full well that the second child might take the larger piece, warily predicts the future and cuts the cake fairly in half.

Beyond the fundamentals of greed or self-interest and into the realm of benevolence, to be fair is to be free from bias or dishonesty. Fairness is related to justice, according to philosophers from Rousseau to Kant. In his work *The Social Contract*, Rousseau sought to describe citizen acceptance of a fair social system as an agreement. Kant's categorical imperative necessitates fairness in the broad sense by actions according to universal laws.

Worldwide distributive justice efforts have gone far in tempering resentment and preventing renewed violence in many regions. From the restitution of land to Native American tribes, from the return of treasures to victims of Nazi invasions, the disputation of objective justice to partially make amends is becoming part and parcel of the history of war and violence.

Philosopher John Rawls believed that the "most reasonable principles of justice are those that would be the object of mutual agreement by persons under fair conditions. Justice as fairness thus develops a theory of justice from the idea of a social contract." Applying his "veil of ignorance" as the criterion for a fair agreement, Rawls contended that impartiality is the only way to find justice.

Rawls came up with two principles of fairness as related to justice. The "equal claim" scheme proposes that every person has basic rights and liberties. The "inequality fairness" scheme accepts that differences are needed to ensure opportunity or to help the disadvantaged.

"Wouldn't it be much worse if life were fair," was a line in the television series *Babylon 5*, "and all the terrible things that happen to us, come because we actually deserve them? So now I take comfort in the general hostility and unfairness of the Universe."

That is the conundrum of society — to know what is fair. We have equity laws to temper strict rules and give leeway when injustices occur. We have "fair measure" and "fair value" to make us humble in our ability to find what is exactly fair. As a society and as good people, we set up systems, pass laws, volunteer and donate to causes, and develop better and better ways to achieve the best balance of fair.

Said Roman poet Ovid, "Fair peace becomes men; ferocious anger belongs to beasts." And so we endeavor.

Synonyms: equity and justice

Skills: consideration, duty, and impartiality

The Virtue of Mindfulness (Witnessing Justice)

To be aware and in the present moment is an extremely difficult practice. Most times, our minds dwell in the future or the past. Sometimes we are simply distracted by the noise and stimuli that clog the contemplative silence of our lives.

The Buddhist monk Bodhidharma attested, "Once you stop clinging and let things be, you'll be free, even of birth and death. You'll transform everything.... And you'll be at peace wherever you are." To think deeply about our lives, to care on a sunny day about the warmth coming with the light, or on a winter day about the coldness and beauty of the snow, has given poets their essential challenge. How do we truly live in a way that lets us absorb the amazing beauty of the moment?

Through our attention and clarity of observation we arrive at an understanding of the moment that gives us the ability to make rational decisions. Mindfulness allows us to be intentional. From being present we find clarity and direction rather than confusion and drifting.

"Between stimulus and response there is a space," said Austrian neurologist Viktor Frankl. "In that space is our power to choose our response. In our response lies our growth and our freedom."

Still, to give us the freedom we need to make decisions, being mindful of the moment does not entail ignoring the past and future. Mindfulness is the opposite of a delusional focus that ignores any aspects of existence. Especially when we witness episodes of violence and war, we keep our eyes open and shed light on what can grow in the dark of ignorance. In many religious practices, mindfulness seems as simple as paying attention to one's breathing, but in that action is the creation of a profound awareness between the physical and spiritual.

Mindfulness is active engagement. Rather than wandering or static, the enlightened mind stays in that place of heedfulness and ardency that eclipses many of the illusion that time and space are fixed and unchanging. Beyond relaxation, mindfulness allows us to transform our perceptions and heal not only our own suffering but alleviate that of those around us. Said Vietnamese monk Thich Nhat Hanh, "When mindfulness embraces those we love, they will bloom like flowers."

Synonyms: attention and alertness

Skills: heedful, vigilant, and circumspect

The Virtue of Equality (Rule of Law)

The Latin phrase *ceteris paribus*, loosely translated as "all things being equal," attests to the causal relationship between two subjects being compared. Indeed, the basis of scientific inquiry is the ability to hold variables constant in order to compare a particular hypothesis with reality.

"All the citizens of a state cannot be equally powerful," said the French philosopher Voltaire, "but they may be equally free." The equality of humankind is a utopian hypothesis that has caused great controversy among philosophers and politicians. As much as we try to develop a theory of equality, we find there are too many variables, or differences, to bring science to bear.

Equalitarianism is the belief that everyone should be treated equally without regard to factors such as religion, sex, race, ethnicity, or economic and social status. What do people deserve in terms of reward for being a member of society? Is it distribution of everything equally, or distribution based on differences?

"From each according to his ability, to each according to his need" was the way Karl Marx tried to reconcile the differences. Whether the system is communist or democratic, socialist or capitalist, statist or anarchic, equality becomes the hinge upon which political philosophy turns. Even with its resistance to definition, equality has become a mainstay of written constitutions around the world. The Enlightenment principle of "inalienable rights endowed by their Creator" was embedded in the United States Constitution by Thomas Jefferson who prefaced it with the immortal words "All men are created equal."

It is the challenge of our governments to find a balance between difference and equality. Social equality, economic equality, and especially equality before the law are expressed differently in every culture and country. Yet there is some consensus that one of the purposes of government is to assure the greatest equality of opportunity for its citizens through rule of law.

"From the equality of rights springs identity of our highest interests," noted German-American politician Carl Schurz, "you cannot subvert your neighbor's rights without striking a dangerous blow at your own."

Without giving others a chance to thrive in their differences, we doom ourselves to the fate of commonality. "Equality is not in regarding different things similarly," wrote the novelist Tom Robbins, "equality is in regarding different things differently."

Synonyms: evenhandedness and similarity
Skills: democratic, balance, and equitable

The Virtue of Resourcefulness
(Alternative Resource Acquisition)

Part inventiveness, part discovery, to be resourceful is to grapple with changing circumstances and difficult situations in a skillful and creative manner. The resourceful person is insightful and thinks out of the box. Innovative options and inspiring discoveries lead to solutions and optimistic new paths.

Alternative resource acquisition is a nonviolent means of living that allows our resourcefulness to prevent war and violence from becoming a dead-end necessity. "Discovery," said physicist Albert Szent-Gyorgyi, "consists of seeing what everybody has seen and thinking what nobody has thought." It is having new eyes, said the novelist Marcel Proust, and not waiting for new landscapes.

Such sightings are found through the powers of observation and learning, seeking out new places and resources, gathering data to experiences. Adventurous actions are often seen as endeavors into the unknown, but often it is having the freedom to explore and come up with new ideas.

Germaine Greer put the necessity of freedom pointedly: "Human beings have an inalienable right to invent themselves; when that right is pre-empted it is called brain-washing." Inventiveness is a creative process that needs freedom of thought and action. Whether it is a better mousetrap or a new technology that delivers a new form of energy, inventiveness may be a radical breakthrough or built upon an old model or idea.

Alternative resource acquisition is the process of creating new opportunities when needs and wants arise. In finding new sources we need open minds as well as the ability to make connections and bring elements from different places to form new relationships. The creativity that allows us to have new visions or sparks for a new idea comes from a moment of insight into a world that had not previously existed.

After the epiphany comes the work. It can be long hours of research and testing. The scientific method has a tried-and-true process, from considering a problem, forming a conjecture, deducing a prediction, then testing to affirm the hypothesis.

Continuous improvement is no less daunting but it increases productivity. Does the original hypothesis hold up under scrutiny? Is it better, cheaper, or faster? Collaboration with others provides the best chance of success. Brainstorming, sharing expenses, getting feedback, all contribute to finding new resources for humanity to share.

In each era or generation, the challenges are daunting. The dangers of war and violence stem from injustice, poverty, and hunger. History has shown the fear these challenges breed is seemingly intransigent and, therefore, must be overcome. That entails working with limited resources, new technologies, and discovering alternatives to what is immediately available.

"If there is no sufficient reason for war," said Senator Robert M. La Follette, "the war party will make war on one pretext, then invent another."

Imagining, discovering, and finding alternative resources is necessary for creating a more habitable world. To serve humanity is the point and the delight of inventions and discoveries. "Somewhere," astronomer Carl Sagan said, "something incredible is waiting to be known."

Synonyms: imagination and inventiveness
Skills: enterprising, adventurous, and clever

The Virtue of Reciprocity (The Golden Rule)

To give a gift of love or monetary value to another can be a one-way action. Yet often the giving has an inherent hope or expectation that the receiver will offer something in return. Far from being an aspect of greed, this reciprocal bond is one of the most important social norms for the survival of our species.

Reciprocity is a two-way action of giving and receiving, a mutual exchange of feelings or things of value. In its most altruistic sense, it is love done alternately, backward and forward.

The maxim of reciprocity is the basis of the Golden Rule, which is the moral philosophy fundamental to all modes of spirituality and religion. Stated generally as "one should treat others as you would like others to treat oneself," the rule of reciprocity keeps us from indulging our pleasures to the detriment of society.

In *Wild Justice* by Bekoff and Jessica Pierce, morality is a "suite of inter-related other-regarding behaviors" that are good for the overall society. Reciprocity entails altruism, cooperation, empathy, and fairness. Whether or not the action of giving a gift is returned, the act of giving is an energy that is bound to have positive repercussions. As a society, reciprocity is a hallowed contract to find our way forward together.

Studies of a variety of mammals such as apes and chimpanzees, coyotes and wolves, and dolphins and whales, show such reciprocity as a natural tendency, certainly along with others less peaceful. Reciprocal actions can, indeed, be positive or negative and great discipline must be used to prevent our mutual exchanges from entering the realm of subjugation and violence.

"By a divine paradox, wherever there is one slave there are two," said poet Edwin Markham. "So in the wonderful reciprocities of being, we can never reach the higher levels until all our fellows ascend with us."

Synonyms: exchange and mutuality
Skills: cooperate, fair, and empowering

The Virtue of Wisdom (Peace Education)

Over 2,500 years ago, Confucius laid down the ways to become wise. "By three methods we may learn wisdom," the Chinese sage proposed, "first, by reflection, which is noblest; second, by imitation, which is easiest; and third, by experience, which is the most bitter."

The wise will never boast to wisdom, being wise themselves. Their next thought, next action will depend entirely on a new set of circumstances that are difficult to know. Peacemaking depends on educating potential adherents about the many ways to create peace. Knowledge of the world and examples of those who have made a contribution is the combination that enables actions that make a positive difference.

No matter how gray the world might be, the ability to discern fact from fiction, true from false, right from wrong is essential but only the first step in an act of wisdom. The next step is applying judgment to action, which can only be appraised in retrospect.

The root word for wise means "to see." Much more than having eyesight, to see is to know. We gain deeper understanding of people and events by observing. With our perceptions and knowledge and experience we gain, the wise among us can choose actions that have optimum chance for successful results.

The difficulty in judging the wise action has given cause to create another phrase for wisdom. "Common sense in an uncommon degree is what the world calls wisdom," said poet Samuel Taylor Coleridge. Common sense is available to anyone regardless of skills or ambition.

Said American philosopher Leo Buscaglia, "We always think of failure as the antithesis of success, but it isn't. Success often lies just the other side of failure."

The maxim "If at first you don't succeed, then try again" gives us the ability to continually endeavor toward wisdom. As a society we give ourselves the flexibility to learn from our failures. In a democracy, the majority has power within the context of minority rights, yet democracy is messy and in a constant search for greater wisdom from its citizens.

"I know of no safe depository of the ultimate powers of the society but the people themselves," said Thomas Jefferson, "and if we think them not enlightened enough to exercise their control with a wholesome discretion, the remedy is not to take it from them but to inform their discretion."

Wisdom may best be viewed from the perspective of an evolving virtue. In the Serenity Prayer we find solace from wisdom's even hand. "God, grant me the serenity to accept the things I cannot change" is one of the paraphrases of a sermon by theologian Reinhold Niebuhr, "the courage to change the things I can, and the wisdom to know the difference."

Synonyms: insight and common sense

Skills: discerning, judgment, and enlightenment

The Virtue of Balance (Global Wellness)

The Greek philosopher Pythagoras and his followers equated mathematics with moral perfection. The Golden Mean was their formula for expressing the beauty and truth in the balance between two extremes.

"Happiness is not a matter of intensity," wrote Thomas Merton, "but of balance, order, rhythm and harmony." The Catholic monk spent his life studying spiritual traditions and was intrigued by the Buddhist concept of the middle way that leads to liberation from suffering.

Balance is equilibrium. Between two opposites which both have their positives and negatives, balance is the desirable point where you can reap the benefits and limit the undesirable effects of both. "It is the harmony of the diverse parts," proposed French philosopher Henri Poincare, "their symmetry, their happy balance; in a word it is all that introduces order, all that gives unity, that permits us to see clearly and to comprehend at once both the ensemble and the details."

In a state of balance, or counterpoise, we seek harmony of thought, spirit, and body. In this counterpoise we find health and happiness. A scale has two pans for weighing, just as our minds are in constant states of measurement between countervailing thoughts. Through emotional stability and calm judgment, we reap the benefits of equilibrium.

"What I dream of is an art of balance," said painter Henri Matisse, "of purity and serenity devoid of troubling or depressing subject matter — a soothing, calming influence on the mind, rather like a good armchair which provides relaxation from physical fatigue."

Balance is the measure of global wellness, part of which is personal, part societal, and part planetary. To have balance in our lives, in what we eat, in our exercise, in the care we take to be free of disease and debilitation, is to find health. In the way we care for the earth and for others, we find balance in the world.

It is also associated with the power between nations of military and economic might. Equity of power can be a positive manifestation of world politics, such as the strides made with "one nation, one vote" in the United Nations General Assembly.

There can be tenuous and dangerous illusion of balance, such as the mutual assured destruction balance that prevented the superpowers from using nuclear arms. "There must be, not a balance of power," warned President Woodrow Wilson, a proponent of the League of Nations, "but a community of power; not organized rivalries, but an organized peace."

Synonyms: equilibrium and stability
Skills: evenness, counterbalancing, and proportioning

The Virtue of Attentiveness (Conflict Resolution)

"To the attentive eye, each moment of the year has its own beauty," said transcendentalist Ralph Waldo Emerson, "and in the same field, it beholds, every hour, a picture which was never seen before, and which shall never be seen again."

To hold attention is to focus, concentrate, and be conscious of a moment's essence. "It is the taking possession by the mind, in clear and vivid form," said pragmatist William James, "of one out of what seem several simultaneously possible objects or trains of thought."

Those who are attentive simply give their attention. They are observant, thoughtful of others, even courteous and polite. Attention is a process of the mind that ignores some things while concentrating on others. Wrote Thornton Wilder, "Those who are silent, self-effacing and attentive become the recipients of confidences."

Attention is the ability to pay attention to the needs of others in order to prevent or alleviate conflict. It is a learned process. In young children, psychologists maintain, conflicts are caused by an inability to hold attention. The young child often lacks the executive controls that allow selection in an appropriate context. To develop attention is to build the sensory neurons in our brains that give us the ability to sequence the overload of input from our senses.

This higher level of attention allows us to resolve conflict between sequences that create fear and distrust. Turning our "spotlight," as William James put it, toward issues of concern allows us to move the resolution of our lenses on the world from the fringes of our perceptions to the focal point of our creative reasoning.

"Geniuses are commonly believed to excel other men in their power of sustained attention," said pragmatist William James. "But it is their genius making them attentive, not their attention making geniuses of them."

Synonyms: alert and observant

Skills: concentration, watchfulness, and vigilance

The Virtue of Unity (Personal Transformation)

More than twenty-five hundred years ago, Aesop espoused a truth that has been paraphrased ever since: "United we stand; divided we fall." Humankind has embraced the cause of unity in our greatest moments, through revolutions and evolutions.

Yet unity, as Albert Einstein understood as he searched for the Unified Field Theory, is encompassing. The physics maven spent his later years trying to find a single formula for the unity of the universe. He sensed a simple harmony beyond relativity and quantum mechanics. "It is a magnificent feeling to recognize the unity of complex phenomena which appear to be things quite apart from the direct visible truth."

Einstein failed to find a single formula for unity. Yet the idea of wholeness in the natural universe has spawned generations of new ideas and inventions through such quixotic searches for a theory of everything.

For those of us with less analytical minds who are just trying to make a positive difference in the world, unity is where we put two and two together to work for peace. We seek to fuse the divisions, experience the harmony, personally transform through deeper understanding of the oneness. We find our spiritual practices and go beyond the confines of conflict and dissonance.

Hard as we try, we sometimes fall short of touching the unity that brings peace. "We have learned to fly the air like birds and swim the sea like fish," wrote Martin Luther King, Jr., "but we have not learned the simple art of living together as brothers."

Unity means wholeness or togetherness. From the Latin *unus* for "one," unity gives us power of the many. It gives us the ability to stand up to an aggressor or oppressor. Unity prevents Aesop's warning of the fall through divisiveness from coming true.

"The moment we break faith with one another, the sea engulfs us and the light goes out," said author James Baldwin, who understood the division that racism and exclusivity can create.

The search for unity is our individual hope for finding harmony in a religion, or government, or personal practice that allows us to find illusive peace. In its societal manifestation, unity can be imagined between two people, or an entire people trying to find the wholeness that brings peace.

"The meeting of two personalities is like the contact of two chemical substances," said psychologist Carl Jung. "If there is any reaction, both are transformed."

Synonyms: wholeness and harmony
Skills: communing, concordant, and universal

The Actionable Virtue of Peace

As individuals, we are gifted and grow with commitment and understanding of our personal virtues of peace. How we succeed as peacemakers depends on which ones we truly embody and their corresponding manifestation in the world of nonviolent action.

With the knowledge that even the greatest icons of peacemaking, such as Mohandas Gandhi and Martin Luther King, Jr., could not have possessed every virtue to the greatest degree should only reaffirm our belief in ourselves. There is hope for all of us to make a difference with what virtues we are blessed to possess.

Then what makes the difference in whether our embodiment of a virtue will have a positive effect? How do friendship and wisdom, forgiveness and empathy take flight?

Peacemaking is a dynamic activity. When the world descends into violence, whether it's a neighborhood shooting or a dictator's oppression, the dynamic peacemaker is moved to act. We witness the violence. We engage the aggression. Finally, if we succeed, we evolve to the state of existence where the way is clear to create peace in our lives.

How we take action is determined, necessarily, by the virtues we hold inside. If we value forgiveness, we can seek reconciliation. If we have tact, we may well succeed as a diplomat. If we embrace generosity, we will give to others in need. Certainly, each of us possesses all of these virtues to a certain degree. Yet which nonviolent methods we choose depends a great deal on the core character skills we possess. Otherwise, our actions will be inauthentic, our energy lost for lack of a true valuation of peace.

Fortunately, the array of nonviolent methods allows for individuality of character. Where some choose mediation or pacifism, others choose artistic endeavors such as painting or journalism. Within the tool chest of peacemaking, thirty powerful virtues correspond to thirty robust methods of nonviolence.

Some believe skill-bearing virtues, such as having compassion or empathy, come from nature, or DNA, or are God-given. Others believe they come from hard work and contemplation, learning and experience, or through the epiphany of a transformative experience.

Virtues can, indeed, be learned, as Confucius knew over two thousand years ago. The skills required for logic are reasoning and deduction. The skills for initiative are eagerness and drive. Like a scholar gaining degrees and accolades, or a girl scout gaining the merit badges that signify great progress, we hold our virtues as personal successes. We build our skills like muscles ready to work.

So equipped with the virtues of peace, we take action. We lobby for the underprivileged. We write exposés and witness injustices. We teach children, nurture teens, help at food banks, run for office, and sit at lunch counters demanding service. The work of peacemaking is necessarily as endless as the incidences of violence. We know we should act, must act, but *HOW* do we act?

What is the activating element for working for peace?

To act is to connect. We give succor to the victims. We engage the oppressors. We join organizations and donate money. We give and give as much as we can to the cause of peace.

And to give is to love. To love is simply finding inside us a good feeling for others, an empathic affection, a deep compassion. To love is to act upon the connections we feel. At times, it is simply walking in the woods. At other times, it is to care for the elderly or support our spouse. The examples of love are as endless as the stories of our lives.

Of course, love has at least two meanings. Romantic love is what we have for our spouses and lovers. It entails an amorous dimension that becomes part of our expressions of marriage, partnership, or union.

On the other hand, platonic love is that love which is extended to our other relationships, brother to sister, friend to friend. From ancient religious texts and rituals to modern utopian philosophies and conservative duty, compassionate love is at the core of our hope for an improved world. As nineteenth century Prime Minister of England William Gladstone said, "We look forward to the time when the Power of Love will replace the Love of Power. Then will our world know the blessings of peace."

Compassionate love is the feeling of shared respect and understanding. Compassionate love is the love that "centers on the good of the other." We all work toward this ideal and, though we fall short, our efforts and valuing of such love is a true measure of our embodiment of peacemaking.

The skills for developing compassionate love have lately gone through the process of definition, especially through the work of the World Health Organization (WHO). Also, the editors of the breakthrough book *The Science of Compassionate Love* have outlined some of the defining features as paraphrased in the following:

- Allowing free choice for the other person
- Endeavoring to understand yourself, the other, and the relationship between
- Valuing the other person at a deep level
- Being open and receptive to the other person
- An outpouring of emotion from the heart

Compassionate love is the essence of the "how" in our work for peace. Love is the active component of peacemaking. It gives us the ability to move our energy to work the good of others. It provides authenticity for the methods we use. When we do mediations, or artwork, or feed the hungry, if we do it with love the results can be astounding. We create more peace in the world through love centered on others.

In the best of circumstances, the compassionate love of peacemaking is reciprocal. We give and receive love. The benefit of doing for others is often returned in kindness and thankfulness and, in many cases, a more peaceful life in our community and family. In fact, the energetic love we express is not only for humans but also for our homelands and our planet with all the plants, animals, and beauty that it contains. Love is expansive. It knows no bounds.

And love is available to all. Even the most despotic ruler is often seen in the bosom of family. The murderer on death row finds solace in the unconditional love of a mother. With love, there are no undeserving persons.

So we hone our skills and grow in our virtues. We ready ourselves with an openness to love. We love. We act. Sometimes we find instant reward. We see the smiles on our children or the victorious dissident freed from prison.

Sometimes we become tired and frustrated. We love so much that our peacemaking exhausts us. We work our empathic fingers to the bone. Each connection requires a vast amount of energy.

And sometimes we fail. Yet we shouldn't be worried. We all fall short of possessing all of the virtues. We get mad at friends. We abandon lovers and get divorces. Many times we lack courage in the face of victimization, especially in blatant misuse of power or the horrors of war.

Yet we don't give up hope. Life gives us precious time to learn from our experiences and understand where we fall short in our virtues as well as where we succeed. Peacemaking is a lively endeavor. We may not be able to transform all the world's challenges into victories, but we move forward. We expend our love until, at times, we have no more to give.

So we choose our battles wisely. We do what we can. To engage, to connect, to love is our greatest solace and our most powerful virtue. The energy of love is always conserved. Love is returned to us as abundance in our lives and as progress through the ages in an increasingly peaceful but challenging world.

To love.

That's all nonviolence is, organized love. — Joan Baez, American singer and songwriter

Omnia vincit amor; et nos cedamus amori. — Virgil, Roman poet

Appendix: The Methods and Virtues of Peace

1. **DIPLOMACY: THE VIRTUE OF TACTFULNESS**
   Synonyms: finesse and subtlety
   Skills: considerate, thoughtful, and discreet

2. **STATECRAFT: THE VIRTUE OF FORESIGHT**
   Synonyms: mental preparedness and insight
   Skills: anticipation, circumspection, and discernment

3. **RECONCILIATION: THE VIRTUE OF FORGIVENESS**
   Synonym: pardon, release
   Skills: compassion, objectivity, and grace

3. **MEDIATION: THE VIRTUE OF INTEGRITY**
   Synonyms: upright and honorable
   Skills: honest, objective, and incorruptible

4. **ARBITRATION: THE VIRTUE OF DECISIVENESS**
   Synonyms: strength of mind and purpose
   Skills: will, certainty, and resolve

5. **PEACEKEEPING: THE VIRTUE OF CALMNESS**
   Synonyms: composure and self-possession
   Skills: patience, serenity, and restraint

6. **ECONOMIC AID: THE VIRTUE OF GENEROSITY**
   Synonyms: benevolence and giving
   Skills: charity, kindness, and hospitable

7. **FAIR TRADE: THE VIRTUE OF JUSTICE**
   Synonyms: fairness and equity
   Skills: judicious, even-handed, and reasonable

8. BOYCOTT: THE VIRTUE OF DISCRETION
   Synonyms: judgment and consideration
   Skills: acumen, discriminate, and measuring

9. UNITED ACTION: THE VIRTUE OF COOPERATION
   Synonyms: collaboration and association
   Skills: helpful, communing, and synergistic

10. CIVIL DISOBEDIENCE: THE VIRTUE OF DISSENT
    Synonyms: disapproval and disagreement
    Skills: refusing, discordant, and contentiousness

11. CONSCIENTIOUS OBJECTION: THE VIRTUE OF CONSCIENCE
    Synonyms: moral sense and inner voice
    Skills: qualms, principles, and scruples

12. SPIRITUAL PRACTICES: THE VIRTUE OF COMPASSION
    Synonyms: tender feelings and empathy
    Skills: commiserate, kind, and conscientious

13. PACIFISM: THE VIRTUE OF MORALITY
    Synonyms: principled and incorruptible
    Skills: decent, righteous, and ethical

14. CULTURAL EXCHANGE: THE VIRTUE OF FRIENDSHIP
    Synonyms: companionship and association
    Skills: affection, affinity, and goodwill

15. CITIZEN DIPLOMACY: THE VIRTUE OF INITIATIVE
    Synonyms: enterprise and enthusiasm
    Skills: eager, active, and enterprising

16. ENVIRONMENTALISM: THE VIRTUE OF SUSTAINABILITY
    Synonyms: ecology and preservation
    Skills: circumspect, defensive, and reasonable

17. ARTISTIC EXPRESSION: THE VIRTUE OF CREATIVITY
    Synonyms: artistry and imagination
    Skills: clever, inventive, and original

18. NONVIOLENT RESISTANCE: THE VIRTUE OF COURAGE
    Synonyms: bravery and fortitude
    Skills: valor, strength, and fearless

19. ARMS REDUCTION: THE VIRTUE OF LOGIC
    Synonyms: reasoning and synthesis
    Skills: argumentative, deductive, and inductive

20. HUMANITARIANISM: THE VIRTUE OF EMPATHY
    Synonyms: deep understanding and affinity
    Skills: appreciation, compassion, and caring

21. **Distributive Justice: The Virtue of Fairness**
    Synonyms: equity and justice
    Skills: consideration, duty, and impartiality

22. **Witnessing Justice: The Virtue of Mindfulness**
    Synonyms: attention and alertness
    Skills: heedful, vigilant, and circumspect

23. **Rule of Law: The Virtue of Equality**
    Synonyms: evenhandedness and similarity
    Skills: democratic, balance, and equitable

24. **Alternative Resource Acquisition: The Virtue of Resourcefulness**
    Synonyms: imagination and inventiveness
    Skills: enterprising, adventurous, and clever

25. **The Golden Rule: The Virtue of Reciprocity**
    Synonyms: exchange and mutuality
    Skills: cooperate, fair, and empowering

26. **Peace Education: The Virtue of Wisdom**
    Synonyms: insight and common sense
    Skills: discerning, judgment, and enlightenment

27. **Global Wellness: The Virtue of Balance**
    Synonyms: equilibrium and stability
    Skills: evenness, counterbalancing, and proportioning

28. **Conflict Resolution: The Virtue of Attentiveness**
    Synonyms: alert and observant
    Skills: concentration, watchfulness, and vigilance

T30. **Personal Transformation: The Virtue of Unity**
    Synonyms: wholeness and harmony
    Skills: communing, concordant, and universal

The Actionable Virtue of Peace: Love

Notes

Citations and bibliographical references for each chapter are listed below. The quotations at the end of each of the Methods sections have been verified with original sources.

Introduction: Real-World Methods of Nonviolence

1. John F. Kennedy, *Legacy of a President: The Memorable Words of John Fitzgerald Kennedy*, Address Before the 18th General Assembly of the United Nations, New York, September 20, 1963 (Delhi: Indian Book Co., 1964), 26.
2. *Journal of the American Medical Association*, April 2001, accessed September 20, 2010, http://www.bullyingstatistics.org/content/bullying-statistics-2010.html.
3. Terry Frei, "Columbine's 'Boy in the Window,'" interview on ESPN, April 15, 2009, accessed September 20, 2010, http://sports.espn.go.com/espn/otl/news/story?id=4069745.
4. "Youth Violence: Facts at a Glance," Center for Disease Control, Summer 2008, accessed March 12, 2009, http://www.cdc.gov/ViolencePrevention/pdf/yv-datasheet-a.pdf.
5. Zbigniew Brzezinski, *Out of Control: Global Turmoil on the Eve of the Twenty-First Century* (Ontario: Macmillan, 1993), 17.
6. Michael W. Sonnleitner, *Gandhian Nonviolence: Levels of Satyagraha* (New Delhi: Shakti Malik, 1985), 22.

Chapter 1. The Art of Diplomacy

1. Derek H. Chollet, *The Road to the Dayton Accords: A Study of American Statecraft* (New York: Palgrave Macmillan, 2005), x.
2. H.E. Dr. Haris Silajdzic, Chairman of the Presidency of Bosnia and Herzegovina, Head of Delegation of Bosnia and Herzegovina, 63rd Session of the General Assembly, on the occasion of General Debate, 2008, accessed September 20, 2011, http://www.un.org/ga/63/generaldebate/pdf/bosniaherzegovina_en.pdf.
3. Robert Mackay, "Revisiting Holbrooke's Last Remarks," *The New York Times*, December 14, 2010.
4. Richard Holbrooke, *To End A War* (New York: Modern Library, 1999), 212.

Chapter 2. The Vision of Statecraft

1. Martin Luther King, Jr., *Stride Toward Freedom* (Boston: Beacon Press, 2010), 208.
2. Mark Roberti, *The Fall of Hong Kong: China's Triumph and Britain's Betrayal* (New York: John Wiley & Sons, 1996), 50.

3. "2009 Index of Economic Freedom," The Heritage Foundation, accessed September 20, 2011, http://www.heritage.org/Index/Ranking.aspx.

4. Miles Goslett, "My Regrets over Hong Kong by Lady Thatcher," *The Telegraph*, June 10, 2007.

Chapter 3. The Process of Reconciliation

1. Lyn S. Graybill, *Truth and Reconciliation in South Africa: Miracle or Model?* (Boulder, CO: Lynne Rienner, 2002), 19.

2. Andrew Rigby, *Justice and Reconciliation: After the Violence* (Boulder, CO: Lynne Rienner, 2001), 124.

3. Briton Hadden, and Henry Robinson Luce, *Time*, Volume 170, Issues 1–11 (New York: Time Inc., 2007), 14.

Chapter 4. Mediation Techniques

1. George J. Mitchell, *Making Peace* (New York: Knopf, 1999). 35.

2. "Sutton Index of Death," Cain Web Service, accessed July 1, 2010, http://cain.ulst.ac.uk/sutton/tables/Year.html.

3. Martin Gansberg, "Thirty-Eight Who Saw Murder Didn't Call the Police," *The New York Times*, March 27, 1964.

4. Tore Frangsmyr, and Irwin Abrams, eds., *Nobel Lectures, Peace 1971–1980* (New York: World Scientific, 1997).

5. "First Declaration of the Peace People," accessed September 20, 2010, http://www.peacepeople.com/PPDeclaration.htm.

Chapter 5. Arbitration Techniques

1. "AIDS Epidemic Update: December, 2007," Joint United Nations Programme on HIV/AIDS (UNAIDS) and World Health Organization (Geneva, Switzerland: UNAIDS, 2007), 6.

2. "TRIPPS: What are Intellectual Property Rights?" United Nations publications, accessed September 20, 2010, http://www.wto.org/english/tratop_e/TRIPS_e/intel1_e.htm.

3. "World Trade Organization, DOHA Declaration, 2005," accessed September 20, 2010, http://www.g77.org/southsummit2/doc/Doha%20Declaration(English).pdf.

4. "Stories from Around the World," Avert, accessed September 12, 2010, http://www.avert.org/aids-hiv-stories.htm.

Chapter 6. Peacekeeping

1. John G. Taylor, *East Timor: The Price of Freedom* (New York: St. Martin's Press, 1999), 71.

2. Ibid., 212.

3. "East Timor demands rebels give up," Al Jazeera, accessed September 20, 2011, http://english.aljazeera.net/news/asia-pacific/2008/04/200861503015444338.html.

4. Conan Elphicke, "A Profile of East Timor's Jose Ramos-Horta," *Solidarity*, first published in *Against the Current*, May-June 2009, accessed September 20, 2011, http://www.solidarity-us.org/current/node/892.

5. "Covering Burma and Southeast Asia," *The Irrawady*, June 2003, Vol. 11, No. 5, http://www.irrawaddy.org/print_article.php?art_id=2986.

6. *Inside Indonesia*, Issues 57–68 (Indonesia Resources and Information Programme, 1999), 103.

Chapter 7. Economic Aid

1. "The Right to Food: Report by the Special Rapporteur on the Right to Food, Mr. Jean Ziegler," United Nations Commission on Human Rights, Resolution, 2000, page 5.

2. "G8 Declaration on Development and Africa," Office of the White House, July 8, 2008, accessed September 20, 2011, http://merln.ndu.edu/archivepdf/AF/WH/20080708-5.pdf.

3. Anup Shah, "World Military Spending," *Global Issues*, May 2, 2011, accessed September 20, 2011, http://www.globalissues.org/article/75/world-military-spending.

4. Lisa C. Smith, and Lawrence Haddad, *Overcoming Child Malnutrition in Developing Countries* (Washington, D.C.: International Food Policy Institute, 2000), vii.

5. Ishbel Ross, *Angel of the Battlefield: the life of Clara Barton* (New York: Harpers, 1956), 179.

6. Tanya Thomas, "For Street Kids in India, School is a Distant Dream," *Media India*, accessed September 20, 2011, http://www.medindia.net/news/For-Street-Kids-in-India-School-is-a-Distant-Dream-85752-1.htm.

Chapter 8. Fair Trade

1. David Ransom, *The No-nonsense Guide to Fair Trade* (Oxford: New Internationalist Publications, 2001), 39.

2. "Fair Trade, and Coffee Social Responsibility," Starbucks Coffee, March 7, 2006, accessed March 12, 2009, http://starbuckscoffee.com.

3. "Secretary General, Accepting Moscow Award, says Strength of Russian Spirit 'is your country's greatest natural asset,'" United Nations Information Service, June 6, 2002, accessed September 20, 2011, http://www.unis.unvienna.org/unis/pressrels/2002/sgsm8262.html.

4. Peter Berger, "The Epistemological Modesty: An Interview with Peter Berger," accessed September 12, 2011, web.pdx.edu/~tothm/religion/Epistemological%20Modest1.pdf.

5. "Speech by President of the Republic of Tarja Halonen at the Main Celebration of the Anders Chydenius Jubilee Year in Kokkola on 1.3.2003," Office of the Republic of Finland, accessed September 20, 2011, http://www.tpk.fi/Public/default.aspx?contentid=174109&nodeid=41417&contentlan=2&culture=en-US.

Chapter 9. Boycott

1. Dan La Botz, *César Chávez and la Causa* (New York: Pearson/Longman, 2006), 136–7.

2. Vithalbhai Jhaveri, *Mahatma: Life of Gandhi 1896–1948, Commentary, Reel 11*, Gandhi National Memorial Fund, 1968, accessed September 20, 2011, http://www.gandhiserve.org/video/mahatma/commentary05.html.

Chapter 10. United Action

1. Lech Walesa, *A Way of Hope* (New York: Henry Holt, 1987), 70.

Chapter 11. Civil Disobedience

1. Frederic O. Sargent, *The Civil Rights Revolution: Events and Leaders, 1955–1968* (Jefferson, NC: McFarland, 2004) 161.

2. George Bernard Shaw, *Man and Superman* (Cambridge: The University Press, 1903), 243.

Chapter 12. Conscientious Objection

1. "Desmond Doss Citation," *Home of Heroes*, accessed September 20, 2011, http://www.homeofheroes.com/moh/citations_living/ii_a_doss.html.

2. Jeffery S. Cramer, *Walden: A Fully Annotated Edition* (New Haven: Yale University Press, 2004), 317.

3. Anthony O. Edmonds, *Muhammad Ali: A Biography* (Westport, CT: Greenwood Press, 2006), 68.

4. "Conscientious Objection to Military Service: Commission on Human Rights resolution 1993/84, 1993," United Nations High Commissioner for Human Rights, accessed March 12, 2009, http://www.unhchr.ch/Huridocda/Huridoca.nsf/0/5bc5759a53f36ab380256671004b 643a?Opendocument.
5. Henry David Thoreau, *Civil Disobedience and other Essays* (Stillwell, KS: Digireads Books, 2009), 9.
6. Ibid., 10.

Chapter 13. Spiritual Practices

1. Thomas D. Hamm, *The Quakers in America* (New York: Columbia University Press, 2003), 25.
2. George Fox, *A Journal on Historical Account of the Life, Travel, Sufferings, Christian Experiences and Labour of Love in the Work of the Ministry of that Ancient, Eminent and Faithful Servant of Jesus Christ, George Fox*, 5th ed., *Vol. 2* (Philadelphia: B and T. Kite, 1808), 483.
3. Peter Kreeft, *Catholic Christianity* (San Francisco: Ignatius Press, 2001), 239.
4. Kahlil Gibran, *The Prophet* (Hertfordshire, England: Wordsworth Editions Limited, 1996), 33.

Chapter 14. Pacifism

1. Charles DeBenedetti, *Peace Heroes in Twentieth-Century America* (Bloomington: Indiana University Press, 1986), 138.
2. "The Russell-Einstein Manifesto: Issued in London, 9 July 1955," Pugwash Conference on Science and Human Affairs, accessed September 20, 2010, http://www.pugwash.org/about/manifesto.htm.
3. Nathan Otto and Heinz Norden, eds., *Einstein on Peace* (New York: Simon & Schuster, 1960), 636.
4. Peter Van den Dungen, *West European Pacifism and the Strategy for Peace* (New York: St. Martin's Press, 1985), 20.
5. Peter Laslett, *John Locke: Two Treatises of Government* (New York: New American Library, 1960), 311.
6. John Offer, *Herbert Spencer: Critical Assessments, Vol. 4* (London: Routledge, 2004), 82.
7. Glenn Paige, "Action Principles," Reprinted with permission from the Global Center for Nonkilling, accessed September 20, 2011, http://www.nonkilling.org/node/40.
8. Gerald Holton and Yehuda Elkana, eds., *Albert Einstein: Historical and Cultural Perspectives* (Princeton: Princeton University Press, 1982) 377.
9. Sonya Bargmann, translation based on *Mein Weltbild*, Carl Seelig, ed., *Albert Einstein: Ideas and Opinions* (New York: The Modern Library, 1994), 120.
10. Ibid., 164.

Chapter 15. Cultural Exchange

1. Anais Nin and Gunther Stuhlmann, *The Diary of Anais Nin: 1934–1939* (Columbus, OH: Swallow Press, 1970), 193.
2. Friendship Force International, accessed September 20, 2010, http://www.thefriendshipforce.org/PressCenter.aspx.
3. Ibid., accessed September 20, 2011, http://www.thefriendshipforce.org.

Chapter 16. Citizen Diplomacy

1. "Waging Peace Through Elections," The Carter Center, accessed March 12, 2009, http://cartercenter.org/peace/democracy/observed.html.
2. Douglas Johnston and Cynthia Sampson, eds., *Religion, the Missing Dimension of Statecraft* (Oxford: Oxford University Press, 1994), 111.

Chapter 17. Environmental Activism

1. Wangari Muta Maathai, *Unbowed: A Memoir* (New York: Knopf, 2006) 175.
2. Laura Westra, *Environmental Justice and the Rights of Ecological Refugees* (London: Dustan House, 2009), xii.
3. "Report of the Brundtland Commission: 'Our Common Future'" (Oxford: Oxford University Press, 1987).
4. Simon Robinson, "Wangari Maathai," *Time Magazine*, Oct. 10, 2004, accessed March 10, 2009, http://www.time.com/time/specials/2007/article/0,28804,1663317_1663320_1669 918,00.html.

Chapter 18. Artistic Expression

1. Rollo May, *The Courage to Create* (New York: W. W. Norton, 1994), 115.
2. "Imagine Peace," interview with Yoko Ono, 1996, accessed March 12, 2009, http://imag inepeace.com/news/wish.

Chapter 19. Nonviolent Resistance

1. Democratic Voice of Burma, "Protests swell as monks receive increasing support," *Democratic Voice of Burma*, September 12, 2007, accessed March 11, 2009, http://english.dvb.no/text only/news.php?id=458.
2. The Buddhist Channel. "Resistance, Not Repression, is the Real Story From Burma," Cynthia Boaz, The Buddhist Channel, Oct. 10, 2007, accessed March 10, 2009, http://www.budd histchannel.tv/index.php?id=8,5147,0,0,1,0.
3. Mahatma Gandhi, *The Essential Gandhi*, Louis Fischer, ed. (New York: Vintage Books, 1983), 180.
4. Ibid., 77.
5. Mahatma Gandhi, *Satyagraha* (Ahmedabad: Naajivan Publishing House, 1958), 87.
6. Gene Sharp, *The Politics of Nonviolent Actions, Vol. 2: the Methods of Nonviolent Action* (Boston: Porter Sargent, 1873).

Chapter 20. Arms Reduction

1. Horizon, University of North Carolina, "Total U.S. and Soviet Nuclear Warheads," accessed March 10, 2009, http://horizon.unc.edu/projects/presentations/Wfs/sld137.html.
2. Corey Hinderstein, *Cultivating Confidence: Verification, Monitoring, and Enforcement for a World Free of Nuclear Weapons* (Stanford: Hoover Institution Press, 2010), 228.
3. Text of a letter from the president to the chairman and ranking members of the House and Senate Committees on Armed Services and Appropriations, the chairman and ranking members of the House Committee on Foreign Affairs and the Senate Committee on Foreign Relations, May 13, 2010.
4. *Public Papers of the Presidents of the United States: Barack Obama, 2009, Book 1* (Washington, D.C. U.S. Government Printing Office, 2009), 442.
5. *Public Papers of the Presidents of the United States: Barack Obama, 2009, Book 1* (Washington, D.C.: U.S. Government Printing Office, 2009) 442.
6. Remarks by the President at the Acceptance of the Nobel Peace Prize, Oslo City Hall, Oslo, Norway, December 10, 2009.

Chapter 21. Humanitarianism

1. University of Michigan, *Remembering Raoul Wallenberg: the University of Michigan Celebrates Twentieth-century Heroes* (Ann Arbor: University of Michigan Press, 2001), 10.
2. Corey Hinderstein, ed., *Cultivating Confidences: Verification, Monitoring and Enforcement for a World Free of Nuclear Weapons* (Stanford: Hoover Institution Press, 2010), ix.
3. Michael Flint and Hugh Goyder, Tsunami Funding Coalition, *Funding the Tsunami*

Response, June 2006, Tsunami Funding Coalition, accessed March 10, 2009, http://www.ifrc.org/docs/pubs/updates/tec-funding-report.pdf.

4. Martin Luther King, Jr., *Where Do We Go from Here: Chaos or Community?* Excerpts from "The World House" Essay (Boston: Beacon Press, 2010), 177.

Chapter 22. Distributive Justice

1. Worldwatch Institute, "Forgive and Forget" Won't Fix Third World Debt, April 26, 2001, accessed March 10, 2009, http://www.worldwatch.org/node/1696.

2. United Nations Press Release, "SG/T/2450: Activities of Secretary-General in France, 13–14 June 2005," accessed March 10, 2009, http://www.un.org/News/Press/docs/2005/sgt2450.doc.htm.

3. Marina Primorac, International Monetary Fund, "F&D Spotlights Widening Gap Between Rich and Poor," accessed Sept. 20, 2010, http://www.imf.org/external/pubs/ft/survey/so/2011/NEW091211A.htm.

Chapter 23. Witnessing Violence

1. W. James Booth, *Communities of Memory: On Witness, Identity, and Justice* (Ithaca: Cornell University Press, 2006), 97.

2. Irwin Abrams, *The Nobel Peace Prize and the Laureates: An Illustrated Biographical History, 1901–1987* (Boston: G.K. Hall, 1988), 220.

Chapter 24. Rule of Law

1. Address by Secretary of State Madeleine K. Albright to the UN Human Rights Commission, Palais des Nations, accessed March 23, 2000, http://geneva.usmission.gov/humanrights/2000/albright.html.

2. Mark David Agrast, Juan Carlos Botero, and Alejandro Ponce. *The World Justice Project: Rule of Law Index, 2010* (Washington, D.C.: World Justice Project, 2010).

3. World Justice Project, Washington, D.C., Press Release, June 24, 2010, accessed Sept. 20, 2010, http://worldjusticeproject.org/MENA%20conference%20press%20release.

4. *Justice of the Peace and Local Government Review*, Vol. 11, 1952, page 492.

Chapter 25. Alternative Resources Acquisition

1. Jimmy Briggs, *Innocents Lost: When Child Soldiers Go To War* (New York: Basic Books, 2005), xii.

2. Water Footprint Network, "FAQ: Why Act Now," accessed Sept. 20, 2011, http://www.waterfootprint.org/?page=files/FAQ_Why_act_and_how.

Chapter 26. The Golden Rule

1. Jeffrey Wattles, *The Golden Rule* (New York: Oxford University Press, 1996), 16.

2. Marnie Jones, *Holy Toledo: Religion and Politics in the Life of "Golden Rule"* (Lexington: University Press of Kentucky, 1998), 223–4.

3. David Bohm, *Wholeness and the Implicate Order* (London: Routledge, 2005), xviii.

4. Norman Vincent Peale, *Stay Alive All Your Life* (New York: Prentice Hall, 1985), 172.

5. John Hagelin, "Shift-Power of the Collective," accessed September 20, 2011, http://www.istpp.org/pdf/Shift-PoweroftheCollective.pdf.

Chapter 27. Peace Education

1. "Nobel Peace Prize," The Norwegian Nobel Committee, accessed September 20, 2011, http://nobelpeaceprize.org/en_GB/about_peaceprize/.

2. "Promoting Human Values and A Sense of Oneness Within Humanity," Dalai Lama Center, accessed March 12, 2009, www.dalailamacenter.org.

Chapter 28. Global Wellness

1. Halbert L. Dunn, *High-level Wellness: A Collection of Twenty-nine Short Talks on Different Aspects of the Theme "High-level Wellness for Man and Society"* (Arlington, VA: Beatty, 1973) 4.
2. "Focus on Women," World Food Programme, accessed March 5, 2009, http://www.wfp.org.
3. *The Millennium Development Goals Report, 2011* (New York: United Nations, 2011), foreword.

Chapter 30. Personal Transformation

1. Andrew B. Newberg, *Why We Believe What We Believe: Uncovering Our Biological Need for Meaning, Spirituality, and Truth* (New York: Free Press, 2006), 209.

Chapter 31. Summary of Methods

1. Walter Wink, *Engaging the Powers: Discernment and Resistance in a World of Domination* (Minneapolis: Fortress Press, 1992), 221.
2. Nelson Mandela, *Long Walk to Freedom: The Autobiography of Nelson Mandela* (Boston: Little, Brown, 1994), 554.

Conclusion: The Virtuoso of Peace

Notes and citations for the quotations in "The Virtuoso of Peace" are included here in the order used with separation for sections. Citation numbers have been removed from the text to enhance readability.

David Starr Jordon, *The Philosophy of Despair* (London: P. Elder and M. Shepard, 1902), 37.

TACTFULNESS

Misattributed to Isaac Newton; widely attributed to Howard W. Newton, advertising executive; source unidentified.
Errick A. Ford, *Iron Sharpens Iron: Wisdom of the Ages* (Mustang, OK: Tate, 2010), 104.
Benjamin Disraeli, *Endymion* (London: Longmans & Green, 1880), 276.

FORESIGHT

James Finlayson, *Sermons by Hugh Blair* (London: A. & R. Spottiswoods, 1822), Sermon XIII, 127.
Ralph Waldo Emerson, *Fate, Prefatory Notice by Walter Lewin* (London: Walter Scott, 1886), 141.
Theodore H. White, *The Making of the President—1968* (New York: Atheneum House, 1969), 200.

FORGIVENESS

Collected Works of Mahatma Gandhi. "Interview to the Press in Karachi, Young India, April 2, 1931" (Delhi: Ministry of Information and Broadcasting, 1972), Vol. 51.
Williamson, Marianne. *A Return to Love: Reflections on the Principles of a Course in Miracles* (New York: HarperCollins, 1996), 228.

(*Conclusion*, continued)

INTEGRITY
R. Buckminster Fuller, *Critical Path* (New York: St. Martin's Press, 1981), xxxvii.
Gary Allan Ratson, *The Meaning of Health: The Experience of a Lifetime* (Victoria, BC.: Trafford, 2003) Not attributed but widely quoted in other texts, here on pg. 59.
Ayn Rand, *Atlas Shrugged* (New York: Penguin, 1992), Chapter VII, 1021.

DECISIVENESS
Erich Sauer: widely quoted but no original source could be identified.
Omar Bongo, accessed September 20, 2011, http://saharanvibe.blogspot.com/2007/04/gabons-omar-bongo-president-for-life.html.

CALMNESS
Norman Vincent Peale, *A Guide to Confident Living* (New York: Simon & Schuster, Fireside Edition, 2003), 79.
James Allen, *As a Man Thinketh* (Bellevue, WA: Emptitude Books, 2009), 33.
Maturin Murray Ballou, *Treasury of Thought* (Boston: Houghton, Mifflin, 1884), 407.

GENEROSITY
The English Digest, Vol. 69 (Mellifont Press, 1962), 18.
Mitch Albom, *Tuesdays with Morrie: An Old Man, a Young Man, and Life's Greatest Lesson* (New York: Doubleday, 1997), from "Taking Attendance."
Rajendra Pillai, *Pocket Book of Quips and Quotes* (Mumbai: Better Yourself Books, 1999), 10.

JUSTICE
Adi Hormusji Doctor, *Sarvodaya: A Political and Economic Study* (London: Asia Publishing House, 1967), 43.
Hailmar Day Gould and Edward Louis Hessenmueller, *Best Thoughts of Best Thinkers* (Cleveland: Best Thoughts, 1904), 447.
"Message of His Holiness Pope Paul VI For the Celebration of the Day Of Peace, January 1, 1972," accessed September 20, 2011, http://www.vatican.va/holy_father/paul_vi/messages/peace/documents/hf_p-vi_mes_19711208_v-world-day-for-peace_en.html.

DISCRETION
The Works of Joseph Addison: Volume 3 (New York: Harper & Brothers, 1842), 329.
John Kleinig and Yurong Zhang, *Professional Law Enforcement Codes: A Documentary Collection* (Westport, CT: Greenwood, 1993), 131.
Herbert Blumer and Ernest Watson Burgess, *The American Journal of Sociology*, Vol. 11, 1906, page 454.
Henri Frédéric Amiel, *Journal: The Journal Intime, Vol. 1*, trans. Mrs. Humphry Ward. (London: Macmillan, 1895), 196.

COOPERATION
Isaac Reed, *The Plays of William Shakespeare: In Six Volumes* (Philadelphia: Charles Williams, 1813), 262.
Einstein, Albert. *Ideas and Opinions* (New York: Crown: Modern Library, 1994), 175.

DISSENT
Dave Patterson, *Green Islands* (Charlottetown, Canada: Green Island Books, 2008) 512.
Howard Zinn quote in an interview with TomPaine.com, accessed September 20, 2011, http://www.tompaine.com/Archive/scontent/5908.html.
AFL-CIO, *The American Federationist*, Vol. 61, no. 7, page 32.
George Bernard Shaw, *Man and Superman: A Comedy and Philosophy* (Cambridge, MA: The University Press, 1903), 124.

CONSCIENCE

Vincent van Gogh, Irving Stone and Jean Stone, *Dear Theo: The Autobiography of Vincent Van Gogh* (London: Constable and Co., 1937), 181.

Henry David Thoreau, *Walden, Or Life in the Woods: With "On the Duty of Civil Disobedience"* (Seattle: Coffeetown Press, 2008), 296.

Edward Conze, *Buddhism: Its Essence and Development*, Dover ed. (New York: Harper Brothers, 1959), 162.

Thomas Merton, *The Nonviolent Alternative* (Toronto: McGrall-Hill Ryerson, 1980), 35.

Norman Cousins, *Present Tense: An American Editor's Odyssey* (New York: McGraw-Hill, 1967), 371.

Immanuel Kant, *Critique of Practical Reason* (Radford, VA: Wilder Publications, 2008), 111.

COMPASSION

Tyron Edwards, *A Dictionary of Thoughts* (New York: Cassell, 1891) 78.

Thomas Browne, *Religio medici*, T. Chapman, ed. (Oxford: J. Vincent, M DCCC XXXI), 114.

Charles H. Dyer, *Character Counts: The Power of Personal Integrity* (Chicago: Moody, 2010), 34.

J. Miller, and Y. Nakagawa, eds., *Nurturing Our Wholeness: Perspectives on Spirituality in Education* (Brandon, VT: Foundation for Educational Renewal, 2002), 305.

MORALITY

Suzy Platt, ed., *Respectfully Quoted: A Dictionary of quotations* (New York: Barnes and Noble, 1993), 71.

Robert Andrews, *The Columbia Dictionary of Quotations* (New York: Columbia University Press, 1993), 719.

Saheed A. Adejumobi, *The History of Ethiopia* (Westport, CT: Greenwood, 2007), 154.

FRIENDSHIP

A. D. Cousins, and Peter Howarth, *The Cambridge Companion to the Sonnet* (Cambridge: Cambridge University Press, 2011), 131.

Mary Cox Garner, *The Hidden Souls of Words* (New York: SelectBooks, 2004), 30.

Chip R. Bell, and Bilijack R. Bell, *Magnetic Services: Secrets for Creating Passionately Devoted Customers* (San Francisco: Berrett-Koehler, 2009), 40.

Peter, Anthony St. *The Greatest Quotations of All Time* (n.p.: Xlibris, 2010), 167.

James French, *The Sociable Story-Teller* (Boston: James French, 1846), 15.

INITIATIVE

Elle Davenport Adams, *This Life and the Next* (London: Grant Richards, 1902), 244.

Jerry Phillips, Andrew Ladd, and Karen H. Myers, *Romanticism and Transcendentalism, 1800–1860*, 2d ed. (New York: Chelsea House, 2006), 24.

Wayne Ashmore, and Jennifer Nault, *Mark Twain: My Favorite Writer* (New York: Weigl, 1909), 12.

Bill Capodagli and Lynn Jackson, *Innovate the Pixar Way* (New York: McGraw Hill, 2009), 125.

SUSTAINABILITY

Rachel White Scheuering, *Shapers of the Great Debate on Conservation* (Westport, CT: Greenwood Press, 2004), 86.

Drury University Sustainability Quotes, accessed September 18, 2011, http://www.drury.edu/multinl/story.cfm?ID=11595&NLID=259.

National Geographic, Vol. 160, National Geographic Society (Washington, D.C.: National Geographic Society, 1981), 791.

John Duane Ivanko and Lisa Kirvirist, *ECOpreneuring: Putting Purpose and the Planet Before Profits* (Gabriola Island, BC: New Society, 2008), 49.

(Conclusion, continued)

Allan K. Smith, quote from press release, accessed September 18, 2010, http://ir.steelcase. com/releasedetail.cfm?ReleaseID=371359.

CREATIVITY

Patrick J. Lewis, *Michelangelo's World* (Mankato, MN: Creative Editions, 2007), 207.
Andy Bryner and Dawna Markova, *An Unused Intelligence* (Berkeley: Conari Press, 1996), 11.
L. Ann Masters and Harold R. Wallace, *Personal Development for Life and Work* (Mason, OH: South-Western Cengage Learning, 2011), 241.
Saint-Exupéry, Antoine de. Translated by Galantiére. *Flight to Arras,* Galantiére, trans. (New York: Harcourte Brace, 1942).

COURAGE

C. S. Lewis, *The Complete C.S. Lewis Signature Classics* (New York: HarperCollins, 2001), 270.
Angela Angelou, *Even the Stars Look Lonesome* (New York: Random House, 1997), 132.
James Neil Hollingworth, "No Peaceful Warriors!" *Gnosis: A Journal of the Western Inner Traditions* #21, Fall 1991, accessed September 18, 2011, http://www.giga-usa.com/gigawebl/quotes 2/quautredmoonambrosehx001.htm.
Mary Anne Redmacher, *Courage Doesn't Always Roar* (San Francisco: Canari Press, 2009), 3.

LOGIC

Ludwig Wittgenstein, *Notebooks, 1914–1916,* G. H. von Wright, ed., 2d ed. (Chicago: University of Chicago Press, 1979), 110.
Ludwig Wittgenstein, *Tractatus Logico-Philosophicus* (Whitefish: Kessinger Publishing: www.kissenger.net), 54.
Gerald F. Lieberman, *3,500 Good Quotes for Speakers* (New York: Doubleday, 1985).
Michael Nesmith, Brainyquote, accessed September 20, 2011, http://www.brainyquote. com/quotes/quotes/m/michaelnes264047.html.
Ambrose Bierce, *The Devil's Dictionary* (n.p.: Plain Label Books, 1925), 179.
Lewis Caroll, *Through the Looking Glass: And What Alice Found There,* Florence Milner, ed. (New York: Rand McNally & Co., 1917), 58.

EMPATHY

Gary P. Guthrie, *1600 Quotes and Pieces of Wisdom That Just Might Help You Out When You're Stuck in a Moment* (Lincoln, NE: iUniverse, 2003), 60.
Daniel Goleman, *Social Intelligence: The New Science of Human Relationships* (New York: Bantam Dell, 2006), 54.
Marshal Rosenberg, *Nonviolent Communication,* accessed September 18, 2011, http://www. freerangelearning.com/index.php/nonviolent-communication.

FAIRNESS

Miguel de Cervantes Saavedra, *The History of Don Quixote de la Mancha* (Boston: Charles H. Peirce, M DCC XLVII), 245.
Widely attributed but no original source could be determined.
John Rawls, *Justice as Fairness: A Restatement,* 2d ed., Erin Kelly, ed. (Cambridge: Belknap Press of Harvard University Press, 2001), xi.
TV Tropes, accessed September 18, 2011, http://tvtropes.org/pmwiki/pmwiki.php/Main/ ptitlebcvjiokg.
William Giddings Sibley, *The French Five Hundred: And Other Papers* (Gallipolis, OH: The Tribune Press, 1901), 276.

MINDFULNESS

Bodhidharma, *The Zen Teaching of Bodhidharma* (New York: North Point Press, 1987), 41.
Alex Pattakos, *Prisoners of Our Thoughts: Viktor Frankl's Principles for Discovering Meaning in Life and Work* (San Francisco: Berrett-Koehler, 2010), 220.

Thich Nhat Hanh, *Be Still and Know: Reflections from Living Buddha, Living Christ* (New York: Riverhead Books, 1996), Mindfulness and the Holy Spirit.

EQUALITY

Voltaire, *A Philosophical Dictionary: From the French* (London: J. & H.L. Hunt, 1824), 379.

Karl Marx and Frederick Engels, *The Communist Manifesto*, Phil Gasper, ed. (Chicago: Haymarket Books, 2005), 33.

Carl Schurz, Frederick Bancroft, and William Archibald Dunning. *The Reminiscences of Carl Schurz: 1852–1863*, vol. 2 (New York: The McClure Company, MCMVII), 123.

Tom Robbins, *Still Life with Woodpecker* (New York: Bantam Dell, 2003), 92.

RESOURCEFULNESS

Servando Gonzalez, *The Nuclear Deception: Nikita Krushchev and the Cuban Missile Crisis* (n.p.: InteliBooks, 2002), 17.

Galen Strawson, *Selves: An Essay in Revisionary Metaphysics* (Oxford: Oxford University Press, 2009), 16.

"Opposing the War Party," *The Progressive*, accessed September 14, 2011, http://www.pro gressive.org/may04/zinn0504.html.

Michael A. Seeds and Dana Backman, *Foundations of Astronomy* (Boston: Brooks/Cole, 2009), 356.

RECIPROCITY

Marc Bekoff and Jessica Pierce, *Wild Justice: The Moral Lives of Animals* (Chicago: University of Chicago Press, 2009), 7.

Edwin Markham, *The Man with the Hoe* (New York: The Doubleday and McClure Co., MDCCC), 45.

WISDOM

Widely attributed to Confucius but unidentifiable in the Whaley version of *The Analytics of Confucius*.

Leo F. Buscaglia, *Born for Love: Reflections on Loving* (New York: Ballantine, 1994), 7.

Condy Raguet, ed., *The Examiner, and Journal of Political Economy, Volume 1* (Philadelphia: The Examiner, 1834), 133.

Reinhold Niebuhr and Robert McAfee Brown, *The Essential Reinhold Niebuhr: Selected Essays and Addresses* (New Haven: Yale University Press, 1986), 251.

BALANCE

Thomas Merton, *No Man Is an Island* (Boston: Shambhala Publications, 2005), 134.

Henri Poincaré, *The Foundations of Science*, George Bruce Halsted, ed. (New York: The Science Press, 1913), 372.

Gérard Durozoi, *Matisse* (London: Studio Editions, 1993), 17.

Albert Edward McKinley, *Collected Material for the Study of the War* (Philadelphia: McKinley, 1918), 10.

ATTENTIVENESS

Ralph Waldo Emerson, *Works of Ralph Waldo Emerson, Vol. 5*, "Beauty" (Boston: Houghton, Osgood and Company, 1880), 23.

William James, *The Principles of Psychology, Volume 1* (London: Macmillan, 1891), 403.

Thornton Wilder, *The Eighth Day* (New York: Harper Perennial Modern Classics, 2007).

William James, *The Principles of Psychology, Volume 1* (London: Macmillan, 1891), 243.

UNITY

Aesop, "The Four Oxen and the Lion," *Aesop's Fables* (electronically developed by Moble Reference from multiple translations).

Ronald W. Clark and Ronald William Clark, *Einstein: The Life and Times* (New York: Avon Books, 1984), 77.

(*Conclusion*, continued)

Martin Luther King, Jr., *Strength to Love* (Philadelphia: First Fortress Press, 1981), 75.

David Adams Leeming, *James Baldwin: A Biography* (New York: Knopf, 1994), 227.

Beverly Fehr, Susan Sprecher, and Lynn G. Underwood, eds., *The Science of Compassionate Love: Theory, Research, and Applications* (Malden, MA: Wiley-Blackwell, 2009), 3–25.

Carl Gustav Jung, *Modern Man in Search of a Soul* (Oxford: Routledge Classics, 2005), 49.

ACTIONABLE VIRTUE

Hugh Rawson and Margaret Miner, *The Oxford Dictionary of American Quotations* (Oxford: Oxford University Press, 2006), 493.

Virgil, *Eclogues of Virgil* (Quebec: Gilbert Stanley, 1847), 47.

Bibliography

Listed here are works consulted in the writing of *The Elements of Peace*. With new ideas, trends, and scholarship, the materials available for the study of nonviolence in general and each method in particular evolve. For extensive study, referencing the bibliography from a book by a specialist in each area of nonviolence is highly recommended.

Abbink, Jon, and Gerti Hesseling, eds. *Election Observation and Democratization in Africa*. New York: St. Martin's Press, 2000.

Ackerman, Peter, and Jack DuVall. *A Force More Powerful: A Century of Nonviolent Conflict*. New York: St. Martin's Press, 2000.

Ackerman, Peter, and Christopher Kruegler. *Strategic Nonviolent Conflict: The Dynamics of People Power in the Twentieth Century*. Westport, CT: Praeger, 1994.

Adelman, Howard, and Astri S. Aldelman. *The Path of a Genocide: The Rwanda Crisis from Uganda to Zaire*. New Brunswick, NJ: Transaction, 1999.

African Development Bank. *African Development Report: 2006: Aid, Debt Relief and Development in Africa*. Oxford: Oxford University Press, 2006.

Amiram Raviv, Lou. *How Children Understand War and Peace: A Call for International Peace Education*. San Francisco: Jossey-Bass, 1999.

Anderlini, Sanam Naraghi. *Women Building Peace: What They Do, Why It Matters*. Boulder, CO: Lynne Rienner, 2007.

Asmal, Kader, et al., eds. *In His Own Words — Nelson Mandela*. New York: Little, Brown, 2003.

Baker, Newton D. Introduction, *The Conscientious Objector*. New York: Da Capo Press, 1970.

Barish, David P., and Charles P. Webel. *Peace and Conflict Studies*. Thousand Oaks, CA: Sage, 2002.

Barrett, Scott. *Environment and Statecraft: The Strategy of Environmental Treaty-Making*. Oxford: Oxford University Press, 2005. Retrieved March 10, 2009, http://ebooks.ohiolink.edu/xtf-ebc/view?docId=tei/ox/0199286094/0199286094.xml&query=&brand=default.

Bausum, Ann. *Freedom Riders: John Lewis and Jim Zwerg on the Front Lines of the Civil Rights Movement*. Washington, DC: National Geographic, 2006.

Beane, Allan. *Protect Your Child from Bullying: Expert Advice to Help You Recognize, Prevent, and Stop Bullying Before Your Child Gets Hurt*. San Francisco: Jossey-Bass, 2008.

Bekker, Peter H. F. *World Court Decisions at the Turn of the Millennium, 1997–2001*. The Hague and New York: M. Nijhoff, 2002.

Bennett, Steven C. *Arbitration: Essential Concepts*. New York: ALM, 2002.

Benton, Barbara, ed. *Soldiers for Peace: Fifty Years of United Nations Peacekeeping*. New York: Facts on File, 1996.

Black, Maggie. *The No-Nonsense Guide to International Development*. London: Verso, 2002.

Blackburn, William R. *The Sustainability Handbook: The Complete Management Guide to Achiev-*

ing Social, Economic, and Environmental Responsibility. Washington, DC: Environmental Law Institute, 2007.

Blakaby, Frank, Joseph Rotblat, et al., eds. *A Nuclear-Weapon-Free World: Desirable? Feasible?* Boulder, CO: Westview Press, 1993.

Bloom, Harold. *Henry David Thoreau.* New York: Bloom's Literary Criticism, 2008.

Bodine, Richard J., and Donna K. Crawford. *The Handbook of Conflict Resolution Education: A Guide to Building Quality Programs in School.* San Francisco: Jossey-Bass, 1998.

Bolten, Jose, and Stan Graeve, eds. *No Room for Bullies: From the Classroom to Cyberspace.* Boys Town, NE: Boys Town Press, 2005.

Booth, W. James. *Communities of Memory: On Witness, Identity, and Justice.* Ithaca: Cornell University Press, 2006.

Bosch, Olivia, and Peter van Ham, eds. *Global Non-Proliferation and Counter-Terrorism: The Impact of UNSCR 1540.* Washington, DC: Brookings Institution Press, 2007.

Briggs, Jimmy. *Innocents Lost: When Child Soldiers Go to War.* New York: Basic Books, 2005.

Brock, Peter. *The Quaker Peace Testimony: 1660–1914.* York, England: Sessions Book Trust, 1990.

Brown, Michael Barratt. *Fair Trade.* London: Zed Books, 1993.

Brown, Nathan. *Palestinian Politics After the Oslo Accords: Resuming Arab Palestine.* Berkeley: University of California Press, 2003.

Buckley, Roger. *Hong Kong: The Road to 1997.* Cambridge: Cambridge University Press, 1997.

Burlingame, Dwight F. *The Responsibilities of Wealth.* Bloomington: Indiana University Press, 1992.

Burns, Stewart, ed. *Daybreak of Freedom: The Montgomery Bus Boycott.* Chapel Hill: University of North Carolina Press, 1997.

Bush, Robert A. Baruch, and Joseph P. Folger. *The Promise of Mediation: Responding to Conflict through Empowerment and Recognition.* San Francisco: Jossey-Bass, 1994.

Carnegie Commission on Preventing Deadly Conflict. *Preventing Deadly Conflict: Final Report.* New York: Carnegie Corporation, 1997.

Carter, Jimmy. *Palestine: Peace, Not Apartheid.* New York: Simon & Schuster, 2006.

Chan, Steve, and A. Cooper Drury, eds. *Sanctions as Economic Statecraft: Theory and Practice.* New York: St. Martin's Press, 2000.

Chernus, Ira. *American Nonviolence: The History of an Idea.* Maryknoll, NY: Orbis Books, 2004.

Chinn, Peggy L. *Peace and Power: Creative Leadership for Building Community.* Boston: Jones and Bartlett, 2004.

Chollet, Derek H. *The Road to the Dayton Accords: A Study of American Statecraft.* New York: Palgrave Macmillan, 2005.

Cloke, Kenneth, and Joan Goldsmith. *Resolving Personal and Organizational Conflict: Stories of Transformation and Forgiveness.* San Francisco: Jossey-Bass, 2000.

Coerr, Elanor. *Sadako and the Thousand Paper Cranes.* New York: Puffin, 1999.

Coffin, William Sloane, and Morris I. Leibman. *Civil Disobedience: Aid or Hindrance to Justice?* Washington, DC: American Enterprise Institute for Public Policy Research, 1972.

Cohn, Ernist J., et al., eds. *Handbook of Institutional Arbitration in International Trade: Facts, Figures, and Rules.* Amsterdam: North Holland, 1977.

Collignon, Stefan, and Robert Taylor, eds. *Burma: Political Economy under Military Rule.* New York: Palgrave, 2001.

Coloroso, Barbara. *The Bully, the Bullied, and the Bystander: From Preschool to High School—How Parents and Teachers Can Help Break the Cycle of Violence.* New York: Collins Living, 2008.

Cornell, Dewey G. *School Violence: Fears Versus Facts.* Mahwah, NJ: Lawrence Erlbaum Associates, 2006.

Craig, Mary. *Lech Walesa and His Poland.* New York: Continuum, 1987.

Daalder, Ivo H. *Getting to Dayton: The Making of America's Bosnia Policy.* Washington, DC: Brookings Institution Press, 2000.

DeBenedetti, Charles. *Peace Heroes in Twentieth-Century America.* Bloomington: Indiana University Press, 1986.

DeChaine, D. Robert. *Global Humanitarianism: NGOs and the Crafting of Community.* Lanham, MD: Lexington Books, 2005.

DePino, Catherine. *Real Life Bully Prevention for Real Kids: 50 Ways to Help Elementary and Middle Schools Students.* Lanham, MD: Rowman & Littlefield Education, 2009.

Dierenfield, Bruce. *The Civil Rights Movement.* New York: Pearson Longman, 2008.

Dill, Vicky Schreiber. *A Peaceable School: Cultivating a Culture of Nonviolence.* Bloomington, IN: Phi Delta Kappa Educational Foundation, 1998.

Dockrill, Michael Lawrence. *Diplomacy and World Power: Studies in British Foreign Policy, 1890–1950.* Edited by Brian McKercher. Cambridge: Cambridge University Press, 1996.

Dreher, Diane. *The Tao of Inner Peace: A Guide to Inner Peace.* New York: Plume Book, 2000.

Drell, Sidney D., and George P. Shultz. *Implications of the Reykjavik Summit on Its Twentieth Anniversary: Conference Report.* Stanford: Hoover Institution, 2007.

Dunn, James. *East Timor: A Rough Passage to Independence.* 3d ed. New South Wales, Australia: Longueville Books, 2003.

Edmonds, Anthony O. *Muhammad Ali: A Biography.* Westport, CT: Greenwood Press, 2006.

Elliott, Michele, ed. *Bullying: A Practical Guide to Coping for Schools.* 3d ed. London: Pearson Education, 2002.

Etzioni, Amitai. *The New Golden Rule: Community and Morality in a Democratic Society.* New York: Basic Books, 1996.

Evans, Alice Frazer, and Robert A. Evans. *Peace Skills: Leaders' Guide.* San Francisco: Jossey-Bass, 2001.

Evans, Patricia. *Controlling People: How to Recognize, Understand, and Deal with People Who Try to Control You.* Avon, MA: Adams Media, 2002.

Falk, Richard A., Robert C. Johansen, and Samuel S. Kim, eds. *The Constitutional Foundations of World Peace.* Albany: State University of New York Press, 1993.

Federer, Juan. *The UN in East Timor: Building Timor Leste, a Fragile State.* Darwin: Charles Darwin University Press, 2005.

Fehr, Beverly, et al., eds. *The Science of Compassionate Love: Theory, Research, and Applications.* Malden, MA: Wiley-Blackwell, 2009.

Fisher, Ronald J. *Interactive Conflict Resolution.* New York: Syracuse University Press, 1997.

Fitzell, Susan Gingras. *Transforming Anger to Personal Power.* Champaign, IL: Research Press, 2007.

Forcey, Linda Rennie, and Ian Murray Harris. *Peacebuilding for Adolescents: Strategies for Educators and Community Leaders.* New York: Peter Lang, 1999.

Forsythe, David P. *Human Rights & World Peace.* 2d ed. Lincoln: University of Nebraska Press, 1989.

Fort, Timothy L. *Business, Integrity, and Peace: Beyond Geopolitical and Disciplinary Boundaries.* Cambridge: Cambridge University Press, 2007.

Freedman, Russell. *Confucius: The Golden Rule.* New York: Arthur A. Levine Books, 2002.

Fuller, Robert C. *Wonder: From Emotion to Spirituality.* Chapel Hill: University of North Carolina Press, 2006.

Garbarino, James, and Ellen DeLara, *And Words Can Hurt Forever: How to Protect Adolescents from Bullying, Harassment, and Emotional Violence.* New York: The Free Press, 2002.

Girard, Kathryn, and Susan J. Koch. *Conflict Resolution in the Schools: A Manual for Educators.* San Francisco: Jossey-Bass, 1996.

Glickman, Lawrence B. *Buying Power: A History of Consumer Activism in America.* Chicago: The University of Chicago Press, 2009.

Goodwyn, Lawrence. *Breaking the Barrier: The Rise of Solidarity in Poland.* New York: Oxford University Press, 1991.

Gosselin, Abigail. *Global Poverty and Individual Responsibility.* Lanham, MD: Lexington Books, 2009.

Graham, Thomas Jr., and Damien J. LaVera. *Cornerstones of Security: Arms Control Treaties in the Nuclear Era.* Seattle: University of Washington Press, 2003.

Graybill, Lyn S. *Truth and Reconciliation in South Africa: Miracle or Model?* Boulder, CO: Lynne Rienner, 2002.

Guogi, Yu. *Olympic Dreams: China and Sports, 1895–2008.* Cambridge, MA: Harvard University Press, 2008.

Hamm, Thomas D. *The Quakers in America.* New York: Columbia University Press, 2003.

Hanlon, Joseph, and Roger Omond. *The Sanctions Handbook.* Middlesex, England: Penguin, 1987.

Harris, Ian M., and Mary Lee Morrison. *Peace Education.* Jefferson, NC: McFarland, 2003.

Hastings, Tom H. *The Lessons of Nonviolence: Theory and Practice in a World of Conflict.* North Carolina: McFarland & Company, 2006.

Hastings, Tom H. *Nonviolent Response to Terrorism.* Jefferson, NC: McFarland, 2004.

Helminiak, Lanham. *Spirituality for Our Global Community: Beyond Traditional Religion to a World at Peace.* Lanham, MD: Rowman & Littlefield, 2008.

Herndon, Booton. *The Unlikeliest Hero: The Story of Desmond T. Doss, Conscientious Objector, Who Won His Nation's Highest Military Honor.* Mountain View, CA: Pacific Press, 1967.

Heydenberk, Warren, and Roberta Heydenberk. *A Powerful Peace: The Integrative Thinking Classroom.* Boston: Allyn and Bacon, 2000.

Holbrooke, Richard. *To End a War.* New York: Modern Library, 1999.

Hope, Ronald H. *Poverty, Livelihoods, and Governance in Africa: Fulfilling the Development Promise.* New York: Palgrave Macmillan, 2008.

Howard, Lisa Morjé. *U.N. Peacekeeping in Civil Wars.* Cambridge: Cambridge University Press, 2008.

The International Bill of Human Rights. Foreword by Jimmy Carter. Introduction by Tom J. Farer. Glen Ellen, CA: Entwhistle Books, 1981.

International Development Research Center. *Cultivating Peace: Conflict and Collaboration in Natural Resource Management.* Ottawa: International Development Research Center, 1999. Retrieved March 10, 2009, http://www.netlibrary.com/Search/BasicSearch.aspx.

Isard, Walter. *Understanding Conflict & the Science of Peace.* Cambridge: Blackwell, 1992.

Iyer, Raghavan, *The Moral and Political Writings of Mahatma Gandhi, Vol. III, Non-Violent Resistance and Social Transformation.* Oxford: Clarendon Press, 1987.

Jaana, Juvonen, and Sandra Graham, eds. *Peer Harassment in Schools: The Plight of the Vulnerable and Victimized.* New York: The Guilford Press, 2001.

Jamner, Margaret Schneider, and Daniel Stokols, eds. *Promoting Human Wellness: New Frontiers for Research, Practice, and Policy.* Berkeley: University of California Press, 2000.

Jefferson, Frederick O. *The Civil Rights Revolution: Events and Leaders, 1955–1968.* Jefferson, NC: McFarland, 2004.

Joint United Nations Programme on HIV/AIDS (UNAIDS) and World Health Organization (WHO) 2007. Retrieved March 10, 2009, from http://www.unaids.org/en/Knowledge-Centre/HIVData/GlobalReport/2008/2008_Global_report.asp.

Jones, Marnie. *Holy Toledo: Religion and Politics in the Life of "Golden Rule."* Lexington: University Press of Kentucky, 1998.

King, Robert Harlen. *Thomas Merton and Thich Nhat Hanh: Engaged Spirituality in an Age of Globalization.* New York: Continuum, 2001.

Kool, V.L. *The Psychology of Nonviolence and Aggression.* New York: Palgrave/Macmillian, 2008.

Korey, William. *NGOs and the Universal Declaration of Human Rights.* New York: St. Martin's Press, 1998.

Kriegel, Blandine. *The State and the Rule of Law.* Translated by Marc A. LePain and Jeffrey C. Cohen. Princeton: Princeton University Press, 1995.

Kurlansky, Mark. *Nonviolence: Twenty-five Lessons from the History of a Dangerous Idea.* New York: Random House, Modern Library, 2006.

LaBotz, Dan. *César Chávez and la Causa.* New York: Pearson/Longman, 2006.

Lanham, Howard N. *The World Court in Action.* Lanham, MD: Rowman & Littlefield, 2002.

Larkin, Ralph W. *Comprehending Columbine.* Philadelphia: Temple University Press, 2007.

Larsen, Jeffrey A., ed. *Arms Control: Cooperative Security in a Changing Environment.* Boulder, CO: Lynne Rienner, 2002.

Lauren, Gordon. *The Evolution of International Human Rights: Visions Seen.* 2d ed. Philadelphia: University of Pennsylvania Press, 2003.

Lederach, John Paul. *The Moral Imagination: The Art and Soul of Building Peace.* New York: Oxford University Press, 2005.

Levi, Michael A., and Michael E. O'Hanlon. *The Future of Arms Control.* Washington, DC: Brookings Institution Press, 2005.

Maathai, Wangari Muta. *Unbowed: A Memoir.* New York: Knopf, 2006.

Macmillan, Margaret. *Nixon and Mao.* New York: Random House, 2007.

Mandela, Nelson. *Long Walk to Freedom: The Autobiography of Nelson Mandela.* Boston: Little, Brown, 1994.

Maslow, Abraham H. *Motivation and Personality.* 2d ed. New York: Harper & Row, 1970.

McArthur, Debra. *Raoul Wallenberg: Rescuing Thousands from the Nazis' Grasp.* Berkeley Heights, NJ: Enslow, 2005.

McFaul, Thomas R. *The Future of Peace and Justice in the Global Village: The Role of World Religions in the Twenty-first Century.* Westport, CT: Praeger, 2006.

Mestrovic, S.G., and Stjepan Gabriel. *The Trials of Abu Ghraib: An Expert Witness Account of Shame and Honor.* Boulder, CO: Paradigm, 2007.

Meyer, Aleta Lynn. *Promoting Nonviolence in Early Adolescence: Responding in Peaceful and Positive Ways.* New York: Kluwer Academic/Plenum Publishers, 2000.

Michelli, Joseph. *The Starbucks Experience: 5 Principles for Turning Ordinary into Extraordinary.* New York: McGraw-Hill, 2007.

Milko, Matthew. *Peaceful Societies.* Oakville, Ontario: CPRI Press, 1973.

Mills, Nicolaus. *Winning the Peace.* Hoboken: John Wiley & Sons, 2008.

Mitchell, George J. *Making Peace.* New York: Knopf, 1999.

Mollin, Marian. *Radical Pacifism in Modern America: Egalitarianism and Protest.* Philadelphia: University of Pennsylvania Press, 2006.

Moore, Christopher W. *The Mediation Process: Practical Strategies for Resolving Conflict.* San Francisco: Jossey-Bass, 2003.

Moore, John Allphin, Jr., and Jerry Pubantz. *The New United Nations: International Organization in the Twenty-first Century.* Upper Saddle River, NJ: Pearson Prentice Hall, 2006.

Moretta, John A. *William Penn and the Quaker Legacy.* New York: Pearson Longman, 2007.

Mortenson, Greg, and David Oliver Renlin. *Three Cups of Tea: One Man's Mission to Promote Peace...One School at a Time.* New York: Penguin Books, 2006.

Muscat, Robert J. *Investing in Peace: How Development Aid Can Prevent or Promote Conflict.* Armonk, New York: M.E. Sharpe, 2002.

Munroe, Alexandra, and Jon Hendricks. *Yes Yoko Ono.* New York: Japan Society; Harry N. Abrams, 2000.

Myers, N., and J. Kent. *Environmental Refugees: A Growing Phenomenon in the 21st Century.* Washington, DC: The Climate Institute, 2001.

Nafziger, E. Wayne, and Juha Auvinen. *Economic Development, Inequality, and War: Humanitarian Emergencies in Developing Countries.* New York: Palgrave Macmillan, 2003.

Nagel, Stuart S., ed. *Handbook of Global Economic Policy.* New York: Marcel Dekker, 2000.

Narlikar, Amrita. *The World Trade Organization: A Very Short Introduction.* Oxford: Oxford University Press, 2005.

Nesbitt, Francis Njubi. *Race for Sanctions: African Americans Against Apartheid, 1946–1994.* Bloomington: Indiana University Press, 2004.

Newberg, Andrew B. *Why We Believe What We Believe: Uncovering our Biological Need for Meaning, Spirituality, and Truth.* New York: Free Press, 2006.

Newton, David E. *Environmental Justice: A Reference Handbook.* Santa Barbara: ABC-CLIO, 1996.

Oliner, Samuel P. *Do Unto Others.* Cambridge, MA: Westview Press, 2003.

Oppenheimer, Martin. *The Sit-In Movement of 1960.* New York: Carlson, 1989.

Osa, Maryjane. *Solidarity and Contention: Networks of Polish Opposition.* Minneapolis: University of Minnesota Press, 2003.

Otto, Nathan, and Heinz Norden, eds. *Einstein on Peace.* New York: Simon & Schuster, 1960.

Phillips, Rick, et al. *Safe School Ambassadors: Harnessing Student Power to Stop Bullying and Violence.* San Francisco: Jossey-Bass, 2008.

Pikas, Anatol. *Rational Conflict Resolution.* Uppsala, Sweden: Stencile Edition, 1973.

Pinkney, Andrea Davis. *Boycott Blues: How Rosa Parks Inspired a Nation.* New York: Greenwillow Books, 2008.

Plante, Thomas G., and Carl E. Thoresen, eds. *Spirit, Science, and Health: How the Spiritual Mind Fuels Physical Wellness.* Westport, CT: Praeger, 2007.

Pogue, Alan, and Roy Flukinger. *Witness For Justice: The Documentary Photographs of Alan Pogue.* Austin: University of Texas Press, 2007.

Ransom, David. *The No-nonsense Guide to Fair Trade.* Oxford: New Internationalist, 2001.

Rao, K. Ramakrishna, ed. *Cultivating Consciousness: Enhancing Human Potential, Wellness, and Healing.* Westport, CT: Praeger, 1993.

Rawls, John. *A Theory of Justice.* Cambridge, MA: Belknap Press of Harvard University Press, 1999.

Reiss, Albert J., Jr., and Jeffrey A. Roth, eds. *Violence: Understanding and Preventing.* Washington, DC: National Academy Press, 1993.

Requejo, William Hernandez, and John L. Graham. *Global Negotiation: The New Rules.* New York: Palgrave Macmillian, 2008.

Reychler, Luc, and Thania Paffenholz, eds. *Peacebuilding: A Field Guide.* Boulder, CO: Lynne Rienner, 2001.

Rigby, Andrew. *Justice and Reconciliation: After the Violence.* Boulder, CO: Lynne Rienner, 2001.

Roberti, Mark. *The Fall of Hong Kong: China's Triumph and Britain's Betrayal.* New York: John Wiley & Sons, 1996.

Roberts, Walter R. *Bully from Both Sides.* Thousand Oaks, CA: Corwin Press, 2006.

Ross, Dennis. *Statecraft: And How to Restore America's Standing in the World.* New York: Farrar, Straus and Giroux, 2007.

Ross, Fiona C. *Bearing Witness: Women and the Truth and Reconciliation Commission in South Africa.* Sterling, VA: Pluto Press, 2003.

Sargent, Frederic O. *The Civil Rights Revolution: Events and Leaders, 1955–1968.* Jefferson, NC: McFarland, 2004.

Schrumpf, Fred, and Donna K. Crawford, and Richard J. Bodine. *Peer Mediation: Conflict Resolution in Schools: Program Guide.* Champaign, IL: Research Press, 1997.

Shannon, Timothy J. *Iroquois Diplomacy on the Early American Frontier.* New York: Viking, 2008.

Shaw, Randy. *Beyond the Fields: Cesar Chavez, the UFW, and the Struggle for Justice in the 21st Century.* Berkeley: University of California Press, 2008.

Shermer, Michael. *The Science of Good and Evil: Why People Cheat, Gossip, Care, Share and Follow the Golden Rule.* New York: Times Books, 2004.

Smith, Michael G., and Moreen Dee. *Peacekeeping in East Timor: The Path to Independence.* Boulder, CO: Lynne Rienner, 2003.

Smoker, Paul, et al., eds. *A Reader in Peace Studies.* Oxford: Pergamon Press, 1990.

Solimano, Andrés, Eduardo Aninat, and Nancy Birdstall, eds. *Distributive Justice and Economic Development: The Case of Chile and Developing Countries.* Ann Arbor: University of Michigan Press, 2000.

Stanford, Karin L. *Beyond the Boundaries: Reverend Jesse Jackson in International Affairs.* Albany: State University of New York Press, 1997.

Starke, J. G. *An Introduction to the Science of Peace (Irenology).* Leyden: A.W. Sijthoff, 1968.

Stegar, Manfred B. *Gandhi's Dilemma: Nonviolent Principles and Nationalist Power.* New York: St. Martin's Press, 2000.

Stiglitz, Joseph E., and Andrew Charlton. *Fair Trade for All: How Trade Can Promote Development.* Oxford: Oxford University Press, 2005.

Stojanovic,' Svetozar. *Serbia: The Democratic Revolution.* Amherst, NY: Humanity Books, 2003.

Tal, Alon, ed. *Speaking of Earth: Environmental Speeches that Moved the World.* New Brunswick, NJ: Rutgers University Press, 2006.

Talbott, Strobe. *Deadly Gambits: The Reagan Administration and the Stalemate in Nuclear Arms Control.* New York: Knopf, 1984.

Taylor, John G. *East Timor: The Price of Freedom.* New York: St. Martin's Press, 1999.

Tariq, Ali, and Susan Watkins. *1968: Marching in the Streets.* New York: The Free Press, 1998.

Thoreau, Henry D. *Walden: A Fully Annotated Edition.* Edited by Jeffery S. Cramer. New Haven: Yale University Press, 2004.

Thoreau, Henry David. *Walden, Civil Disobedience, and Other Writings: Authoritative Texts, Journal, Reviews and Posthumous Assessments, Criticism.* New York: W.W. Norton, 2008.

Tov, Yaacov Bar-Siman, ed. *From Conflict Resolution to Reconciliation.* New York: Oxford University Press, 2004.

Troester, Rod. *Jimmy Carter as Peacemaker: A Post-Presidential Biography.* Westport, CT: Praeger, 1996.

Truth and Reconciliation Commission of South Africa report. Foreword by Desmond Tutu. London: Macmillan Reference, 1999. 10 March 2009, http://www.netlibrary.com/Details.aspx.

United States Institute of Peace. *Dialogues on Conflict Resolution: Bridging Theory and Practice.* Washington, DC: United States Institute of Peace, 1993.

United States Institute of Peace. *Whither the Bulldozer? Nonviolent Revolution and the Transition to Democracy in Serbia*. Washington, DC: U.S. Institute of Peace, 2001.

United States Senate, One Hundred Ninth Congress, Second Session. *Energy Diplomacy and Security: A Compilation of Statements by Witnesses before the Committee on Foreign Relations*. Washington, DC: U.S. Government Printing Office, 2006.

University of California. *The New Wellness Encyclopedia*. Boston: Houghton Mifflin, 1995.

University of Michigan. *Remembering Raoul Wallenberg: The University of Michigan Celebrates Twentieth-Century Heroes*. Ann Arbor: University of Michigan Press, 2001.

Van den Dungen, Peter. *West European Pacifism and the Strategy for Peace*. New York: St. Martin's Press, 1985.

Walesa, Lech. *A Way of Hope*. New York: Henry Holt, 1987.

Walker, Geoffrey de Q. *The Rule of Law: Foundation of Constitutional Democracy*. Carlton, Victoria: Melbourne University Press, 1988.

Wang, Enbao. *Hong Kong, 1997: The Politics of Transition*. London: Lynne Rienner, 1997.

Wattles, Jeffrey. *The Golden Rule*. New York: Oxford University Press, 1996.

Weber, David, ed. *Civil Disobedience in America: A Documentary History*. Ithaca: Cornell University Press, 1978.

Weddle, Meredith Baldwin. *Walking in the Way of Peace: Quaker Pacifism in the Seventeenth Century*. Oxford: Oxford University Press, 2001.

Wilford, Rick, ed. *Aspects of the Belfast Agreement*. Oxford: Oxford University Press, 2001.

Williams, Oliver F. *Peace Through Commerce: Responsible Corporate Citizenship and the Ideals of the United Nations Global Compact*. Notre Dame: University of Notre Dame Press, 2008.

Williamson, Sue. *Resistance Art in South Africa*. New York: St. Martin's Press, 1989.

Wilson, Mike, ed. *World Religion*. Detroit: Greenhaven Press, 2006.

Wilson, Richard Ashby. *Humanitarianism and Suffering: The Mobilization of Empathy*. Cambridge: Cambridge University Press, 2009.

Wink, Walter. *Engaging the Powers: Discernment and Resistance in a World of Domination*. Minneapolis: Fortress Press, 1992.

Wohlforth, William, ed. *Witnesses to the End of the Cold War*. Baltimore and London: The Johns Hopkins University Press, 1996.

Worthington, Everett L., Jr., ed. *Handbook of Forgiveness*. New York: Routledge, 2005.

Wylie, Diana. *Art + Revolution: The Life and Death of Thami Mnyele, South African Artist*. Charlottesville: University of Virginia Press, 2008.

Yale, Richmond. *Cultural Exchange and the Cold War: Raising the Iron Curtain*. University Park: Pennsylvania State University Press, 2003.

Young-Eisendrath, Polly, and Melvin E. Miller, eds. *The Psychology of Mature Spirituality: Integrity, Wisdom, Transcendence*. London: Routledge, 2000.

Zifcak, Spencer, ed. *Globalisation and the Rule of Law*. New York: Routledge, 2005.

Zinsser, William, ed. *Paths of Resistance: The Art and Craft of the Political Novel*. Boston: Houghton Mifflin, 1989.

Zucker, Ross. *Democratic Distributive Justice*. Cambridge: Cambridge University Press, 2001.

Index